The State of the Environment

United Nations Environment Programme

The State of the Environment

Prepared by

Essam El-Hinnawi and Manzur H. Hashmi

Butterworths
London Boston Durban Singapore Sydney Toronto Wellington

First published 1987
Reprinted 1988

© **United Nations Environment Programme, 1987**

British Library Cataloguing in Publication Data

El-Hinnawi, Essam E.
   The state of the environment.
   1. Human ecology
   I. Title   II. Hashmi, Manzur H.   III. United Nations.
   Environment Programme
   333.7   GF141

   ISBN 0-408-02183-7

Library of Congress Cataloguing in Publication Data

Hinnawi, Essam E.
   The state of the environment.

   At head of title: United Nations Environment
Programme.
   Includes bibliographies and index.
   1. United Nations Environment Programme.   2. Environ-
mental protection.   3. Pollution Environmental aspects.
4. Environmental policy.   I. Hashmi, Manzur-ul-Haque.
II. United Nations Environment Programme.   III. Title.
TD 170.2.H56   1987   363.7   87–11639

   ISBN 0–408–02183–7

Photoset by Mid-County press, London SW15
Printed and bound in Great Britain by Anchor Brendon, Tiptree, Essex

Contents

Foreword

The 15 years after the United Nations Conference on the Human Environment convened in Stockholm in 1972 brought into focus the general realization that the different physical components of the environment have limited assimilative and carrying capacities and that pollution control measures must be instituted to safeguard the environment and the quality of human life. More important has been the growing realization that the natural environmental resources of water, soil, plant and animal life constitute the natural capital on which man depends to satisfy his needs and achieve his aspirations for development. The wise management of these resources has demanded positive and realistic planning that balances human needs against the potential the environment has for meeting them.

It is gratifying to note that environmental policies are no longer focusing simply on the control of pollution and the abatement of nuisances but on more positive actions directed at the improvement of the quality of life that depends on the health and viability of the natural and man-made environments. Preventive rather than curative actions have been gaining momentum and wide acceptance. Good management avoids pollution and the wastage of resources by irreversible damage; to prevent such types of environmental degradation is more challenging and certainly more efficient than to redress them after they have occurred.

The 15 years after Stockholm also brought into focus the importance of international cooperation not only to solve world development problems but also to safeguard the environment for future generations. It is true that countries are at many stages of development with different economic, social and environmental priorities. But it is not enough to deduce that poverty defiles the environment in many developing regions; it is necessary to know exactly how this happens and how overconsumption creates other threats elsewhere. Moreover, nations are not isolated; the actions of one country may affect the environment in a neighbouring one.

Since its establishment in 1972, the United Nations Environment Programme has been keeping under review the world environmental situation to ensure that environmental problems of wide significance receive appropriate consideration. In this respect, UNEP has produced over the past years a number of in-depth reviews of different environmental issues and an annual state of the environment report which focused on selected emerging topics. The present volume consolidates and updates this material in what can be considered as a state of the world environment report. In this respect, I must emphasize that it has never been the intention to present an encyclopaedic study, but to highlight contemporary and future environmental issues, especially those of global significance.

I hope that this volume will be found to give a balanced review of the state of the environment, and it is my sincere hope that the scientific community will pick up the different inadequacies in our knowledge and accelerate the efforts to fill these gaps. In this respect, it is appreciated that several policy makers faced with long-term environmental problems often argue that they cannot afford to worry about the remote and abstract when surrounded by the immediate and concrete; that potential climatic and genetic instabilities are of academic interest in a world full of actual war, famine, disease and ignorance. This thesis cannot be fully accepted. The problems which overwhelm us today are precisely those which, through a similar approach, we failed to solve decades ago; problems which have built-in perceptual and response delays of many years. These delays ensure that such an approach can only defer or disguise problems, not solve them.

Mostafa Kamal Tolba
Executive Director
United Nations Environment Programme

Nairobi, January 1987

Preface

One of the main functions assigned to the Governing Council of the United Nations Environment Programme by the General Assembly in Resolution 2997 (XXVII) of 15 December 1972 is 'to keep under review the world environmental situation in order to ensure that emerging environmental problems of wide international significance receive appropriate and adequate consideration by Governments'. Accordingly, the United Nations Environment Programme issues each year a report on the state of the environment. The first reports published in 1974, 1975 and 1976 discussed a broad spectrum of environmental issues, such as climatic changes, the condition of the biosphere, stress and social tension and pollution. Subsequent annual state of the environment reports focused on some selected specific environmental issues.

Since 1976 we have been responsible for the preparation of most of the annual state of the environment reports published by UNEP. We were assisted in this task by many scientists and we drew heavily on information gathered from the United Nations system and major scientific institutions. Dr Mostafa Kamal Tolba, Executive Director of UNEP, found that the time was ripe to consolidate and update the annual state of the environment reports in one text to be published 15 years after the Stockholm Conference. He entrusted us with this task. When we started the preparation of the present text we realized that our work would be much more than mere scientific editing. The process of consolidation and updating of the different issues dealt with involved the complete rewriting of several parts of the annual state of the environment reports to eliminate duplication and to present the material in a coherent manner. Therefore, the presentation of the material in the present text is our responsibility.

In the course of the preparation of the present volume we received help and contributions from several colleagues at the United Nations Environment Programme and other United Nations bodies; their efforts are gratefully acknowledged. We are particularly indebted to Dr Mostafa Kamal Tolba, Executive Director of UNEP, for entrusting us with this assignment and for his valuable guidance and comments. We would like also to express our thanks to the following institutions for providing us with information and/or permission to use material and figures from their publications: the Stockholm International Peace Research Institute (SIPRI), the World Bank, the World Health Organization, the World Meteorological Organization, the Food and Agriculture Organization of the United Nations, the Organization for Economic Cooperation and Development (OECD), the Economic Commission for Europe, Earthscan, the International Institute for Environment and Development, the World Resources Institute and the Worldwatch Institute.

Essam El-Hinnawi   *Manzur H. Hashmi*
Cairo, February 1987   *Lahore, February 1987*

Chapter 1

Introduction

The environment – defined as the total outer physical and biological system in which man and other organisms live – is a whole, albeit a complicated one with many interacting components. The wise management of that environment depends upon an understanding of those components: of its rocks, minerals and waters, of its soils and their present and potential vegetation, of its animal life and potential for livestock husbandry and of its climate. It demands positive and realistic planning that balances human needs against the potential the environment has for meeting them. Too many people think only of pollution when they consider environmental problems. Good management avoids pollution, erosion and the wastage of resources by irreversible damage. To prevent such types of environmental degradation is even more challenging and certainly more efficient than to redress them after they have occurred.

Both the creation and the recognition of environmental problems depend closely on the way society is organized and on its values and objectives. Changes in the relationship between man and his physical environment depend to a large degree on changes in the organization and aims of society. If man is to escape from a situation in which much energy and resources are devoted to correcting past mistakes, his aim must be to build a society which is intrinsically compatible with its environment.

The fundamental needs of a human being are hard to define. Our perception of them varies according to our culture, time and technological progress. But some may be considered 'basic' because unless they are sufficiently satisfied, dignified and active human life is impossible. They are food, shelter, health, clothing, education and creative productive work and they are felt by every human being irrespective of culture, race or sex. Closely linked with them there is another group of 'social' or 'cultural' goals such as entertainment, artistic and musical expression, participation in social affairs, travel, choice of employment and the like. It is hard to draw the line between human needs and desires. Once basic human needs are satisfied – and this in itself will be difficult to achieve throughout the world – people still have wants which relate not only to individual standards but also strongly reflect cultural influences. Aspirations and expectations increase as societies develop and economic growth proceeds; they are never fully attained.

The greatest challenge of today is to design development so that it satisfies basic needs – beginning with the eradication of poverty – but is environmentally realistic and does not transgress the 'outer limits' imposed by the capacities of the biosphere. These limits still cannot be defined accurately. It is easy enough to see that the earth is of finite size, receives a finite amount of radiation from the sun, has a finite potential plant productivity and in consequence can meet only the basic needs of a finite number of people. But we do not know what the 'carrying capacity' of the earth is, or which factors are most likely to constrain the processes of social development. One thing is evident. The world is not environmentally uniform. Nations differ in their environmental resources. Some may always have to struggle against poor soils, unpredictable climates or extremes of heat and cold, just as others lack indigenous energy resources or access to sea fisheries. No single solution will work everywhere and development to meet basic needs and social aspirations will be much easier in some countries than in others. Some may never be fully self-sufficient in food, just as others see no way of becoming self-sufficient in energy or raw materials. Development will demand interdependence.

Different parts of the biosphere differ in their 'resilience', that is their resistance to changes in the nature and intensity of human impact. It used to be thought that diverse and dominant systems like tropical forests were also relatively stable, while species-poor systems evidently under the continuing stress of a harsh environment, like the deserts, were fragile. New research suggests that the relationship between diversity and stability is far less simple. In tropical forests a high proportion of the essential nutrients in the system is commonly present within the trees, and if cutting and burning disperses these nutrients and at the same time bares the soil to erosion, much of the fertility in the system may be rapidly lost. On the other hand the temperate zones of the world, with their more equable climate, have large areas where despite millennia of continuous agricultural use, the robust soils remain fertile. These differences in the capacities of different systems to sustain their biological productivity when manipulated by man may set local outer limits to land development in various regions – or at least indicate which methods of development are most appropriate.

Environmental problems can be classified according to the nature of the damage to human beings, as follows:

1. direct assaults on human welfare, including obvious damage to health (for example, lead poisoning or aggravation of lung disease by air pollution), social disruption (for example, displacement of persons from their living areas by mining operations and hydroelectric projects) and other direct effects on what human beings perceive as their 'quality of life' (for example, congestion, noise and litter);
2. indirect effects on human welfare through interference with services provided for society by natural biological systems (for example, diminution of ocean productivity by the filling of estuaries and the pollution of coastal waters and acceleration of erosion by logging or overgrazing).

Most of the attention devoted to environmental matters by scientists, politicians and the public alike has been concerned with the direct effects and, more particularly, acute rather than chronic manifestations. This is only natural. It would be wrong, however, to interpret limited legislative and technical progress towards alleviating the direct, acute symptoms of environmental damage as evidence that society is on its way to an orderly resolution of its environmental problems. The difficulty is not merely that the discovery, implementation and enforcement of treatment for those obvious symptoms is likely to be expensive and difficult. Unfortunately, the long-term consequences for human beings of chronic exposure to low concentrations of environmental contaminants may be more serious – and the causes less amenable to detection and removal – than those of acute pollution as it is perceived today. The most serious threats of all, however, may well prove to be the indirect ones generated by mankind's disruption of the functioning of the natural environment – the second category mentioned above.

In the past decade, speculation about what biophysical constraints might impose boundaries on man's activities has become bewilderingly diverse, reflecting both the diversity of the world scientific community and the blurring of distinctions between technical, ethical and ideological conclusions. Governments, rather reluctant to assume the worst in cases of scientific uncertainty (especially on a timescale of decades or centuries), have tended to discount the rising concern behind these speculations, and hence may have to overlook important long-term pragmatism.

Yet this very emphasis on dealing with acute and immediate problems has focused attention not merely on how man might approach these boundaries but also on why man cannot approach some of them. As we identify biophysical constraints, the avoidance or evasion of which will require social and institutional change, we begin to see the difficulty of that change through our everyday efforts to overcome not ultimate biophysical constraints but more proximate managerial constraints. In short, even as we become aware of boundaries, inner limitations or constraints rise to crowd them from our thoughts.

This dichotomy, or rather continuum, of limits can be discussed in a different way. The amount of most resources theoretically available under perfect management is extremely large; this is as true of food as of energy and minerals. However, the gap between theoretical and practical availability also tends to be extremely large because of various constraints – geopolitical, social, technical, biological, economic and so on. The rate, difficulty and side effects of overcoming these constraints will vary widely from case to case and will be assessed differently by different people (this is partly because perceptions vary in the sphere of purely social or political constraints, which are of course no less real or effective than biophysical constraints). In many cases and places, the constraints which stand between us and the more remote boundaries are so hard to overcome in good time that these boundaries are of purely academic interest. Thus while we must bear in mind their long-term implications, our immediate task is to assess the nature and permeability of the far more obvious constraints. In order not to undertake this task on false assumptions, we may have to reason backwards from the ultimate boundaries, however remote they may seem on the short timescale of much political action; we may have to ask what options we must retain for the long term and what we can do now if we are to retain those options.

This long-range planning approach is commonly rejected in favour of reliance upon short-term technological remedies. One must therefore ask whether technology is inherently addictive, forcing society into further crises demanding further technological remedies until the habit becomes socially unsustainable. This might occur if, for example, remedies are prescribed for biophysical symptoms rather than for underlying social disorders – a common result of misdefining a problem and then supposing it to have a solution. If technology evades, obscures or defers social problems rather than resolving them, then its ever increasing use must eventually lead to social disequilibria without technical remedy. Likewise, if technical change involves social change, then the pace of required social change must soon become excessive. Many thoughtful analysts are uneasy about these trends and about the rising dependence of all societies on rapidly devised and deployed technologies whose complex side effects are unpredictable, unpredicted or (most often) simply ignored. Yet this unease seldom crystallizes into explicit consideration of the option of technological restraint, into trying to root out the underlying social problem rather than attacking its symptoms with technical zeal. This option – assessing the wisdom of intervening at all with our technical tools – is generally submerged by more 'practical' assessment of the nature and hazards of *ad hoc* solutions to immediate problems. Thus the possibility of social adjustment, eg of stimulated changes in social norms and goals, is generally dismissed by technologists – dismissed even as they strive to suppress the symptoms that might bring it about, and even as they assume that the equally difficult social adjustments that technical innovation requires will indeed occur on schedule.

It may well be said that the problems must be sorted into a hierarchy of decreasing imminence and tackled as they arise. Such a hierarchy does indeed exist; but it is a rather incomplete tool for decision making, a tool whose use has led to many of our present difficulties. Constraints are now in general most imminent in food supply, then in energy supply and lastly in mineral supply; but the imminence of grave food/population problems in some regions does not make other kinds of constraints irrelevant anywhere. On the contrary, it means that, while preparing as best we can for those situations which it is too late to avoid, we should be dealing with the problems that will arise next – problems which we may have time to solve if we start now. In other words, we must break the cycle of short-term planning that has got us into our present acute difficulties.

Progressive social thinkers faced with long-term environmental problems often argue that they cannot afford to worry about the remote and abstract when surrounded by the immediate and concrete, that potential climatic and genetic instabilities are of academic interest in a world full of actual war, famine, disease, injustice and ignorance. This thesis cannot be fully accepted. The problems which overwhelm us today are precisely those which, through a similar approach we failed to solve decades ago; problems which have built-in perceptual and response delays of many years. These delays ensure that such an approach can only defer or disguise problems, not solve them.

Chapter 2

Air quality and atmospheric issues

Air quality

Life on earth depends on the atmosphere, which is subject to wide natural variation and to human modification. Air pollution and the need to protect the health and welfare of the general public from it are not new issues: there have been laws passed since the Middle Ages to reduce atmospheric emissions. However, the occurrence of air pollution was not perceived as a major problem in most countries until the late 1950s and 1960s. It was then usually still seen as a local problem in urban and industrialized areas. Only in recent years have air pollution and other atmospheric issues evolved as problems of regional and international importance.

Air pollution comes from natural and man-made sources. Natural sources include smoke from forest fires, wind blown dust and, on occasion, large scale volcanic eruptions. Man-made sources include emissions from stationary or mobile sources and are generally more abundant in urban and/or industrial areas than in the countryside. The most common emissions are sulphur oxides, nitrogen oxides, particulate matter, hydrocarbons, carbon monoxide, lead and other trace compounds. The concentration of air pollutants depends not only on the quantities that are emitted but also on the ability of the atmosphere to either absorb or disperse excess amounts.

On a global basis, the amounts of common air pollutants emitted into the atmosphere by human activities were about 110 million tonnes (t) of sulphur oxides, 59 million t of particulate matter, 69 million t of nitrogen oxides, 194 million t of carbon monoxide and 53 million t of hydrocarbons in 1980 (OECD, 1985). On a regional and/or national basis, the amounts of pollutants emitted into the atmosphere vary from one area to another depending on the density and type of human activity and on the measure adopted to reduce such emissions. The countries of the Organization for Economic Cooperation and Development (OECD) account for about half of the total global amounts of pollutants emitted each year into the atmosphere (Figure 1).

Most air pollutants enter the body by inhalation, thus making the respiratory system the main organ directly affected. Exposure to more than one pollutant at the same time (which is normally the case) can further aggravate health effects; for example, the effects increase synergistically on exposure to both sulphur oxides and particulate matter at the same time. Air pollution also has adverse effects on agriculture, forest growth, water resources and different buildings and structures. Estimates of total annual damage resulting from air pollution have reached 1% of

5

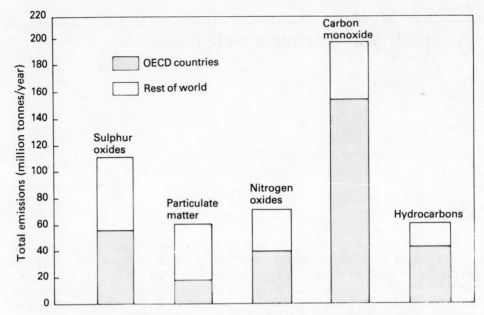

Figure 1 Total emissions of common air pollutants from human activities in the world in 1980
Drawn from data given by OECD, 1985

the gross domestic product (GDP) in France and 2% of GDP in the Netherlands, for example (OECD, 1985). Although it is difficult to determine the exact impacts of different air pollutants on human health and the environment, ambient guidelines have been established as indicative values for the protection of human health and the environment. The United Nations Environment Programme (UNEP) in cooperation with the World Health Organization (WHO) have established environmental health criteria for the common air pollutants (see, UNEP/WHO, 1977, 1979a,b).

Concern about the different impacts of air pollution has triggered a number of national and international actions in recent years. Programmes have been established, especially in developed countries, to routinely monitor and assess air quality conditions, to observe trends and to assess the relationship between air pollution and human health. A global programme of air quality monitoring was established by WHO in 1973. Its objectives are to assist countries in operational air pollution monitoring, to improve the practical use of data in relation to the protection of human health and to promote the exchange of information. In 1976 the air monitoring project became a part of the Global Environmental Monitoring System (GEMS). At present, some 50 countries are participating in the GEMS air monitoring project in which data are obtained at approximately 175 sites in 75 cities (Bennett *et al*, 1985), 25 of which are located in developing countries (GEMS, 1984).

Measurements at the GEMS project sites have so far been limited to sulphur dioxide (SO_2) and suspended particulate matter (SPM) as indicators of industrial pollution in urban areas. The data obtained from national air monitoring systems and from the GEMS project give indications of certain general trends in urban air quality.

Trend analyses of carbon monoxide (CO) emissions in OECD countries for the period 1970 to 1979 show that the total emissions have declined significantly in North America and Japan and that the picture in OECD Europe is mixed. In the period 1979 to 1984, there was a decline in, or at least a stabilization of, CO emissions and concentrations in urban areas in the OECD countries. This can be attributed to a levelling off or a slower rate of increase in the total number of vehicle-kilometres travelled by motor vehicles and to environmental controls introduced in the 1970s (OECD, 1985).

In the period from 1970 to 1979, the nitrogen oxides (NO_x) emissions from transport sources have tended to increase in most OECD countries; emission of NO_x from stationary sources remained, however, relatively stable. From 1979 to 1984 there was a decline in, or at least a stabilization of, NO_x emissions in most OECD countries. This has been attributed to stagnation in GDP or reduced rates of economic growth, greater efficiencies of national economies with regard to fossil fuel requirements resulting from energy savings and/or greater reliance on alternative sources of energy and to environmental control measures introduced in the 1970s. The level of NO_x emissions is likely to remain stable up to 1990; the emissions may be more significantly reduced in many OECD countries by 1993, following the resolution adopted at the Multilateral Conference on the Causes and Prevention of Damages to Forests and Waters by Air Pollution in Europe (Munich, June 1984). Negotiations are also underway between member states of the Economic Commission for Europe (ECE) to conclude a protocol on the control of NO_x emissions within the framework of the Transboundary Air Pollution Convention.

Over the period from 1970 to 1979 sulphur dioxide (SO_2) emissions fell significantly in most OECD countries. The downward trend in SO_2 emissions has continued in most of these countries from 1979 to 1984. This has been attributed to stagnation of economic growth, energy savings and environmental control measures introduced since the 1970s. Ambient concentration levels of SO_2 have also decreased in most cities of the OECD with the exception of Rome, Italy, where ambient SO_2 concentration increased from 74 micrograms per cubic metre ($\mu g/m^3$) in 1980 to about 90 $\mu g/m^3$ in 1983 (OECD, 1985), which is well above the upper exposure limit established by WHO (Figure 2). As a result of the recent protocol on the control of SO_2 emissions signed in Helsinki in 1985, it is likely that by 1993 many of the OECD countries will have reduced their SO_2 emissions from the 1980 levels by at least 30%.

On a global basis, trend analyses carried out for data obtained from 63 sites of the GEMS air monitoring project (all sites with data for five or more years) showed downward trends in SO_2 concentrations at 54% of the sites, upward trends in 16% and stationary levels of SO_2 in 30% of the sites, over the period 1973–80 (GEMS, 1984). The mean values of SO_2 taken from the measurement period 1975–80 from all sites indicate that 49% of the sites are below the lower exposure limit established by WHO (40 $\mu g/m^3$), 25% of the sites are within the WHO guideline values (40–60 $\mu g/m^3$) and 26% of the sites are above the upper exposure limit (60 $\mu g/m^3$). Examples of the latter are Milan (with a high composite average of SO_2 of 207 $\mu g/m^3$), Sao Paulo, Zagreb, London, Brussels, Glasgow, Tehran, Madrid and Manila (65 $\mu g\ SO_2/m^3$).

As for suspended particulate matter (SPM), emissions showed a significant decline in most OECD countries from 1970 to 1984. Trend analyses of data obtained from 62 sites of the GEMS air monitoring project show that for the period 1973–80, the average annual concentration of SPM decreased in 43% of the sites, increased in 10% and remained stationary in 47% of the sites (GEMS, 1984). The average SPM taken from the measurement period 1975–80 from all sites at the GEMS project show that 24% of the sites are below the lower exposure limit established by WHO (40 $\mu g/m^3$), 34% of the sites are within the guideline values (40–60 $\mu g/m^3$), and 42% of the sites are above the upper limit (60 $\mu g/m^3$). Examples of the latter are Calcutta (with a high

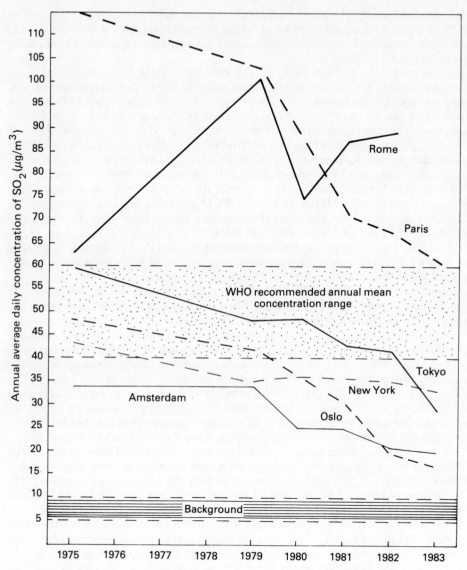

Figure 2   Trends of ambient SO$_2$ concentration in selected urban areas in the OECD region
Drawn from data given by OECD, 1985

composite average of SPM of 360 μg/m^3), Tehran, Zagreb, Hamilton, Houston, Manila, Sydney, Toronto, Montreal, Vancouver, Osaka and New York (62 μg SPM/m^3).

The data obtained from the GEMS air monitoring project show that most cities in the developing countries are more polluted with SO$_2$ and SPM than most of the cities in the developed countries. However, the data do not allow for trend analyses since most of the data available cover only a short period of time (generally less than five years).

In some countries seasonal changes in the concentration of air pollutants occur. For example, in Hungary most urban areas show higher concentrations of sulphur dioxide, nitrogen oxides and SPM in winter than in summer due to extensive use of fossil fuels (especially coal) for heating in winter (KSH, 1986).

Several countries have been installing air pollution control equipment at industrial enterprises, with marked successes in reducing industrial emissions. For example, in Bulgaria it has been possible to reduce emissions of SPM by 1.6 million tonnes annually between 1976 and 1980 and toxic substances in gaseous emissions were cut down by 70% over the same period. By 1985, toxic substances in gaseous emissions were reduced by 81% (Pavlov, 1982). Comparable reductions in air pollutants have also been recorded in Hungary and USSR.

Indoor air pollution

Contaminated indoor air is not new. Soot found on ceilings of prehistoric caves provides evidence of the high levels of pollution associated with inadequate ventilation of open fires. Elevated indoor pollutant concentrations continue to be a fact of life for people who live in impoverished areas and cook over open fires fuelled by charcoal, wood, dung or agricultural residues.

Indoor air quality in non-occupational settings in urban areas has recently attracted the attention of scientists, policy makers and the public. Many people spend more than 90% of their time indoors and it has been shown that indoor exposure to environmental pollutants can be substantial (NRC, 1981; Spengler et al, 1982; Spengler and Sexton, 1983).

Indoor air pollution in residences, public buildings and offices is created for the most part by the occupants' activities and their use of appliances, power equipment and chemicals; by wear and tear and emission of vapours from some structural or decorative materials; by thermal factors; and by the intrusion of outdoor pollutants (Table 1). The most important indoor contaminants are tobacco smoke, radon decay

TABLE 1. Main indoor pollutants

Source and type	Indoor concentration	Indoor/outdoor ratio
I Pollutants from outdoors		
Sulphur oxides	0–15 $\mu g/m^3$	< 1
Ozone	0–10 ppb	≪ 1
II Pollutants from indoors and outdoors		
Nitrogen oxides	10–700 $\mu g/m^3$	≫ 1
Carbon monoxide	5–50 ppm	≫ 1
Carbon dioxide	2 000–3 000 ppm	≫ 1
Particulate matter	10–1 000 $\mu g/m^3$	1
III Pollutants from indoors		
Radon	0.01–4 pCi/litre	≫ 1
Formaldehyde	0.01–0.5 ppm	> 1
Synthetic fibres	0–1 fibre/ml	1
Organic substances		> 1
Polycyclic hydrocarbons		> 1
Mercury		> 1
Aerosols		> 1
Micro-organisms		> 1
Allergens		> 1

Source: Spengler and Sexton (1983)

products, formaldehyde, asbestos fibres, micro-organisms, aeroallergens and combustion byproducts (such as nitrogen oxides, sulphur oxides, carbon monoxide and polycyclic aromatic hydrocarbons). These pollutants are associated with a range of health problems, from mild irritation of nasal and mucous membranes to irreversible toxic and carcinogenic effects (Berglund *et al*, 1986).

Combustion of tobacco generates a large variety of organic and inorganic chemicals in both the gaseous and particulate phases. The nature of the emissions can vary greatly depending on such variables as temperature of combustion, smouldering rate, frequency of puffs, depth of inhalation, etc. The mainstream combustion products have been found to be significantly associated with adverse health effects in smokers, eg chronic obstructive lung disease and lung cancer (see Chapter 6). In recent years, there has been an increasing concern that exposure to 'sidestream' smoke in enclosed spaces may pose some risk to non-smokers. Current efforts to reduce ventilation rates, especially in public buildings, in order to conserve energy could amplify the presence of sidestream contaminants indoors (Leaderer *et al*, 1984).

Another important source of pollution indoors is the combustion of fuels, whether for cooking, water or space heating. In urban homes elevated concentrations of carbon monoxide have been recorded in kitchens having water heaters that are gas-fired (see, for example, Brunekreef *et al*, 1982). Unvented portable kerosene-fired space heaters emit carbon monoxide, carbon dioxide, nitrogen oxides, formaldehyde and fine particulate matter (Traynor *et al*, 1983). Wood-burning fireplaces produce several pollutants, the quantities of which depend on the type of wood burned and the design of the fireplace. Dasch (1982) reported the following emissions for 1 kg of wood burned: 10g particulates, 110g of carbon monoxide, 1.5g hydrocarbons, 0.7g of nitrogen oxides, and 370 μg of benzo-a-pyrene. Lipari *et al* (1984) found that the total aldehyde emissions from fireplaces range from 0.6 to 2.3 g/kg of wood burned. Formaldehyde, acetaldehyde and p-tolualdehyde are the major aldehydes emitted with formaldehyde comprising 21–42% of the total.

Biomass fuels are used by about half of the world's population as a major, often the only, source of domestic energy for cooking and heating. The emissions from these fuels are an important source of indoor air pollution, especially in rural communities in developing countries. These emissions contain important pollutants that adversely affect health – suspended particulate matter and polycyclic organic matter which includes a number of known carcinogens, especially benzo-a-pyrene, as well as gaseous pollutants such as carbon monoxide and formaldehyde (WHO, 1984; Smith, 1986).

The most important identified adverse consequences for human health from burning biomass fuels are chronic obstructive pulmonary disease and nasopharyngeal cancer (WHO, 1984). The particular adverse effects that are prevalent vary from one country and culture to another and so does the composition of the affected population. When infants and children are exposed, acute bronchitis and pneumonia occur because respiratory defences are impaired. These cause many infant and child deaths in some countries. If the emissions contain high concentrations of carcinogens, nasopharyngeal cancer is common among adults who have been exposed to emissions since infancy. In a few places, chronic carbon monoxide poisoning has been observed. In addition to its effects on the heart and nervous system, this exposes the developing foetus to the risk of birth defects. However, chronic obstructive pulmonary disease, the most commonly observed end result in India, is probably the most prevalent in almost all other settings too (WHO, 1984; Smith, 1986).

Several problems exist in attempting to regulate indoor air quality. It is essential to realize that a fundamental difference exists between indoor and outdoor air. Outdoor air is a public good in the sense that members of a community breathe the same ambient air. The rationale for government regulation of outdoor air pollution is the protection of the health of the members of the community on an equal basis. The situation is quite different for some indoor environments, especially private residences. If occupants foul the air in their own home, they are forced to breath it. If they attempt to improve its quality, by increasing ventilation for example, they bear the costs and enjoy the benefits. The problem of regulating indoor air quality is, therefore, highly dependent on public perception and awareness of the different risks involved.

Changes in atmospheric ozone and its environmental impact

Ozone, the triatomic molecule of oxygen (O_3), is present in the upper atmosphere in small amounts. If all of the ozone in the atmosphere was distributed uniformly over the surface of the earth at sea level, it would form a layer only about 3 mm thick. Most of the atmospheric ozone (about 95%) is found in the stratosphere, between 25 and 40 km above the earth's surface. Ozone in the stratosphere is the natural filter that absorbs and blocks the sun's short wavelength ultraviolet radiation that is harmful to life.

Ozone is a highly reactive chemical. It is produced by a complex photochemical process that begins with the photolysis of oxygen. Ozone is destroyed in several complex series of chemical reactions (as many as 200 reactions have been identified) involving oxygen, hydrogen, chlorine and nitrogen compounds, with the last three acting as catalysts at very small concentrations. To understand how easily the ozone layer can be disturbed, it is useful to recognize that ozone is actually only a trace constituent of the stratosphere; at its maximum concentration ozone makes up only a few parts per million of the air molecules. Furthermore, ozone destruction mechanisms are based on chain reactions in which one pollutant molecule may destroy many thousands of ozone molecules.

Life on earth is directly and indirectly dependent on solar radiation as its source of energy. All living organisms require energy in a usable chemical form for metabolic activities associated with growth, development and reproduction. The process of photosynthesis in green plants converts solar energy, carbon dioxide and water into carbohydrates rich in energy. Organisms that cannot produce their own energy through photosynthesis must participate in a food chain that includes plants that can. The spectrum of solar radiation is divided into three different parts: visible light (from 400 to 800 nm in wavelength; a nanometre (nm) is one-billionth of a metre), infrared radiation (from 800 to 20 000 nm) which is sensed as heat, and ultraviolet radiation (200 to 400 nm). The latter is divided into three regions: UV-A, with wavelengths in the range of 320 to 400 nm, UV-B, from 280 to 320 nm and UV-C, from 200 to 280 nm. Ecologically the most important part of the UV radiation is the UV-B, which causes sunburn in man and has other marked biological effects.

In general, ozone absorbs radiation strongly in the UV-C band and little, if at all, in the UV-A range. In the UV-B band, absorption by ozone is a sensitive function of wavelength, increasing as wavelength decreases (NRC, 1984). Other mechanisms besides that of ozone are involved in absorbing UV radiation in the stratosphere, which complicates analysis of the precise amount of harmful UV-B to reach ground level. The net result of these factors, however, is that, averaged over the year, more than 70% of the total UV-B to reach the planetary surface falls on the equatorial regions between latitudes 30°N and 30°S.

It has been realized that human activities result in the addition of certain compounds to the atmosphere, upsetting the balance between production and destruction processes of ozone, leading to changes in the total amounts of ozone above the earth's surface. The detection of a particular trend in ozone has become more complicated with the recognition that ozone in the stratosphere is actually under the simultaneous influence of a number of compounds of known or suspected anthropogenic origin. Among these are chlorofluorocarbons (CFCs) and nitrous oxide (each of which can act to reduce ozone) and nitrogen oxides from commercial subsonic aircraft, methane and carbon dioxide (each of which can increase ozone).

Chlorofluorocarbons (CFCs) are compounds used extensively in diverse applications, mainly because of their favourable physical and chemical characteristics. Their principal uses are as propellants and solvents in aerosol sprays, fluids in refrigeration and air-conditioning equipment; foam blowing agents in plastic foam production; and solvents, mainly in the electronics industry. Although there is a range of compounds called chlorofluorocarbons, trichlorofluoromethane (CFC-11) and dichlorodifluoromethane (CFC-12) are by far the most commonly used. These account for about 80% of world production of CFCs (Figure 3). In addition to chlorofluorocarbons, carbon tetrachloride and methyl chloroform are also important pollutants in relation to possible changes in the ozone layer. All these substances are relatively chemically inert in the lower atmosphere, but in the stratosphere they are converted by UV radiation to form the ozone-destroying catalyst, atomic chlorine.

At present, the concentration of chlorine in the stratosphere is set mainly by anthropogenic sources of CFC-11, CFC-12, carbon tetrachloride and methyl chloroform. The release rates of these gases have been estimated at about 260 million kg, 420 million kg, 120 million kg and 500 million kg per year, respectively (Prather et al, 1984). The atmospheric concentrations of CFC-11, CFC-12, CCl_4 and CH_3CCl_3 as of late 1985 were about 230 parts per trillion by volume (pptv), 400 pptv, 125 pptv and 130 pptv and are observed to be increasing at annual rates of about 5% for CFC-11 and CFC-12, 1% for CCl_4 and 7% for CH_3CCl_3 (WMO/NASA, 1985). The atmospheric residence times for CFC-11, CFC-12, CCl_4 and CH_3CCl_3 are calculated to be approximately 65, 110, 25–50, and 8 years, respectively (Ramanathan et al, 1985). Global chlorine budget formulations set an upper limit of about 3 parts per billion (ppbv) for tropospheric organic chlorine that, in turn, sets an approximate chlorine maximum value for the stratosphere. The values of total chlorine measured by Gallagher et al (1985) at altitudes of 15, 20, 25 and 30 km (2.6 ppbv at 15 km and 2.2–2.5 ppbv at higher altitudes) are consistent with model predictions and remain approximately constant with increasing altitude. The concentration of stratospheric chlorine is expected to rise eventually to about 10 ppbv if the release rates of chlorocarbons remain constant at the above mentioned rates. Although such chlorine emissions are thought to influence ozone primarily in the region above 30 km, Prather et al (1984) argue that important reductions in ozone could also take place below 30 km if the concentration of chlorine were to rise above that of nitrogen oxides (which cause an increase in ozone).

Emissions of bromine could also lead to a significant reduction in stratospheric ozone (Prather et al, 1984). The concentration of organic bromine is now between 0.025 and 0.030 ppbv, with methylbromide accounting for 30–70% of the present atmospheric burden. The lifetime of methylbromide is about three years and known industrial sources account for about half of the current releases. The gases ethylene

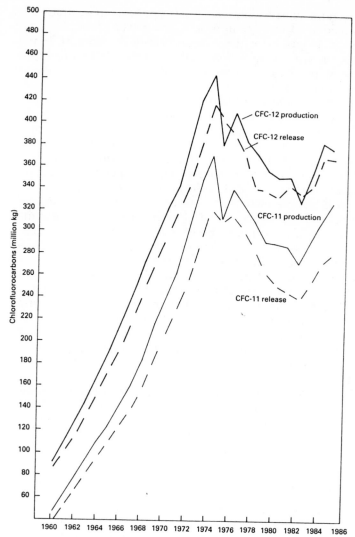

Figure 3 Production and release to the atmosphere of chlorofluorocarbons
After data given by UNEP, 1987

dibromide and bromofluorocarbons (FC-1301 and FC-1211) are mainly anthropogenic in origin and account for about 15% of the current bromine content of the atmosphere. The concentration of industrial bromocarbons is likely to rise in the future. Production of methylbromide has increased four- to fivefold since 1972 and may be anticipated to rise further if it replaces ethylene dibromide as a fumigant. The use of FC-1301 and FC-1211 as fire extinguishers is growing, and concentrations of these gases in the atmosphere appear to have increased at a rate higher than 10% per year from 1978 to 1983 (Prather *et al*, 1984). Residence times for FC-1301 and FC-1211 are long, about 110 years and 25 years, respectively. Associated concentrations may therefore be expected to increase to levels of about 0.010 and 0.003 ppbv in steady state, if release rates remain constant. Under present concentrations of chlorine and nitrogen oxides, an increase in bromine from 0.020 to 0.100 ppbv is calculated to cause a 4% reduction in the column density of ozone. Effects of chlorine and bromine are nearly additive. For a chlorine concentration of 16 ppb, the reduction in ozone is predicted to grow from 18% to 23%, as bromine is increased from 0.020 to 0.100 ppbv.

In the early 1970s it was thought possible that several hundred civil supersonic transport aircraft would eventually fly in the stratosphere and that these would be sufficient to reduce the average global ozone cover by 10% or more (through the release of nitrogen oxides in their exhaust gases). The abandonment of civil supersonic projects has removed this threat; there is little information on the frequency of stratospheric flights by military aircraft. The use of chlorine containing gases in space shuttles may also lead to a small reduction in ozone (NAS, 1975).

There is also the possible production of nitrogen oxides from fossil fuels combustion and from the production and use of nitrogen fertilizers on a sustained and intensive scale for raising agricultural production. To raise yields, nitrate fertilizer is often added to the soil or leguminous and other plants are grown which fix nitrogen from the atmosphere. Eventually, soil nitrate is converted back to nitrogen or nitrous oxide by the bacteria in soils and water. Several sets of data indicate that nitrous oxide concentration has been increasing at a rate of about 0.2% per year since about 1960 reaching a value of 300 ppbv in 1980. It is uncertain whether the increase is due to increased rate of combustion of fossil fuels or to denitrification of an increased fertilizer consumption. Nitrous oxide is important since it controls the concentration of nitrogen species in the stratosphere which in turn is crucial in controlling the effects of the chlorine cycle in the catalytic destruction of ozone (UNEP, 1984).

Finally, there are the risks related to nuclear explosions in the atmosphere. Such action would result in 'punching a hole' in the tropopause, propelling nitrogen oxides and ozone-attacking chlorine into the stratosphere. One of the environmental consequences of a global nuclear war that has been predicted is the significant reduction in the ozone layer (see Chapter 7).

Has the ozone layer been depleted?

Observing the changes in the chemistry of the stratosphere caused by the release of trace gases is difficult. The substances of interest are present in only trace amounts and many of them are difficult to measure. The approach to the problem has been to develop theoretical models of the physical and chemical processes thought to be important in the stratosphere. These models are used to calculate the concentrations of various species as a function of position and time.

Over the past few years research has led to considerable improvement in our understanding of the effects on stratospheric ozone of releases of chlorofluorocarbons and oxides of nitrogen. Concern regarding the possibility of a depletion of atmospheric ozone due to CFCs remains, although current estimates of such a reduction are lower than those reported a few years ago (WMO/NASA, 1985). The latest scientific findings (see for example, NRC, 1984; WMO/NASA, 1985; UNEP, 1986) indicate that if production of CFCs were to continue into the future at the current rate, the steady state reduction in total global ozone could be about or less than 3% over the next 70 years. If the release rate of CFCs should become twice the present level or if stratospheric chlorine reaches 15 ppbv, it has been predicted that there will be a 3% to 12% reduction of the ozone column, assuming that the annual rates of increase in the atmospheric concentrations of CO_2, N_2O and CH_4 continue at their present rate. It should be noted, however, that the calculated effects over longer periods are sensitive to assumed source gas scenarios and future changes in relative concentrations of these gases may significantly alter current estimates (WMO/NASA, 1985).

Current models of combinations of pollutants suggest that the reduction in total ozone to date resulting from human activities is less than 1%. Examination of historical data has not yet shown a significant trend in total ozone that can be ascribed to human activities. However, an ozone depletion of 2-3% per decade was observed in the upper stratosphere over the period 1970 to 1980. The impact of CFCs should be assessed in the context of a broad understanding of the variety of ways in which human activity can alter stratospheric composition. Ozone may be reduced by increasing levels of CFCs and nitrous oxide, but reductions might be offset in part by higher concentrations of carbon dioxide and perhaps methane.

Recent measurements have, however, indicated a considerable decrease (about 40%) in the total column of ozone in the lower stratosphere between 15 and 20 km above Antarctica during the spring period, mid-August to mid-November, since 1957, with most of the decrease occurring since the mid-1970s (Farman et al, 1985). Measurements have also indicated that there has been a significant decrease of ozone in the latitude belt between 45°S and 70°S. Such large decreases in ozone have not been observed at other latitudes nor during other seasons at Antarctica. However, recent analyses of data received from instruments aboard the Nimbus-7 Satellite show that the northern hemisphere is experiencing a decline in atmospheric ozone. The area of greatest decline is centred over Spitzbergen, halfway between Scandinavia and the North Pole. The average annual decline of ozone has been estimated at 1.5% to 2% (UNEP, 1986). Crutzen and Arnold (1986) suggest that nitric acid cloud formation in the Antarctic stratosphere is the major cause of the springtime 'ozone hole'.

Consequences of changes in atmospheric ozone

Substantial reductions in upper stratospheric ozone and associated increases in ozone in the lower stratosphere and upper troposphere might lead to undesirable global perturbations in the earth's climate. The vertical redistribution of ozone may warm the lower atmosphere and reinforce the greenhouse effect associated with an increase in carbon dioxide. A projected increase in global surface temperature of 1.5°C to 4.5°C could occur by as early as 2030. About half of this increase would be caused by greenhouse gases (including chlorofluorocarbons and ozone in the lower atmosphere); the other half by increase in carbon dioxide concentration in the atmosphere (Ramanathan et al, 1985; UNEP/ICSU/WMO, 1986).

Not all the effects of solar radiation are beneficial to humans, other animals or plants. Light in the UV-B band has been found to be absorbed by cells and to be associated with diverse and often deleterious biological effects. It is predicted that a 1% reduction in the amount of stratospheric ozone will lead to an increase of approximately 2% in UV-B radiation.

UV-B radiation can kill micro-organisms outright and in plants and animals it can destroy individual cells. The molecular structures of proteins and nucleic acids, which are the building blocks of plant and animal tissue and together make up the greater part of its dry weight, are damaged by UV radiation so that they can no longer properly perform their biological functions. Proteins are most sensitive to

UV radiation at 280 nm, and nucleic acids at 260 nm; but in each case radiation around these peak wavelengths produces similar, though lesser, damage (Nachtwey and Murphy, 1975).

Over a long period of time, organisms have evolved mechanisms to withstand the amounts of UV reaching the surface of the planet under normal conditions – that is, under the protection of the ozone layer. They use four principal means: protective covering and pigmentation, which screens off the UV radiation; behavioural adaptation to avoid the sunlight; photoreactivation or photoprotective mechanisms; and dark repair mechanisms. In these ways, nature may have adjusted to a fairly high degree of short-term variability in UV exposure (there are 10% to 20% fluctuations in ground level UV from one year to another); but any significant and sustained increase of UV could be expected to disturb the existing balance of life.

When plants are subjected to increased UV-B radiation in the laboratory, some crop species such as peanut and wheat prove fairly resistant, while others such as lettuce, tomato, soybean and cotton are sensitive. In general, seedlings are much more sensitive than vegetative structures like leaves (NAS, 1973). Where the amount of UV-B radiation is increased to simulate the effects of a 35% to 50% ozone reduction in the stratosphere, minor changes in leaf anatomy, disruption of photosynthesis and decreases in growth rates are observed in about half of the wild and crop species studied. One variety of soybean showed a yield loss of up to 25% following exposure to UV-B radiation simulating a 20% reduction in the ozone layer. UV-B radiation alters the reproductive capacity of some plants and also the quality of harvestable products (UNEP, 1986). The long-term biological implications, especially genetic changes, may be far reaching (Brabbam et al, 1975).

Preliminary investigations with phytoplankton, the microscopic floating plants which are the basis of the food chain in marine ecosystems, show that UV-B radiation reduces photosynthesis. Experiments off the coast of Africa suggest that under increased UV-B radiation photosynthesis of plankton may be inhibited by as much as 60% (Calkins and Nachtwey, 1975). Increased levels of UV-B radiation may also modify freshwater ecosystems by destroying micro-organisms, thus reducing the efficiency of natural water purification (Van Dyke and Thomson, 1975). UV-B radiation damages larval stages of fish, shrimp and crab. Studies show about 8% loss of the larval anchovy population for a 9% decrease in the ozone column (UNEP, 1986).

The effects of increased UV-B on animals other than man have received little attention, as it has generally been assumed that the radiation is absorbed by hair, feathers, scales, shells and normal skin pigments. Presumably these factors will continue to provide some degree of protection, but some animals may already be at their UV-B tolerance limit and further increases may produce harmful effects in animals that at present show no damage (Hsiao, 1975). Unlike humans, most animals will not expose themselves to full sunlight unless they have a way of preventing excessive amounts of light from reaching sensitive tissues. Most marine species hide during the day, in crevices in rocks, burrows or in deep water, coming out by night to browse on seaweed. Most terrestrial wild animals are nocturnal in habit, or keep in the shade of a forest during the day (Porter et al, 1975).

Human health is influenced by UV radiation in many ways, for example, by occurrence of sunburn, eye diseases, immunological changes and photoallergic reactions and skin diseases including skin cancer. Skin cancer stands out as one problem that will increase with increased UV-B irradiation. Epidemiological studies have shown that the incidence of non-melanoma skin cancer correlates with exposure to sunlight. While non-melanoma skin cancers occur in people with all skin types, the incidence is highest in light skinned people. Animal experiments have revealed that UV-B is the most effective wavelength region for carcinogenesis by UV radiation. The data indicate that increased incidence of non-melanoma skin cancer is to be expected to result from increased UV-B radiation. It has been estimated that for every 1% decrease in total ozone (ie 2% increase in UV-B), the incidence of basal cell carcinomas will increase by about 4% and the incidence of squamous cell carcinomas by about 6% (UNEP, 1986). Although the incidence of squamous cell carcinomas is only about 20% of the total, it is more invasive and lethal than basal cell carcinomas.

There are several indications that sunlight may also be one of the causative factors in the pathogenesis of malignant melanoma, which affects people of all skin types. These indications come from epidemiological and clinical observations which, because they deal with exposure to total sunlight, do not point to any particular wavelength range in the solar spectrum. Animal experiments indicating the effective wavelength range are not available. In cases where UV-B is involved, a decrease in stratospheric ozone might be expected to increase the incidence of melanoma. Epidemiological studies indicate that a 1% ozone depletion could increase the incidence of melanoma by 2%, assuming that the relationship between UV-B radiation and melanoma is causal (UNEP, 1986).

Recent research indicates that UV-B radiation alters several responses of the immunological system. The doses of UV-B radiation causing these changes are much smaller than those which are associated with an increased incidence of tumours. Some experimental results indicate that infectious diseases with a cutaneous component could be exacerbated by the increased UV-B radiation associated with ozone depletion. Herpes and the tropical skin disease leishmaniasis are two such diseases for which some evidence exists. Some evidence supports the hypothesis that melanoma of the eye could be increased by sunlight. Studies on animals and epidemiological data support the conclusion that UV-B is one of the causes of cataracts. Epidemiological studies indicate that a 1% ozone depletion would result in between 0.2 and 0.6% increase in cataract prevalence (UNEP, 1986).

Efforts to address the possible threats of the depletion of the ozone layer culminated in the adoption of the Vienna Convention for the Protection of the Ozone Layer at a Conference of Plenipotentiaries sponsored by the United Nations Environment Programme and by the Austrian Government on 22 March 1985. The Convention is the first global instrument to address an environmental threat to the earth's atmosphere that has been under debate in scientific and political circles for the past decade. The Convention's purpose is to promote exchanges of information, research and data on monitoring to protect human health and the environment against activities that have an adverse effect on the ozone layer. Further work concerning the formulation of a protocol on the control of chlorofluorocarbons is underway.

The impact of carbon dioxide and other trace gases on climate

For more than a hundred years scientists have been suggesting that slight changes in the chemical composition of the atmosphere could bring about major climatic changes. Until recently, focus has been particularly on worldwide release of carbon dioxide, as a result of burning fossil fuels and changes in land use that release carbon dioxide from forests and soils. It is now appreciated, however, that other trace gases, besides carbon dioxide, could also be responsible for climatic changes.

Carbon dioxide, along with water vapour, ozone and a variety of other trace gases, is a key factor in determining the thermal structure of the atmosphere. These so-called greenhouse gases are fairly transparent to solar radiation but relatively opaque to longer wavelength thermal radiation from the earth's surface. Thus, as the concentration of these gases increases in the air, the theory holds that the receipt of solar radiation at ground level will be but little reduced, whereas the loss of the thermal radiation from land and water surfaces to space will be significantly reduced, with the net result that there will be a surplus of energy available at the ground and surface air temperatures will rise.

Emission of carbon dioxide

Combustion of fossil fuels, especially coal, constitutes the main source of man-made carbon dioxide emissions. Current annual emissions of carbon dioxide due to fossil fuels have been estimated at about 5×10^9 tonnes of carbon (NRC, 1983). Terrestrial biota, especially forests and their soils, have been a net source of carbon dioxide for the atmosphere over the past century and are currently releasing between 1.8×10^9 and 4.5×10^9 tonnes of carbon annually, of which nearly 80% is due to deforestation, especially in the tropics (Woodwell et al, 1983). The annual release of carbon from the biota and soils exceeded the release from fossil fuels until about 1960.

Estimates of future carbon dioxide emissions vary widely according to future scenarios of energy consumption and the state of the biosphere, especially forests. It has been estimated that annual emissions of carbon dioxide due to fossil fuels might range between about 7 and 13×10^9 tonnes of carbon in the year 2000, and between 10 and 30×10^9 tonnes in 2030 (NRC, 1983). If deforestation increases in proportion to population, the biotic release of carbon would reach 9×10^9 tonnes per year early in the next century (Woodwell et al, 1983).

In the unperturbed atmosphere, the concentration of carbon dioxide is determined by the partitioning of CO_2 among the atmosphere, the oceans and the biosphere. Carbon circulates naturally among these reservoirs driven by physical and biological processes; this circulation is known as the geochemical cycle of carbon. The injection of carbon dioxide into the atmosphere by human activities may be viewed as a disturbance of this cycle. It has been estimated that between 40% and 60% of all carbon dioxide emitted into the atmosphere remains air borne; the rest finds its way into the different sinks, especially into the ocean.

The concentration of CO_2 in the atmosphere has varied over the ages; for example, there is evidence that it may have been about 200 parts per million by volume (ppmv) during the last ice age, some 18 000 years ago. Estimates of preindustrial CO_2 concentration in the atmosphere are in the range of 250 to 290 ppmv. Recent analyses of air trapped in glacier ice cores have revealed that the atmospheric CO_2 concentration aroung the year 1750 was 280 ppmv (Neftel et al, 1985). Precise and continuous measurements of atmospheric CO_2 concentration have been made at Mauna Loa Observatory, Hawaii, since 1958 and show a clear increase from 315 ppmv to 343 ppmv in 1984 (Figure 4). Similar records of increase in atmospheric carbon dioxide have also been obtained from other monitoring stations that started operation in later years.

In view of the uncertainties about future fossil fuel emissions, the biotic contribution and uptake of carbon dioxide by different sinks, several models have

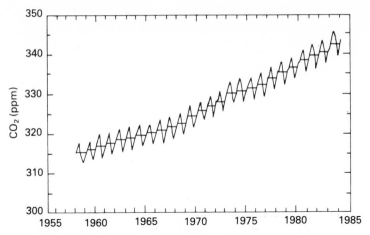

Figure 4 Concentration of atmospheric CO_2 at Mauna Loa Observatory, Hawaii
After WMO/NASA, 1985

been developed to estimate future atmospheric CO_2 concentrations. According to the different scenarios used in these models, the mean concentration of CO_2 in the atmosphere has been estimated to vary from 370 ppmv to as high as 2 100 ppmv in the year 2100 (NRC, 1983). However, if the present increase of CO_2 emission (an average of 1–2% per year since 1973) continues over the next four decades with a slackening of the rate of increase thereafter, a doubling of the preindustrial CO_2 concentration (ie 600 ppmv) would be reached towards the end of the next century (UNEP/ICSU/WMO, 1986).

Emission of other trace gases

Although there are many trace gases in the atmosphere that would contribute to the greenhouse effect, the most important ones are nitrous oxide (N_2O), methane (CH_4), chlorofluorocarbons (CFC-11 and CFC-12), ozone and water vapour (Ramanathan *et al*, 1985; Rasmussen and Khalil, 1986).

Nitrous oxide emissions result primarily from biological denitrification processes in soil and in the oceans. Human activities add indirectly to such emissions by increasing the use of nitrogen fertilizers. The annual total emissions of N_2O have been estimated at about 30 million tonnes, 25% of which are anthropogenic (Rasmussen and Khalil, 1986). Measurements of N_2O concentration in the atmosphere show an increase from 289 parts per billion by volume (ppbv) in 1970 to 303 ppbv in 1984 (Seidel and Keyes, 1983; NRC, 1983; WMO/NASA, 1985). It has been estimated that the N_2O concentration might reach 375 ppbv in the year 2030 (Ramanathan *et al*, 1985).

Chlorofluorocarbons, especially CFC-11 and CFC-12, have been emitted from industrial sources to the atmosphere during the past 50 years. It has been estimated that the annual emission of each of the CFCs is about 0.4 tonnes (Rasmussen and Khalil, 1986). Photochemical destruction, mainly in the stratosphere, and very slow uptake by the oceans are the only known significant sinks for chlorofluorocarbons. The concentration of CFC-11 in the atmosphere was about 150 parts per trillion by volume (pptv) in 1977; in 1985, the concentration reached about 230 pptv (Figure 5). The CFC-12 concentration rose from 260 pptv in 1977 to 400 pptv in 1985

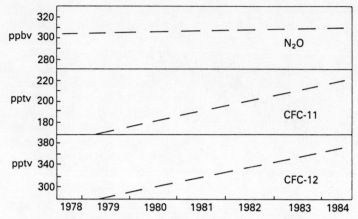

Figure 5 Concentration of N₂O, CFC-11 and CFC-12 in the atmosphere
After WMO/NASA, 1985

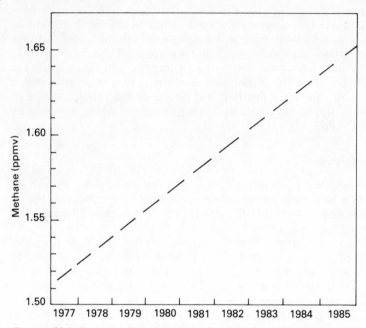

Figure 6 Globally averaged concentrations of methane from 1977 to 1985
After UNEP, 1986

(WMO/NASA, 1985). Ramanathan *et al* (1985) estimated that the concentration of CFC-11 and CFC-12 in the atmosphere might reach 1 100 pptv and 1 800 pptv respectively in the year 2030.

The principal sources of methane in the atmosphere appear to be enteric fermentation in ruminant animals, release from organic-rich sediments below shallow water bodies and rice paddies and production by termites and biomass burning. The total amount of methane emitted annually into the atmosphere has been estimated at about 550 million tonnes, about half of which comes from anthropogenic activities (Ehhalt, 1985; Rasmussen and Khalil, 1986). Most of the methane emitted into the atmosphere (about 90%) is removed through oxidation, the balance (about 40–50 tonnes annually) remains air borne. The concentration of methane in the atmosphere in 1980 was about 1.64 ppmv in the northern hemisphere and about 1.55 ppmv in the southern hemisphere (Ehhalt, 1985; Ramanathan *et al*, 1985). This approximate 7% difference between the two hemispheres indicates that much of the atmospheric methane originates in northern latitudes. Globally averaged concentrations of CH_4 (Figure 6) increased from about 1.52 ppmv in 1977 to about 1.65 ppmv in 1985 (UNEP, 1986). Ehhalt *et al* (1983) concluded that the atmospheric concentration of methane increased by about 0.5% per year between 1965 and 1975 and by 1–2% per year between 1978 and late 1980. Ramanathan *et al* (1985) estimate that the methane concentration in the atmosphere might reach 2.34 ppmv in the year 2030.

Changes in climate

The results obtained from most numerical models suggest that a doubling of the carbon dioxide concentration in the atmosphere would lead to an increase in the mean global air temperature of about 1.5°C to 4.5°C (NRC, 1983). The doubling of other trace gases in the atmosphere would lead to an additional increase in the temperature of about 2.6°C (as calculated from data given by NRC, 1983).

An evaluation of results from recent climate models indicates that the increase in global mean equilibrium surface temperature caused by increases of CO_2 and other

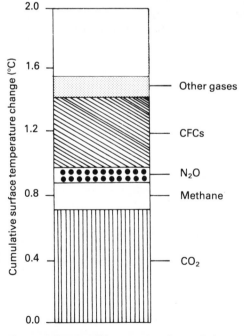

Figure 7 One possible scenario of cumulative surface warming by 2030 due to increase in carbon dioxide and other greenhouse gases

greenhouse gases equivalent to a doubling of the atmospheric CO_2 concentration is likely to be in the range of 1.5°C to 4.5°C (UNEP/ICSU/WMO, 1986). Values beyond this range exist but are now usually discarded as non-feasible (Figure 7).

An analysis of surface temperature records during the past 100 years indicates a global warming from the late 19th century to about 1940 and a cooling until the mid-1960s. Since then, the world as a whole appears to have warmed. These analyses suggest that the global mean temperature has increased 0.3–0.7°C in the past 100 years. This increase in temperature cannot be ascribed in a statistically rigorous manner to the increasing concentration of CO_2 and other greenhouse gases in the atmosphere, although the magnitude is within the range of predictions (UNEP/ICSU/WMO, 1986). Seidel and Keyes (1983) pointed out that during 1970–80, the temperature increased by a total of 0.24°C. Of that increase, 0.14°C was attributed to a 12 ppmv rise in CO_2. The remaining 0.10°C was attributed to other greenhouse gases. However, Idso (1985) pointed out that the net warming of the northern third of the globe over the period 1880–1980 has been about an order of magnitude less than the predicted 3–6°C warming and that for the last half of this period – when concentrations of both CO_2 and other trace gases were rapidly increasing – the temperature trend has been generally downward.

Environmental impact of changes in climate

Changes in climate that may result from increases in atmospheric carbon dioxide and other trace gases may affect the environment in a number of ways. However, the question of how climate interacts with environment and society is complex. Since it is not possible at present to make a detailed and accurate prediction of future climate, without such prediction it is only possible to make speculations about the impact of changes in climate (Lemons, 1985; UNEP/ICSU/WMO, 1986).

Two of the consequences of climate warming could be a melting of the drifting sea ice in the Arctic Ocean and a melting of the West Antarctic ice sheet. The effects of the former would be to substantially increase sea surface temperature and consequently shift major climatic zones 200 km or more northward. It has been estimated that a global warming of 1.5°C to 4.5°C would lead to a sea level rise of 20 to 140 cm (UNEP/ICSU/WMO, 1986). The major contributing factor to such a rise would be the thermal expansion of ocean water. The consequences of this rise of the world's sea level would be the flooding of many coastal and lowland areas. Considerable debate exists concerning the likelihood of the Antarctic ice sheet melting. Recent studies conclude that a catastrophic collapse of the West Antarctic, which could further contribute to a rise in sea level, is not judged to be imminent (UNEP/ICSU/WMO, 1986).

The distribution of the world's biomass depends primarily on climate, particularly temperature and precipitation. Long-term climatic changes would be significant for the tropics and the Arctic tundra. In semiarid regions, trees are susceptible to decreases in precipitation. In wet forests, trees are vulnerable to insect pests and infestations are influenced by temperature and precipitation. In the Arctic tundra a warming trend would cause a reduction in the permafrost; consequently, trees would grow further poleward. Further, the upper layers of the tundra peat would dry out and oxidation and decay of organic matter would increase. The additional carbon dioxide released would enhance warming, thereby creating a positive feedback (Lemons, 1985). Although the understanding of ecosystem ecology is sufficient to predict these types of general changes, such changes may have to be evaluated in the context of increasing human intervention in natural ecosystems.

The stability and distribution of food production could be greatly affected by climate warming. In general, the direct effects of enhanced CO_2 concentrations on crop yield are beneficial. It is estimated from laboratory experiments that, in the absence of climatic change, a doubling of the CO_2 concentration would cause a 0–10% increase in growth and yield of maize, sorghum and sugar cane, and a 10–50% increase for wheat, rice and soya bean, depending on the specific crop and growing conditions (see, eg Kimball, 1983; UNEP/ICSU/WMO, 1986). Kimball and Idso (1983) found that a doubling of CO_2 concentration could reduce transpiration by 34%, or in other words, plant water use efficiency would double for a doubling of the atmospheric CO_2 content. On the other hand, crops are substantially affected by changes in climate. Crop impact analyses show that warmer average temperatures are detrimental to both wheat and maize yields in the mid-latitude core crop regions of North America and Western Europe. Given current technology and crop varieties, a sudden warming of 2°C with no change in precipitation might reduce average yields by 3% to 17% (UNEP/ICSU/WMO, 1986). Warmer and longer growing seasons induced by climatic changes could enable many insect pests to pass through an additional one to three generations. The exponential increase of some pest populations under the new favourable environments could increase losses due to insects and make control more difficult.

Models of agricultural production and trade suggest that numerous feedback mechanisms exist in many regions through which agriculture can adjust and adapt to environmental change. Over the long term, food production in such areas appears more sensitive to technology, price or policy changes than to climatic changes, and these factors are largely controllable, whereas climate is not. However, for some regions, particularly the lands marginal for food production in the developing world, agriculture may be acutely sensitive to climatic changes, as evidenced by the tolls taken by year to year variation in climate. If these regions can adopt measures to reduce further the ill effects of current, short-term climatic variability, it is likely that they will be better prepared to adapt to any adverse effects of future changes in climate, should they occur (UNEP/ICSU/WHO, 1986; UNEP/IIASA, 1986).

Acidic deposition

During the past decade we have become increasingly aware of both the atmospheric and ecological impacts of air pollution. The products of fossil fuel combustion, vehicular traffic and other industrial processes have been linked to visibility reduction, to long-range and transboundary transport of air pollution and to acid precipitation. Further, many of these emissions are of acidic nature and on deposition at the surface of the earth, they are having adverse effects on man-made structures and on sensitive aquatic and terrestrial ecosystems. Resulting damage and losses are significant from an economic, environmental, cultural and aesthetic point of view. Acidic deposition ranks high among such important environmental issues as the global increase of carbon dioxide in the atmosphere and the effect of chlorofluorocarbons on the ozone layer. However, the acidic deposition problem is somewhat unusual among these, in that its consequences are already evident, its adverse effects are already documented and its impact is very real to those living in affected regions.

Acidic deposition means the input from the atmosphere to the surface of the earth of substances which cause, or have the potential to cause, increased acidity and associated effects in the environment. The term 'acidic deposition' is scientifically more accurate than the catchword 'acid rain' commonly used, since pollutants can be transferred from the atmosphere to the earth in a 'wet' and/or 'dry' form. Wet deposition refers to material transferred from the atmosphere by rain, snow or other precipitation forms, while dry deposition refers to all material deposited from the atmosphere in the absence of wet precipitation (eg in the form of fine particles etc). Acidification of the environment can occur in different ways. Some compounds, like sulphuric and nitric acids in precipitation, contribute free hydrogen ions, or 'acidity', directly to receptors on which they fall. Other pollutants, such as sulphur dioxide or ammonium ion in deposition (wet or dry), may cause an increase in hydrogen ions through chemical or biological reaction in receptors. In other cases, pollutant ions may displace hydrogen ions from soil mineral lattices; these hydrogen ions subsequently find their way into surface or groundwaters increasing their acidity.

Acidic deposition is not a new phenomenon – the term 'acid rain' was first coined by a chemist, Robert Angus Smith, who described pollution in Manchester, England, over a century ago (McCormick, 1985). What is new is that perception of the acidic deposition problem has changed over the years. Until recently the impact of air pollution was considered to be primarily local. Damage in the neighbourhood of large power plants and smelters was relatively easy to detect. Little thought was given to more distant effects. But changes in precipitation composition and ecological damage far from sources, accompanying increasing emissions and the building of taller stacks, have focused attention strongly on the larger scale aspects of pollution in recent years. Pollutants from a particular source are deposited from the near source region out to a distance which depends on the pollutant's atmospheric residence time. In the case of sulphur and nitrogen compounds, deposition occurs out to at least a few thousand kilometres and the impacts of that deposition may be felt over the entire distance.

Acidic deposition was first raised as an international problem by the Scandinavian countries at the United Nations Conference on the Human Environment in Stockholm in 1972; it has now developed into a major international environmental issue. A great deal of research has been carried out over the last decade and ample information has been available through the activities of the Cooperative Programme for Monitoring and Evaluation of Long-range Transmission of Air Pollutants in Europe (EMEP), under the Convention on Long-range Transboundary Air Pollution of 1979 and through activities conducted in accordance with the Memorandum of Intent Between the Government of Canada and the Government of the United States of America concerning Transboundary Air Pollution. Furthermore, a special conference on acidification of the environment was held in Stockholm in 1982, followed by a second major international conference held in Munich in 1984. Both conferences reviewed and assessed a large amount of up to date scientific information.

The formation and distribution of acidic deposition

The sulphur and nitrogen compounds emitted from power plants, industrial processes, vehicular transport, domestic sources (mainly from the burning of fossil fuels) etc are the main sources of acidifying substances in the atmosphere. Natural processes also put sulphur and nitrogen compounds into the air, besides man-made sources. Estimates of such natural contribution vary between 50 and 284 million tonnes of sulphur per year in the form of sulphur oxides (Cullis and Hirschler, 1980; Bolin and Cook, 1983; Möller, 1984a) and between 20 and 90 million tonnes of nitrogen a year in nitrogen oxides (Bolin and Cook, 1983). In comparison, human activity results in emissions of sulphur oxides between 75 and 100 million tonnes of sulphur a year (Bolin and Cook, 1983; Möller, 1984b). Fossil fuel combustion and industrial activities yield about 20 million tonnes of nitrogen a year. So, despite the differences in estimates on natural sources, it can be concluded that man-made and natural emissions of sulphur are, globally, of the same order of magnitude, although in areas of concern in Europe and North America the ratio of natural to man-made emissions may be as high as 1 to 20. Similarly, pollution from nitrogen oxides is also of the same order compared to natural emissions (see eg Brady and Selle, 1985).

The mechanisms by which the emitted pollutants, mainly sulphur dioxide and nitrogen oxides, are transformed into acidifying substances in both the gaseous and

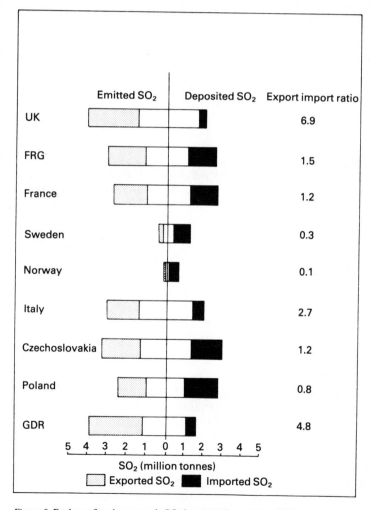

Figure 8 Budget of anthropogenic SO_2 in selected countries, 1981

liquid phases are complex and incompletely understood. The concentration and distribution of acidic deposits, wet and dry, are determined by many interacting processes, eg the transport and dispersal of the parent pollutants, the role of oxidizing agents such as hydrocarbon derivatives and ozone, meteorological factors such as solar radiation, cloud and rainfall etc.

Not all the pollution is acid rain, ie sulphuric and nitric acids dissolved in precipitation. Some of it happens when the sulphur and nitrogen oxides as such fall out on the land as dry deposition. In general this tends to be the main form of the pollution near its source and the longer the gases stay in the air, the more likely they are to go through the complex changes that will turn them into wet deposition, to fall perhaps thousands of kilometres from where they began their journey. Wet deposition rates are fairly well known, but dry deposition is harder to assess and rates remain more uncertain. Both types of deposition can be intercepted by vegetation canopies. The canopies of evergreen forests, in particular, can be subjected to high deposition rates.

Each country gets part of its acid fall-out from its own pollutants, but receives the rest on the winds from neighbouring countries. EMEP has worked out estimates of how much sulphur is emitted, and how much deposited, in individual European countries (Figure 8). This reveals which of them are net importers and which are net exporters of air pollutants (EMEP, 1981). Several European countries, the USA and Canada have established monitoring stations in the last decade to determine the composition of acidic precipitation. On a more global scale, the WMO Background Air Pollution Monitoring Network (BAPMoN), which started operation in 1972 and is now supported by GEMS, involved 95 participating countries at the end of 1986. About 70 of these had operational stations and 55 were regularly reporting data related to precipitation chemistry. One outcome of such intensive monitoring activity has been the improved delineation of areas receiving acidic precipitation (Figure 9). Georgii (1982) reviewed the chemical composition of precipitation as measured by BAPMoN. He pointed out that the spatial distribution of pH of precipitation over Europe and Eastern USA did not change significantly between 1972 and 1976. In the period from 1976 to 1979 no change was detected in the pH of precipitation in Europe, while in the USA an increase in acidity of precipitation was recorded. Since about 1980, average annual patterns for wet deposition in the USA have shown few significant changes, reflecting the fact that emissions have remained relatively constant (EPA, 1984). Recent studies have indicated that acidic precipitation occurs also in Japan, India, China and some developing countries in Asia and Africa (see Harte, 1983; McCormick, 1985; Zhao and Sun, 1986). In Hungary, both wet and dry acidic deposition occur, especially in winter (KSH, 1986).

The impact of acidic deposition

The effects of acidic deposition on the environment vary from certain to speculative. But there is a considerable body of evidence to show that acidic deposition poses a threat to various economic resources: fisheries, forestry, agriculture and wildlife. All areas subject to acidic deposition, however, are not equally susceptible. To a large extent, the capacity of a particular area to remain relatively unaffected by acidic deposition is determined by the composition and natural acidity or alkalinity of the soil and underlying geological formations. The higher the capacity for natural buffering in the soil and water, the greater the ability to neutralize acidic compounds. It is possible, therefore, to define regions of high, moderate or low

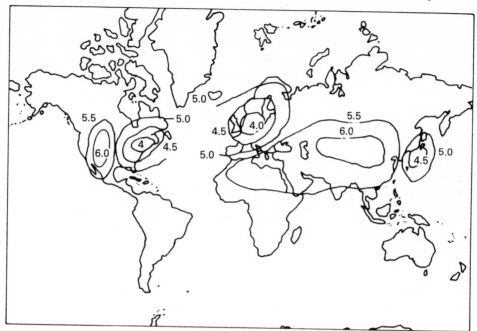

Figure 9 Estimated distribution of precipitation pH in the northern hemisphere for the late 1970s
After Whelpdale, 1983

sensitivity to acidic deposition. Effects will, of course, be greatest in high sensitivity areas exposed to high deposition.

Lakes and rivers were the first victims of acidic deposition to become evident. Hundreds of lakes in parts of Scandinavia, the north-east USA, south-east Canada and south-west Scotland have turned acidic. In Sweden damage to fisheries attributed to acidification has been observed in 2 500 lakes. Out of 5 000 lakes in southern Norway, 1 750 have lost all their fish and 900 others are seriously affected. In the USA damage from acidic deposition has occurred in roughly 50% of the 219 high elevation lakes surveyed in the Adirondacks (Brady and Selle, 1985). In Ontario, Canada, over 300 000 hectares of about 11 400 lakes are considered to be at moderate to high risk, representing a potential loss of 30% or more of the total provincial resource of at least five major fish communities. Most vulnerable were brook trout, lake trout and bass (Environment Canada, 1986).

Acidification of sensitive water bodies has serious biological consequences. Decomposition rates of some organic substrates (eg lignin, cellulose) are reduced. Substratal changes in the species composition of communities of primary producers occur. The richness of phytoplankton species is reduced, while biomass and productivity of phytoplankton are not reduced by acidification. The biomass of herbivorous and predaceous zooplankton is probably also reduced because of reductions in numbers of organisms and/or reductions in their average size. Many benthic invertebrates such as species of snails, clams, crayfish etc are intolerant of low pH and are seldom found in acidified lakes (Dillon *et al*, 1984). At early stages of acidification there are increases in rates of accumulation of trace metals in fish tissue. The ultimate effect, the loss of fisheries, is preceded by changes at the population level, such as reduction in abundance and failure in recruitment of particular age classes (Dillon *et al*, 1984).

The impact of acidic deposition on drinking water quality involves the potential for acidified waters to leach toxic and other metals (eg lead, mercury, cadmium, aluminium and copper) from watersheds (eg soils) and water distribution systems. The presence of these metals in drinking water can result in a number of serious human health impacts (Middleton and Rhodes, 1984; McDonald, 1985; Grimvall *et al*, 1986). Acidification of groundwater supplies has been reported from many countries. In some areas subject to acidic deposition, the pH of groundwater is less than 4.5 and concentrations of aluminium, copper, zinc and cadmium are often 10 to 100 times larger than in neutral groundwater (ECE, 1984).

Soils are normally much better able to resist acidification than lakes, rivers and streams, and so can take much more acid without noticeable ecological drawbacks. Their vulnerability differs depending on their type, the kind of bedrock they cover and the use to which man puts them. The most vulnerable lands are those that have bedrocks poor in lime, covered with shallow layers of soil containing low amounts of protective substances. The acidification of soils is not merely due to acidic deposition; it arises from a natural process as well as the result of biological processes within the soils. Normally the acids thus produced are neutralized during the weathering of mineral soil particles but, depending on the composition of the soils, their capacity to neutralize more than a definite amount of acidity is limited. Acidification of soils may cause nutrients like potassium, magnesium, calcium and other micronutrients to leach more rapidly out of the soil, decreasing soil fertility. Aluminium concentrations would rise, just as they do in water, thus damaging plants and reducing the availability of phosphorus to them. Metals like cadmium, zinc, lead, mercury, iron and manganese spread through the environment more readily with acidification.

Interpretation of available research results suggests that the net response of a crop to acidic deposition is the result of the interaction between the positive effects of sulphur and nitrogen fertilization, the negative effects of acidity and the interaction between these factors and other environmental conditions such as soil type and the presence of other pollutants. Available experimental results appear to indicate that the effects of acidic deposition on crops are minimal and that when a response occurs it may be positive or negative (Irving, 1983).

Acidic deposition can affect forests directly by acting on the foliage or indirectly by changing the properties of the soil supporting forest growth. Sensitivity varies with species and the buffering capacity of soils. Coniferous forest soils are believed to be especially vulnerable (Environment Canada, 1986). Visible injuries to pine forests in Canada have been observed in connection with growing season concentrations of around 45 μg of sulphur dioxide per m^3. Similar effects have been reported in Czechoslovakia (ECE, 1984).

In FR Germany, it was estimated in 1984 that about 50% of the total forest area (3.7 million ha) was damaged to varying degrees. About 33% is slightly damaged, 16% damaged and 1.5% severely damaged and dead (Blank, 1985). This 'die-back' of the forests (mainly spruce) in FR Germany has been attributed to different reasons: acidic deposition, soil acidification, effects of atmospheric sulphur oxides and nitrogen oxides, ozone (and possibly other photo-oxidants), climate, pathogens and the effect of ammonium and other nitrogen compounds (ECE, 1984; Blank, 1985; Binns, 1985; Nihlgard, 1985). Similar die-back of forests has been reported from other European countries. At the end of 1985, it was estimated that about seven million hectares of forests in 15 European countries had been affected to varying degrees (McCormick, 1985). FR Germany is the most seriously affected country followed by Switzerland, Austria, the Netherlands, France, Belgium, Denmark and Sweden. In Eastern Europe, Czechoslovakia is the most seriously affected country (between 200 000 and 300 000 hectares of forests are severely damaged and destroyed). Extensive forest damage has also been reported from Poland, the German Democratic Republic, Romania and Hungary.

Acidic deposition accelerates corrosion in most materials used in the construction of buildings, bridges, dams, industrial equipment, water supply networks, underground storage tanks, hydroelectric turbines and power and telecommunications cables. It can also severely damage ancient monuments, historic buildings, sculptures, ornaments and other important cultural objects. Some of the world's greatest cultural treasures, including the Parthenon in Athens and Trajan's Column in Rome, are being eaten away by acidic fall-out. Tests have shown that materials corrode between twice and ten times as fast in polluted urban and industrial atmospheres as they do in the countryside. Carbon steel, zinc and galvanized steel, copper, nickel and nickel-plated steel, sandstone and limestone all corrode faster as the amount of sulphur dioxide in the air increases (ECE, 1981). On the other hand, materials such as aluminium and stainless steel are only slightly affected. A number of national and international studies have shown that economic losses due to atmospheric corrosion caused by sulphur compounds are considerable. Some studies carried out in the 1970s have estimated such losses to range from $2 to $10 per capita per year or between about 0.10 to 0.23% of GNP (ECE, 1981, 1984).

From the standpoint of human health, acidic deposition is of little direct significance (Moghissi, 1986). The data available indicate a minimal risk to healthy individuals associated with inhalation of sulphuric acid aerosols at ambient concentrations. In sensitive groups (eg asthmatics, children and adults with a hypersensitive respiratory system) the possibility of diverse pulmonary effects from short-term exposures to 0.1 mg/m^3 of sulphuric acid aerosols cannot be excluded (WHO, 1986). Acidic deposition may, however, indirectly affect human health by two main pathways: a possible deleterious effect on drinking water quality or possible altered intake of certain trace elements caused by increased trace element content in fish, shellfish, game or crops (Moghissi, 1986; WHO, 1986).

Reducing and controlling acidic deposition

The damage to water can be alleviated by adding lime to lakes, rivers and streams and/or their catchment areas. Many chemicals such as caustic soda, sodium carbonate, slaked lime, limestone or dolomite can be used to counteract the acidity. Slaked lime and limestone are the most popular. Sweden began a liming programme in 1976 and by 1986 about 3 000 Swedish lakes had been limed at a total cost of about $25 million (McCormick, 1985).

Liming alleviates some of the symptoms of acidification; but it is no real cure, it is not practicable for many lakes and running waters and does not attack the causes of the problem. It should, however, be considered as an interim measure which offers some defence until the emissions of pollutants can be reduced to a satisfactorily low level. Liming can also be used to counterbalance the increasing acidification of cropland. Lime has, of course, been used to improve acidic and calcium-poor soils for centuries. A Swedish test programme was launched in 1982 to study ways of countering soil and groundwater acidification.

The only lasting solution to the acidic deposition problem is to control the emission of pollutants causing the acidity. There are four main routes to cutting such emissions: using low pollutant fuels, preventing the formation of pollutants during combustion, screening pollutants from exhaust and flue gases and energy conservation. Using low sulphur coal and oil is the simplest way of reducing sulphur emissions from fossil fuels, but supplies of low sulphur fuels (especially oil) are limited. Taking sulphur out of fuel oils would cost about $20 to $40 for every tonne of oil, depending on the type of the oil and the size of the plant, among other factors. This would add about $5–10 to the cost of every megawatt/hour of electricity produced (in 1980 prices), adding up to 10% to 20% to the cost of electricity. Industry, on the other hand, puts the costs at $40 to $85 for every tonne of oil (CONCAWE, 1981). To look at it another way, the estimated cost of removing each tonne of sulphur from oil ranges from $1 202 to $2 265, at 1980 cost level (ECE, 1984).

Coal contains two kinds of sulphur – pyrite (iron sulphide) and organic sulphur. Washing coal, after first crushing and grinding it, removes pyrite sulphur. The cost of this mechanical process is estimated to be $1 to $6 per tonne of coal (OECD, 1982; Torrens, 1982). On average it will remove about half of the pyrite, though at best the process can be made to remove up to 90% of it from some coals. The chemical methods are more effective, but also more expensive and have not yet been fully developed. They can remove organic sulphur as well as pyrite. The cost of getting rid of 90% to 95% of the pyrite and half of the organic sulphur would be around $20 to $30 per tonne of coal. The extra costs of coal washing range from less than $1 to about $3 per megawatt/hour, adding about 1–6% to electricity costs. Chemical desulphurization would cost much more, about $8 to $12 per megawatt/hour, and this would add between 15% and 25% to electricity costs.

The burning of fuels can be controlled to reduce the amounts of sulphur and nitrogen compounds released into the gas stream. Methods developed so far have been aimed to reducing both sulphur and nitrogen oxides emissions. Most have just been introduced, or are about to be introduced commercially. Nitrogen oxide emissions can be reduced by changing the ways of burning fuel, particularly in heat and power stations. One of the main ideas for doing this is to reduce the combustion temperature to below 1 500°C and/or to allow only low intakes of air. Such changes could cut in half the amount of nitrogen oxides emitted.

Various 'fluidized bed' technologies offer a promising way of reducing pollution by both sulphur and nitrogen oxides in heat and power plants. Coal is burned in a 'bed' of tiny particles that bubbles like a boiling fluid. Sulphur dioxide emissions can be controlled effectively by adding limestone or dolomite to the bed. And because the fuel is burned at a much lower temperature than in conventional boilers, nitrogen oxide emissions are substantially reduced.

Another approach is to remove the pollutants created when the fuel is burned from the gases just afterwards, before they are pushed out into the air. Sulphur oxides can be taken out by a process called scrubbing. Wet scrubbing, the kind predominantly used at present, typically costs between $5 and $10 per megawatt/hour at 1982 prices, depending on how efficiently the pollution is removed (Rubin, 1982), and would normally increase the cost of electricity by around 8% to 18% (Highton and Chadwick, 1982).

Removing sulphur from fuel and gases creates waste products – solids and slurries – which have to be disposed of properly to avoid pollution of surface and groundwaters and/or soils. This problem grows as emission controls are increased.

Several studies have been carried out to estimate the costs and benefits of controlling emissions that lead to acidic deposition (see, for example, ECE, 1984, 1985). These suggest that the benefits would outweigh the costs, but the uncertainties surrounding the estimates are so wide that they cannot be used to provide a quantitative and reliable evaluation of the balance between costs and benefits. Moreover, there are other factors that complicate such analyses. One – common to many other instances of damage to shared natural resources – is that the countries which would benefit from the reduced pollution would often be different from those that would have to bear the cost of cutting it back. Another is that all the estimates of benefits assume that the damage caused by acid rain can readily be reversed if enough pollution control is implemented – and in reality this may not be so. It may be a long time before the ecological damage, in particular, begins to be reversed. Unfortunately, scientific information on the recovery process is extremely scanty.

So far the acidification of the environment has been seen as a regional problem, restricted to parts of Europe and North America. But other industrialized areas are exposed to the same problem, although there is too little information to assess the magnitude of the impacts. Besides, the problem may well spread to new areas as a result of rapid industrialization and the growth of cities in other parts of the world, particularly developing countries. So it is important that areas affected by acidic deposition (wet or dry) and susceptible to damage from acidification are identified as soon as possible. If they are, the damage could be mitigated, or even avoided, at a minimum cost to society by initiating research and applying what we already know about pollution control and environmentally appropriate energy production technologies at an early stage.

Evidence of the determination of different countries to work together and take the measures needed to cut back emissions to an acceptable level has already been provided by the signing of the Convention on Long-range Transboundary Air Pollution in Geneva in 1979. By March 1985, 30 countries and the European Community had ratified the convention. The Ministerial Conference on Acidification of the Environment, held in Stockholm in 1982, helped to speed up the ratification of the convention and to undertake a number of activities to control sulphur and nitrogen emissions. One of the most substantive results of the Stockholm Conference was the Nordic proposal for a mutual 30% reduction of SO_2 emissions in the 10 years 1983–93, calculated from emission levels in 1980. In 1985, a protocol to the 1979 Convention on Long-range Transboundary Air Pollution on the reduction of sulphur emissions or their transboundary fluxes by at least 30% was signed in Helsinki.

References

BENNETT, B. G. *et al* (1985). Urban air pollution worldwide, *Environmental Science and Technology*, **19**, 298

BERGLUND, B. *et al* (1986). Indoor air quality, *Environment International*, Special issue, **12**, 1-4

BINNS, W.O. (1985). Effects of acid deposition on forests and soils, *The Environmentalist*, **5**, 279

BLANK, L.W. (1985). A new type of forest decline in Germany, *Nature*, **314**, 311

BOLIN, B. and COOK, R. B. (1983). *The Major Biogeochemical Cycles and their Interactions*, SCOPE Report No 21, J. Wiley, Chichester

BRABBAM, D. *et al* (1975). Plant Responses to UV Radiation,*Climatic Assessment Programme*, Monograph 5, Department of Transportation, Washington, DC, Part 1, Chapter 4

BRADY, G.L. and SELLE J.C. (1985). Acid rain: the international response, *International Journal of Environmental Studies*, **24**, 217

BRUNEKREEF, B. *et al* (1982). Indoor carbon monoxide pollution in the Netherlands, *Environment International*, **8**, 193

CALKINS, J. and NACHTWEY, D.S. (1975). UV effects on bacteria, algae, protozoa, and aquatic invertebrates, *Climatic Assessment Programme*, Monograph 5, Department of Transportation, Washington, DC, Part 1, Chapter 5/1.

CONCAWE (1981). *Direct Desulphurization of Residual Petroleum Oil: Investments and Operating Costs*, Study Group for Conservation of Clean Air and Water of Oil Companies (CONCAWE), The Hague

CRUTZEN, P.J. and ARNOLD, F. (1986). Nitric acid cloud formation in the cold Antarctic stratosphere; a major cause for the springtime ozone hole, *Nature*, **327**, 651

CULLIS, C.F. and HIRSCHLER, M.M. (1980). Atmospheric sulphur: natural and man-made sources, *Atmospheric Environment*, **14**, 1262

DASCH, J.M. (1982). Particulate and gaseous emissions from wood-burning fireplaces, *Environmental Science and Technology*, **16**, 639

DILLON, P.J. *et al* (1984). Acidic deposition: effects on aquatic ecosystems, *Critical Reviews in Environment Control*, **13**, 167

ECE (1981). *The Influence of Sulphur Pollutants on Atmospheric Corrosion of Important Materials*, Report ENV/IEB/WG.1/R1 and Add. 1, Economic Commission for Europe, Geneva

ECE (1984). *Airborne Sulphur Pollution*, Air Pollution Studies No 1, Economic Commission for Europe, Geneva

ECE (1985). *Air Pollution Across Boundaries*, Air Pollution Studies No 2, Economic Commission for Europe, Geneva

EHHALT, D.H. (1985). Methane in the global atmosphere, *Environment*, **27**, 6

EHHALT, D.H. *et al* (1983). On the temporal increase of tropospheric methane, *Journal of Geophysical Research*, **88**, 8442

EMEP (1981). *Fourth Technical Report from the Western Meteorological Synthesizing Centre*, Norwegian Meteorological Institute, Oslo, Report MSC.W/81

ENVIRONMENT CANADA (1986). *State of the Environment Report for Canada*, Environment Canada, Ottawa

EPA (1984). *The Acidic Deposition Phenomenon and its Effects*, US Environmental Protection Agency, Washington, DC

FARMAN, J.C. *et al* (1985). *Nature*, **315**, 207

GALLAGHER, C.C. *et al* (1985). Total chlorine content in the lower stratosphere, *Journal of Geophysical Research*, **90**, D6, 10747

GEMS (1984). *Urban Air Quality: 1973-1980*, World Health Organization, Geneva

GEORGII, H.W. (1982). *Review of the Chemical Composition of Precipitation as Measured by the WMO BAPMoN*, World Meterological Organization, Geneva

GRIMVALL, A. *et al* (1986). Quality trends of public water supplies in Sweden, *Water Quality Bulletin*, **11**, 6

HARTE, J. (1983). An investigation of acid precipitation in Qinghai Province, China, *Atmospheric Environment*, **17**, 403

HIGHTON, N.H. and CHADWICK, M.J. (1982). The effects of changing patterns of energy use on sulphur emissions and deposition in Europe, *Ambio*, **11**, 324

HSIAO, T.H. (1975). Effect of UV radiation on insects, *Climatic Assessment Programme*, Monograph 5, Department of Transportation, Washington, DC, Part 1, Chapter 5/3

IDSO, S.B. (1985). The search for global carbon dioxide, etc 'Greenhouse Effects', *Environmental Conservation*, **12**, 29

IRVING, P.M. (1983). Acidic precipitation effects on crops, *Journal of Environmental Quality*, **12**, 442

KIMBALL, B.A. (1983). Carbon dioxide and agricultural yield: an assemblage and analysis of 430 prior observations, *Agronomy Journal*, **75**, 779

KIMBALL, B.A. and IDSO, S.B. (1983). Increasing atmospheric carbon dioxide: effects on crop yield, water use, and climate, *Agricultural Water Management*, **7**, 55

KSH (1986). *State and Protection of the Environment*, Központi Statisztikai Hivatal, Budapest

LEADERER, B.P. *et al* (1984). Ventilation requirements in buildings. II. Particulate matter and carbon monoxide from cigarette smoking, *Atmospheric Environment*, **18**, 99

LEMONS, J. (1985). Carbon dioxide and the environment: a problem of uncertainty, *Journal of Environmental Science*, March/April, 60

LIPARI, F. *et al* (1984). Aldehyde emissions from wood-burning fireplaces, *Environmental Science and Technology*, **18**, 326

McCORMICK, J. (1985). *Acid Earth*, Earthscan, International Institute for Environment and Development, London

McDONALD, M.E. (1985). Acid deposition and drinking water, *Environmental Science and Technology*, **19**, 772

MIDDLETON, P. and RHODES, S.L. (1984). Acid rain and drinking water degradation, *Environmental Monitoring Assessment*, **4**, 99

MOGHISSI, A.A. (1986). Potential public health impacts of acidic deposition, *Water Quality Bulletin*, **11**, 3

MÖLLER, D. (1984a). On the global natural sulphur emissions, *Atmospheric Environment*, **18**, 29

MÖLLER, D. (1984b). Estimation of the global man-made sulphur emissions, *Atmospheric Environment*, **18**, 19

NACHTWEY, D.S. and MURPHY, T.M. (1975). General aspects of UV radiation effects on biological systems, *Climatic Assessment Programme*, Monograph 5, Department of Transportation, Washington, DC, Part 1, Chapter 3,

NAS (1973). *Biological Impacts of Increased Intensities of Solar Ultra-violet Radiation*, National Academy of Sciences, Washington, DC

NAS (1975). *Environmental Effects of Stratospheric Flight*, National Academy of Sciences, Washington, DC

NEFTEL, A. *et al* (1985). Evidence from polar ice cores for the increase in atmospheric carbon dioxide in the past two centuries, *Nature*, **315**, 45

NIHLGARD, B. (1985). The ammonium hypothesis – an additional explanation to the forest die back in Europe, *Ambio*, **14**, 2

NRC (1981). *Indoor Pollutants*, National Research Council, National Academy Press, Washington, DC

NRC (1983). *Changing Climate*, Report of the Carbon Dioxide Assessment Committee, National Research Council, National Academy Press, Washington, DC

NRC (1984). *Causes and Effects of Changes in Stratospheric Ozone: Update 1983*, National Research Council, National Academy Press, Washington, DC

OECD (1982). *Pollution Abatement Costs for Coal Energy Technologies*, Organization for Economic Cooperation and Development, Paris

OECD (1985). *The State of the Environment – 1985*, Organization for Economic Cooperation and Development, Paris

PAVLOV, G. (1982). *The Protection and Improvement of the Environment in Bulgaria*, CMEA, Committee for Scientific and Technological Cooperation, Moscow

PORTER, W.P. *et al* (1975). Effects of ultraviolet radiation on animals, *Climatic Assessment Programme*, Monograph 5, Department of Transportation, Washington, DC, Part 1, Chapter 6/1, 2

PRATHER, M.J. *et al* (1984). Reductions in ozone at high concentrations of stratospheric halogens, *Nature*, **312**, 227

RAMANATHAN, V. *et al* (1985). Trace gas trends and their potential role in climate change, *Journal of Geophysical Research*, **90**, D3, 5547

RASMUSSEN, R.A. and KHALIL, M.A. (1986). The behaviour of trace gases in the troposphere, *The Science of the Total Environment*, **48**, 169

RUBIN, E.S. (1982). *Summary of International Symposium on the Economic Aspects of Coal Pollution Abatement Technologies, Held 24-28 May 1982 at Patten, the Netherlands*, Report ENV/EN/82.13, Organization for Economic Cooperation and Development, Paris

SEIDEL, S. and KEYES, D. (1983). *Can We Delay Greenhouse Warming?*, US Environmental Protection Agency, Washington, DC

SMITH, K.R. (1986). Biomass combustion and indoor air pollution, *Environment Management*, **10**, 61

SPENGLER, J.D. and SEXTON, K. (1983). Indoor air pollution: a public health perspective, *Science*, **221**, 9

SPENGLER, J. *et al* (1982). Indoor air pollution, *Environment International*, Special issue, **8**

TORRENS, I.M. (1982). Cleaning up coal pollution: costs and benefits, *OECD Observer*, September, 118

TRAYNOR, G.W. *et al* (1983). Pollutant emissions from portable kerosene-fired space heaters, *Environmental Science and Technology*, **17**, 369

UNEP (1984). *Report of the 7th Session of the Coordinating Committee on the Ozone Layer*, UNEP/CCOL/ VII, United Nations Environment Programme, Nairobi

UNEP (1986). *Report of the 8th Session of the Coordinating Committee on the Ozone Layer*, UNEP/CCOL/ VIII, United Nations Environment Programme, Nairobi

UNEP (1987) *Environmental Data Report*, Blackwell Scientific, Oxford

UNEP/ICSU/WMO (1986). *Report of the International Conference on the Assessment of the Role of Carbon Dioxide and of other Greenhouse Gases in Climate Variations and Associated Impacts*, World Climate Programme, Report WMO-661, World Meteorological Organization, Geneva

UNEP/IIASA (1986). *Climate Impact on Agriculture*, J. Wiley, London

UNEP/WHO (1977). *Oxides of Nitrogen*, Environmental Health Criteria No 4, World Health Organization, Geneva

UNEP/WHO (1979a). *Carbon Monoxide*, Environmental Health Criteria No 13, World Health Organization, Geneva

UNEP/WHO (1979b). *Sulphur Oxides and Suspended Particulate Matter*, Environmental Health Criteria No 8, World Health Organization, Geneva

VAN DYKE, H. and THOMSON, B.E. (1975). Response of model estuarine ecosystems to UV-B radiation, *Climatic Assessment Programme*, Monograph 5, Department of Transportation, Washington, DC, Part 1, Chapter 5/1

WHELPDALE, D.M. (1983). Acid deposition: distribution and impact, *Water Quality Bulletin*, **8**, 72

WHO (1984). *Biomass Fuel Combustion and Health*, Report EEP/84, 64, World Health Organization, Geneva

WHO (1986). Health impact of acidic deposition, Report of a WHO working group, *The Science of the Total Environment*, **52**, 157

WMO/NASA (1985). *Atmospheric Ozone – 1985*, Global Ozone Research and Monitoring Project Report No 16, World Meteorological Organization, Geneva

WOODWELL, G.M. *et al* (1983). Global deforestation: contribution to atmospheric carbon dioxide, *Science*, **222**, 1081

ZHAO, D. and SUN, B. (1986). Air pollution and acid rain in China, *Ambio*, **15**, 2

Chapter 3

Land, water and food production

Only a small part of the productivity of natural terrestrial ecosystems is used by man. Over history, the development of agriculture and forestry has altered the structure and composition of selected systems so as to increase their yield of food, fibre, timber and other biological products. However, despite their modification by cultivation, irrigation, fertilizer use, plant and animal breeding, control of predators and pests and other management techniques, these systems are (with limited exceptions such as greenhouse horticulture) not wholly controlled by man. The natural processes of the biosphere, and especially climatic extremes like droughts and unseasonable frosts, can still interfere with their production.

Several basic criteria govern the management of ecosystems for sustained productivity. Efficient use of water and the maintenance of soil fertility are crucial. The need for protection against damaging pollution is self-evident. A third need is to regulate the harvest man takes from the system. If overcropping depletes the nutrients in circulation so that they are not fully replenished by natural processes or by the addition of fertilizers, if pastures are grazed so heavily that palatable forage species can no longer sustain themselves, or if harvested organisms are depleted beyond optimal sustainable yield, the system becomes at best inefficient and at worst may change through relatively rapid processes of ecological degradation to one no longer useful to man. Several issues pertaining to land use, water management and food production systems have emerged in the last decade. The main issues are discussed in the following sections.

Land and soil loss

The total land area in the world is about 14 477 million hectares (13 251 million ha is the total ice free land area). Land use patterns are mainly determined by the interaction between climate, geography, geology and human and economic pressures. In recent decades man's modification of land use patterns has been governed by accelerating requirements for food, fuelwood and land to build on. The FAO (1984a, 1985) classifies land use into four categories: arable and permanent cropland, permanent pasture (rangeland), forests and 'other' land which includes unused land, urban areas, waste land and barren land etc. Very little of the earth's land surface – only 11%, about 1 500 million ha – is currently under cultivation

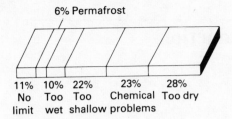

6% Permafrost

11%	10%	22%	23%	28%
No	Too	Too	Chemical	Too dry
limit	wet	shallow	problems	

Figure 10 Suitability of the world's land area for
agriculture
After FAO, 1984a

(Figure 10). Permanent pasture, forests and woodlands and 'other' land constitute 24%, 31% and 33% of the earth's land surface respectively (FAO, 1984a, 1985). The world's potentially cultivable land has been estimated at about 3 200 million ha; at present about half of this area is already under cultivation. In the developed countries, about 70% of the potentially cultivable land is already in use; in the developing countries, 36% of it is in use. But the situation varies greatly from region to region: in South-east Asia, 92% of cultivable land is being used while the figure for South America is only 15% (FAO, 1984a).

The productivity of farmland overwhelmingly depends on the capacity of the soil to respond to management. The soil is not an inert mass. It is a very delicately balanced assemblage of mineral particles, organic matter and living organisms in dynamic equilibrium. Soils are formed over very long periods of time, but if their environments are changed (for example by the removal of vegetation cover), the delicate balance is upset. This can be compensated for by careful use and management (for example by the addition of organic matter), but all too often it is not, and a process of deterioration or degradation begins. The degradation of soil, under excessive human pressure or misguided human activity, can occur over a few decades or even years, and is often irreversible.

In recent decades, man's management of agroecosystems has been steadily intensified, through irrigation and drainage, heavy inputs of energy and chemicals and improved crop varieties increasingly grown as monocultures (see below). Although bringing some general recent growth in agricultural production, this has made agroecosystems more and more artificial and often unstable, with the growing risk of such sudden failures as major pest outbreaks. Various forms of agricultural rotation – grass to crop to fallow, for instance – have become less and less used to remedy the soil fatigue which uninterrupted growth of one crop often brings. The organic humus content of the soil has declined as a result. At the same time, urbanization and the explosive growth of populations have led to the development of two distinct types of human settlement, urban and rural, with the rural settlements providing the food for the industrialized urban settlements. The closed cycle of the traditional agroecosystem has become open ended. The near natural recycling of materials that characterizes subsistence farming has been broken; nutrients and organic materials drain away into the urban sewerages and are no longer returned to farm soil, which instead receives a heavy input of industrial chemicals.

Throughout human history, there have been two aspects to agricultural development: the extension of farming to virgin soil and the intensification of agriculture on land which is already farmed. On the one hand, low productive land, such as deserts, solonchak, swamps and fenlands, has frequently become highly productive through heavy and costly ameliorations. A further major expansion of food producing land is the object of large scale programmes all over the world: the present 1 500 million ha of crop producing land represent about one half of the 3 200 million ha of land considered potentially suitable for agriculture, although the virgin soil left for potential expansion of agriculture is more difficult and much more costly to reclaim and to make productive, as the best soil has already been utilized throughout the world. On the other hand, the productivity per unit area has been increased through more intensive management.

Pressure to expand the area under farming has resulted in more and more utilization of marginal land. Often, the appropriate technology for farming this land on a sustained basis does not exist; where such technology is available, it has frequently been disregarded for social or economic reasons or reasons of political expediency. Overgrazing and overcultivation on steep hillsides everywhere has led to serious erosion; increasing pressure of slash and burn agriculture and forest industry is destroying tropical forests in South-east Asia, Central Africa and Latin America, leading to soil erosion; deforestation in the Himalayas is contributing to the increase in frequency and severity of flooding in India, Pakistan and Bangladesh; and overgrazing and deforestation is contributing to the southward march of the Sahara in the Sudano-Sahelian zone of Africa (see El-Hinnawi, 1985, for a discussion of these phenomena in relation to environmental refugees).

Unfortunately, at the same time as these trends are becoming apparent, the food producing system is steadily losing vast areas of productive land. It has been estimated that, against the 1 500 million ha of land currently used for crop production, nearly 2 000 million ha have been lost in historical times. At present 5–7 million ha of cultivated land (0.3–0.5%) are being lost every year through soil degradation (UNEP/FAO, 1983). If present trends continue, it seems that all the programmes for adding more land to the food producing system may not compensate for the areas lost as a result of soil degradation and through competing land uses. In other words, cultivated land is being lost at nearly the same rate as new land must be brought under cultivation – which means we are running fast to stand still. The FAO *Agriculture : Toward 2000* study calculated that to mitigate this, soil and water conservation measures should be extended to a quarter of all farmland by the end of the century, and that flood control should be extended to 20 million ha. This would cost an estimated US$2 500 million over the next 20 years.

Soil degradation is usually a complex process in which several features can be recognized as contributing to a loss of productive capacity. It is convenient to divide these into two main types: first, erosion and actual removal by water and wind and second, loss of fertility due to chemical, physical, or biological changes (UNEP/FAO, 1983). Soil erosion is a natural process, one that is as old as the earth itself. However, erosion is often greatly increased when human activities cause the disappearance of the protective cover of natural vegetation (so-called 'accelerated erosion'). Under normal agricultural conditions the average erosion rate is estimated to be about 0.5 to 2.0 tonnes per hectare per year (WRI/IIED, 1986). The rate of erosion depends on soil type, slope, nature and intensity of rainfall and wind etc. As the demand for food climbs, the world is beginning to mine its soils, converting a renewable resource into a non-renewable one. In the USA, for example, the loss of soil through erosion exceeds tolerable levels on some 44% of the cropland (Brown and Wolf, 1984). In El Salvador, 77% of the land area is suffering from accelerated erosion, and the silt load of the Citarum river in Java, whose basin is badly eroding through excessive cultivation, has increased sevenfold in three years (Eckholm, 1976). In the eastern hills of Nepal, 38% of the land area consists of fields which have had to be abandoned because the topsoil has washed away, while downstream in the plains of the Nepalese Terai, the same topsoil causes the river beds to rise by 15–30 cm a year. In India, about 150 million ha out of 328 million ha of farmland are affected by erosion to varying degrees (Jalees, 1985). As a matter of fact, soil erosion has been reported from almost every country in the world. It has been estimated that excessive erosion of topsoil from world cropland is about 25 400 million tonnes per year (Brown and Wolf, 1984). A measure of the rapidity of soil erosion is often given by the speed at which new irrigation and power generation reservoirs fill with silt. The Achicaya dam in Colombia lost almost one quarter of its storage capacity through siltation within 21 months of opening in 1955, and was nearly three-quarters full of silt within a decade (Farvar, 1973). Pakistan's Tarbela dam, completed in 1975, is expected to have a life of no more than 50 years because of silt washed down from the deforested and eroded Himalayas (Eckholm, 1976).

A decline in soil fertility or even a total loss of land to agriculture, caused by increase in salinity or alkalinity, is a common problem in many parts of the world. Without adequate drainage, excessive or unwise irrigation can lift salts to the soil surface and even in the absence of subsurface salts, waterlogging may reduce fertility. A study of major irrigation schemes in the Punjab shows that seepage from unlined canals has, in the first 10 years of operation, raised the water table 7–9m above previous levels. In Pakistan in the early 1960s, 22% of all irrigated land was seriously damaged by waterlogging or salinity (Farvar, 1973), while in India it has been estimated that 13 million ha out of a total cultivated area of 328 million ha are degraded by salinization and alkalinization (Jalees, 1985). Salinization is currently affecting large areas of Syria, Iraq, Mexico, USA, Argentina, etc (UNEP, 1982a).

There are other ways, too, in which soil structure, fertility and productivity may be damaged. Overuse of pesticides and inorganic and other fertilizers, for example, can damage the natural microflora and microfauna of the soil. Excessive or inappropriate cultivation can also reduce the soil's agricultural potential. In Tunisia tractor drawn ploughs and disc harrows are breaking up the surface soil and thereby causing wind erosion far more than did the animal drawn ploughs they have replaced, while in parts of the UK drainage and thus crop yields have been reduced by compaction and loss of soil structure caused by the use of heavy machinery in unsuitable weather.

Although several countries are adopting certain measures to halt soil degradation and the loss of agricultural land, most of these efforts are not within formulated national land use and/or soil protection policies. For example, in Egypt construction on agricultural land has been prohibited by law. In Bulgaria, Hungary and other East European countries protection of agricultural land is embodied in national development plans and/or nature protection strategies. In the period from 1976 to 1980, more than 740 000 ha of land in Bulgaria were protected from erosion, and over 1.4 million ha were treated to reduce soil pollution (Pavlov, 1982). In Hungary, soil erosion has caused land degradation in a total area of about 2.3 million ha and efforts are underway to ameliorate this degradation (KSH, 1986).

Desertification

Soil degradation ultimately leads to desertification. The definition of desertification used in this book is necessarily that accepted at the United Nations Conference on Desertification (1977), namely, 'Desertification is the diminution or destruction of the land, and can lead ultimately to desert-like conditions'. A recent assessment by

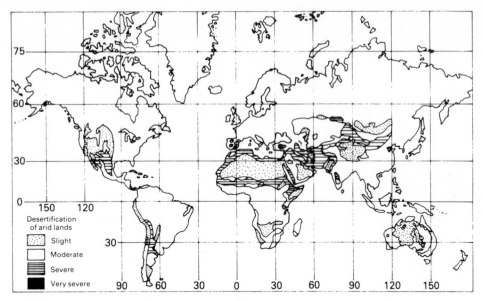

Figure 11 Desertification of arid lands
After UN Conference on Desertification, 1977, and Dregne, 1984

the United Nations Environment Programme (1984) indicates that about 4 500 to 4 700 million ha of land are affected by desertification to varying degrees (Figure 11, Table 2). Estimates indicate that, of this area, 70% to 80% is already slightly to moderately desertified, and 20% to 30% is severely to very severely desertified (Dregne, 1984; Mabbutt, 1984). The population moderately affected by desertification totals about 470 million, while those severely affected total about 190 million. Currently each year some 21 million ha are reduced to a state of near or complete uselessness (Tolba, 1984).

Desertification must be seen as a human problem rather than one concerned solely with the deterioration of ecosystems. Desertification is caused almost entirely by human misuse of the environment, particularly fragile marginal areas with erratic and low annual rainfall. This misuse takes the form of felling trees to provide fuel, overgrazing by domestic animals and harmful agricultural practices such as planting crops on river banks and thereby enhancing soil erosion.

While people are the main agents of desertification, they are also its victims. The most important aspect of desertification lies in its impact on people – on the individual, the family, the community and the nation. The environmental degradation and the biological and physical stress described as desertification in the different dryland livelihood systems have their direct counterparts in physical, emotional, economic and social consequences for man.

As with other environmental hazards, the impact of desertification on human beings shows a chronic or progressive effect, upon which are superimposed those critical periodic stresses that result in human disaster. The effects of desertification on man appear most dramatically in the mass exodus that accompanies a drought crisis. In Africa, widespread famine, malnutrition and deaths arising from drought and desertification affecting some 21 countries have constituted a major crisis that has persisted over the past few years. At the peak of the crisis, in 1984/85, an estimated 30–35 million people were seriously affected, of whom about

TABLE 2. Land area in four desertification classes by continent

Continent	Desertification class	Land area (km^2)	Per cent of arid lands
Africa	Slight	12 430 000	71.7
	Moderate	1 870 000	10.8
	Severe	3 030 000	17.5
	Total	17 330 000	100.0
Asia	Slight	7 980 000	50.9
	Moderate	4 480 000	28.6
	Severe	3 210 000	20.5
	Total	15 670 000	100.0
Australia	Slight	2 330 000	36.6
	Moderate	3 510 000	55.2
	Severe	520 000	8.2
	Total	6 360 000	100.0
North America	Slight	440 000	9.9
	Moderate	2 720 000	61.5
	Severe	1 200 000	27.1
	Very severe	67 000	1.5
	Total	4 427 000	100.0
South America	Slight	1 340 000	43.6
	Moderate	1 050 000	34.1
	Severe	680 000	22.1
	Very severe	6 000	0.2
	Total	3 076 000	100.0
Europe (Spain)	Moderate	140 000	70.0
	Severe	60 000	30.0
	Total	200 000	100.0
All continents	Slight	24 520 000	52.1
	Moderate	13 770 000	29.3
	Severe	8 700 000	18.5
	Very severe	73 000	0.1
	Total	47 063 000	100.0

Source: Dregne (1984)

10 million were displaced (El-Hinnawi, 1985). These figures have been significantly reduced with the recent recovery in crop production in several countries. However, chronic malnutrition affecting 150 million Africans, and the general problems of poverty, loss of possessions and resources for meeting minimum needs, which have been building up over the years, remain acute for nearly 20 million severely affected persons in Africa.

Land conversion from agricultural to other uses

The growth of urban areas and intercity infrastructures has led to a significant conversion of land from agricultural to urban uses in many countries over the past few decades. In the USA, for example, about one million hectares of arable cropland are annually lost to highways, urbanization and other non-farming uses, although this loss is partially offset by the addition each year of half a million hectares of newly developed cropland (Pimentel *et al*, 1976). Over the period 1970 to 1980, between 1% and 3% of agricultural land in OECD countries was converted to urban use. A large proportion of this land lost to agricultural production was prime farmland of high productivity, on fertile plains or in valleys. The proportion of agricultural land converted to urban uses during the same period reached 2.8% in the USA, 1% in France, 2.5% in Italy and 1.2% in the UK (OECD, 1985). It is stated in the USA that the economic and environmental cost of continued conversion of the nation's most productive agricultural land to urban uses could be very high within 20 years. This is in view of the projected increases in demand for US agricultural products in the coming years, particularly for exports, and the uncertainty regarding future gains in crop yield per hectare. Similar concerns are expressed in Canada (OECD, 1985).

The absence of land use policies and land use planning in many countries, especially in the developing ones, make it difficult to study the changes in land use with time. One of the objectives of the World Soils Policy launched by UNEP has been the formulation of land use plans and the monitoring of changes in land use.

Water quality

Various estimates have been made of the total volume of water on earth, and its distribution between the oceans, ice caps, surface streams, rivers and lakes, and underground aquifers (Baumgartner and Reichel, 1975; Van Dam, 1978). It is commonly stated that some 97% of the earth's water is in the oceans and that 3% is on land. Of the latter some 77% is stored in ice caps and glaciers, 22% in groundwater and the remaining tiny fraction is present in lakes, rivers and streams. A substantial proportion of the groundwater stock, which represents the accumulation of centuries of recharge trickling down through soil pores from the overlying ecosystems, lies below 800m depth and is beyond man's present capacity to exploit.

Global water use breaks down into three broad categories: irrigation (73%), industrial uses (21%) and public use (6%). However, water use patterns differ significantly from one country to another. In the developed countries, industries account for 40% or more of all water use, while in the developing countries, the overwhelming bulk of water goes to irrigation. Total water use in 1980 was estimated at 2 600 to 3 000 km^3/y (UNEP, 1982a); it reached about 3 500 to 4 000 km^3/y in 1985; the average annual rate of increase in water use was about 6%.

Surface and groundwaters are subject to pollution from different sources. The basic type of water pollution is the pollution caused by the discharge of untreated or inadequately treated waste water into rivers, lakes and reservoirs. With increase in industrialization, industrial waste waters discharged into water bodies have created new pollution problems. Toxic chemical compounds have killed aquatic biota in many water bodies and have rendered waters useless. Another water quality problem is the increasing eutrophication of rivers and lakes caused mainly by the run-off of fertilizers from agricultural lands.

Although water quality monitoring has been initiated in several countries (the GEMS water quality monitoring project was initiated in 1976; at present it has about 450 stations in 59 countries), the data obtained do not allow trends to be established in most cases. This is particularly true for data obtained from developing countries (in most cases the data are incomplete). However, the data obtained from several monitoring stations in the OECD countries allow for some conclusions to be drawn.

The overall quality of the water in rivers and streams of the OECD countries (as measured by the amount of dissolved oxygen in a river or lake and the amount of biological oxygen demand (BOD) from the introduced waste) has improved since the 1970s. For example, the BOD level in the Mississippi dropped from 2.4 mg/l in 1970 to 1.1 mg/l in 1983; in the Rhine, it dropped from 6.1 mg/l in 1970 to 2.0 mg/l in 1983 (OECD, 1985). This has been attributed to the effects of the clean water legislation introduced, particularly the introduction of secondary (biological) and tertiary (chemical) treatment of waste water, and the reduction in the discharge of untreated or partially treated waste water into different surface water bodies. The 42 rivers monitored in the OECD countries since 1970 have also shown improvement as regards certain other pollutants. For example, the amount of lead in the Rhine dropped from 24 μg/l in 1970 to 8 μg/l in 1983; the amount of chromium dropped from 40 μg/l to 9 μg/l in the same period, and the amount of copper dropped from 24 μg/l to 19 μg/l (OECD, 1985). On the other hand, the concentration of nitrates increased in most rivers. In the Mississippi, for example, the nitrates increased from 0.98 mg nitrogen/l in 1975 to 1.58 mg nitrogen/l in 1983; in the Rhine, nitrates increased from 1.82 mg nitrogen/l in 1970 to 3.88 mg nitrogen/l in 1983 (OECD, 1985).

As for water quality of rivers and lakes in the developing countries the situation differs markedly from one country to another. The scattered data available indicate that water pollution is a growing problem in many countries. In India, for example, about 70% of total surface waters are polluted. China's rivers also seem to be suffering from increasing pollution loads. Of the 78 monitored rivers in the People's Republic of China, 54 are reported to be seriously polluted with untreated sewage and industrial wastes. Reports indicate that more than 40 major rivers in Malaysia are so polluted that they are nearly devoid of fish and aquatic mammals; the primary pollutants were identified as oil palm and rubber processing residues, sewage and wastes from other industries (WRI/IIED, 1986).

The state of water supply and sanitation

The large number of people with no access to safe, clean water and no sanitary services continues to be a matter of deep concern to the world. Shortages are particularly pronounced in developing countries, especially in rural areas. A recent survey by WHO (Deck, 1986) revealed that in developing countries in 1970 only 14% of people in rural areas had access to safe water supplies; by 1980 that proportion had risen to 31% and in 1983 it reached 39%. Rural people were even worse off for sanitary facilities: in 1970, 9% of the people had sanitary facilities; in 1980, the figure became 13% and in 1983, it was 14%. The picture was different for urban dwellers: in 1970, 68% had access to safe water supplies; in 1983, the percentage rose to 74. On the other hand, in 1970, 73% of urban people had sanitary facilities; in 1980, the percentage dropped to 53 and remained so in 1983 (Figure 12).

This continuing grave situation of water supply and sanitation is the main cause of prevalence of communicable diseases in developing countries. Diarrhoeal diseases are endemic throughout the developing countries and are the world's major cause of infant mortality. Cholera, typhoid fever and different intestinal parasites also affect hundreds of millions of people. Studies estimate that the provision of clean water and basic sanitation would reduce the incidence of diarrhoea by 50%, cholera by 90%, sleeping sickness by 80% and Guinea worm infestation by 100%.

The International Drinking Water Supply and Sanitation Decade (1981–90), launched by the United Nations in 1980, is creating a global awareness among policy makers of

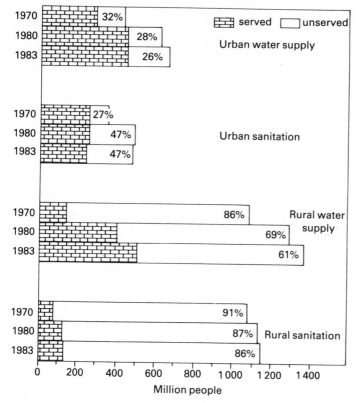

Figure 12 Population reached by water supply and sanitation in developing countries
Drawn from data give by Deck, 1986 for reporting countries

the importance of safe water supplies and appropriate sanitation in the fight against such diseases. The main objective of the IDWSSD has been to provide clean water supplies and adequate sanitation facilities to all people by 1990. However, a mid-decade assessment shows that the original goals set up may not be achieved. By 1990 only about 79% of urban people and 41% of those living in rural areas will have access to clean water. As for sanitation, 62% of urban people and only 18% of those in rural areas will have sanitary facilities.

Groundwater

Groundwater is extensively used in some parts of the world. For example, in the USA, more than 50% of the nation's drinking water supply and 80% of its rural domestic and livestock water needs are supplied by groundwater (NRC, 1986a). According to the US Geological Survey, groundwater use increased in the USA from about 133 million m^3 per day in 1950 to about 360 million m^3 per day in 1985. This represents about one-fifth of the fresh water usage in USA, the other four-fifths being from surface water sources.

Overexploitation of groundwater in some areas has caused a disturbance of the state of equilibrium of the reservoirs, resulting in, for example, a lowering of the water table, decreased pressure in the aquifers and changes in the speed and direction of flow of water etc, all of which could disturb the hydrological cycle in the region, triggering several negative environmental impacts. Land subsidence is an important one; subsidence rates range from about 1 to 50 cm per 10m drop in groundwater level depending on thickness and compressibility of the water bearing formations (Bouwer, 1977). Desertification could be enhanced by the deterioration of plantations due to the reduction in the moisture and/or water coming to their roots from the water table. In coastal areas, overexploitation of groundwater would lead to a rapid intrusion of salt water from the sea, with considerable detrimental effects on soils and plantations.

Groundwater, in its percolation through soil and rocks, leaches out soluble salts; it is thus typically mineralized, and sometimes heavily so (El-Hinnawi and Abdel Mogheeth, 1972; El-Hinnawi and Atwa, 1973; Freeze and Cherry, 1979). Until recently thought of as a pristine resource, groundwater is now known to be vulnerable to contamination because soils and natural processes do not remove many pollutants from surface water as it percolates downward to recharge the groundwater aquifers.

Of all the activities of man that influence the quality of groundwater, agriculture is probably the most important; it is a diffuse source of pollution from fertilizers, pesticides and animal wastes (Freeze and Cherry, 1979; FAO, 1979). Of the main nutrients in nitrogen, phosphorus and potassium fertilizers, nitrogen in the form of nitrate is the most common cause of degradation of groundwater near agricultural lands. Nitrate nitrogen concentrations in water percolating to the groundwater are dependent on the rate and amount of application and the amount of organic and inorganic nitrogen already in the soil, as well as on physical factors such as soil permeability, soil moisture and the amount of water applied in irrigation (FAO, 1979). Nitrate in groundwater has recently become a cause of concern, for example in the UK (White, 1983), the Netherlands (Duyvenbooden and Loch, 1983), Denmark (Forslund, 1986) and the USA (NRC, 1984a, 1986a). In Denmark the overall level of nitrate concentration in groundwater has trebled within the last 20–30 years because of the increase in application of fertilizers and manure in agriculture (Figure 13). Water becomes unsuitable for potable use by infants when nitrate concentrations exceed 45 mg/l, and such levels can at times be reached in shallow groundwaters in agricultural areas.

Despite their low solubility, organochlorine pesticides are toxic and groundwater containing even a few parts per billion of these compounds may be unsafe for drinking purposes. By the early 1980s, several incidents of groundwater contamination resulting from the field application of pesticides had been confirmed in California, New York, Wisconsin and Florida (Holden, 1986). The most widespread problems involved the insecticides/nematocides aldicarb and DBCP (dibromochloropropane). Overall, the emergence of the problem of pesticide residues in groundwater adds a new dimension to the whole array of public health, environmental protection, pesticide innovation and marketing, and agricultural management.

Biochemical processes convert organic nitrogen compounds in animal manures to nitrate and in many agricultural areas this has also led to local degradation of groundwater from farm middens, slurry ponds and feedlots and other intensive livestock units. However, unless these sources are directly above aquifers, this is not usually a significant source of pollution.

The natural processes of leaching, through which groundwaters generally come to contain more dissolved salts than surface freshwaters, can be accentuated in irrigated

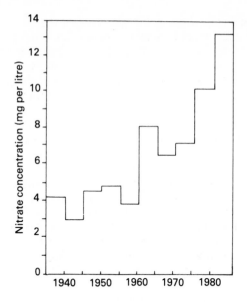

Figure 13 Distribution of nitrate in groundwater
in Denmark
After Forslund, 1986

areas, where soluble salts may be concentrated in the upper soil layers and around plant roots. Such a degradation in groundwater quality has become a serious problem in many areas of the world (FAO, 1979). However, it is not an inevitable consequence of irrigation development and can be alleviated by good water management systems, especially the reduction of seepage losses from irrigation channels and better farm water management (irrigation schedules, control of water quantities through special irrigation technologies, and good drainage system design).

Septic tanks and cesspits contribute filtered sewage effluent directly to the ground and are the most frequently reported sources of groundwater contamination, especially in rural, recreational and suburban areas (Freeze and Cherry, 1979; Yates, 1985). In the USA, for example, an estimated 19.5 million septic tanks and cesspits serving single family homes may release microbial contaminants and pathogens to groundwater (Burmaster, 1986). An increasing percentage of the municipal sewage is, however, now being processed in primary and secondary sewage treatment plants. In many areas, the solid residual material known as sewage sludge – which contains a large number of potential contaminants – is spread on agricultural land. In some regions liquid sewage that has not been treated or that has undergone only partial treatment is sprayed on the land surface. Such application of liquid sewage and sewage sludge to the land provides valuable nutrients such as nitrogen and phosphorus to the soil, with benefits to agriculture. However, the waste water or sludge can add to the contamination of groundwater. The soil profile shows a considerable ability to remove or detoxify several of the compounds found in the waste water; but some may none the less affect groundwater quality. The soil may also effectively eliminate the pathogenic bacteria through filtration and soil microbiological processes; but the survival of viruses is still an open question.

Industrial wastes reach groundwater from impoundments or lagoons, spills, pipeline breaks and land disposal sites. Recent estimates revealed that in the USA there are 76 000 active industrial landfills, mostly unlined, from which contaminants may leach to groundwater (Burmaster, 1986). Abandoned landfill sites have also been found in some European countries. For example, in Denmark, 3 200 sites have been found, 500 of them containing chemical wastes; in the Netherlands there are 4 000 abandoned sites, 350 of which require immediate remedial action (OECD, 1985). Furthermore, at gasoline stations and industrial facilities in several countries, millions of underground steel storage tanks for petroleum products are without corrosion protection. Leaking underground gasoline tanks may be losing millions of litres of gasoline each year, some of which contaminates groundwater (Foegen, 1986). The US Environmental Protection Agency found that chemical contamination of groundwater has already closed more than 1 100 wells, and that there are about 7 700 sites where groundwater has been fouled to varying degrees (Foegen, 1986).

Solid wastes (industrial or urban) were formerly disposed of in open dumps, but are now generally placed in engineered systems known as landfills. Buried refuse in sanitary landfills and dumps is subject to leaching by percolating water, and the leachate may contain several inorganic and organic contaminants. If the landfills are located in relatively permeable strata such as sandstone or fractured rock, leachate migration may cause groundwater contamination over large areas. Such problems can be avoided only by careful evaluation of the hydrogeological features of sites before they are licensed for disposal or by the development of new techniques of waste disposal, such as incineration, which is being used increasingly in developed countries for the destruction of the most toxic substances.

Deep well disposal of liquid wastes can cause serious degradation of the quality of groundwater. Escape of wastes through the well bore into freshwater aquifers can occur as a result of insufficient casing or of casing failures due to corrosion or other causes. Wastes can also escape because they are not confined by truly impermeable strata. Where such wells are permitted, detailed geological and geotechnical studies must be undertaken to avoid possible contamination of groundwater (as well as possible seismic hazards). Well casing methods, rates of injection of wastes and the characteristics of the wastes are among the important factors that should be considered.

Containers of low and intermediate level radioactive wastes resulting from nuclear facilities have been disposed of by burial in shallow excavated trenches, covered with soil. The past history of shallow low level waste burial in the USA is less than satisfactory; leakage of radioactive constituents to the environment has occurred at some sites (Freeze and Cherry, 1979). Although at present this leakage to subsurface flow systems does not present a hazard to potable water supplies, it is striking evidence that undesirable consequences of inadequate hydrogeologic studies of waste management sites can become evident many years or decades after site use begins. The problem facing hydrogeologists now is to ensure, through use of proper site search and evaluation methodologies, that sites for shallow burial of low level wastes, or deeper disposal of long lived wastes in vitrified form, have adequate radionuclide containment capabilities and that proper subsurface monitoring facilities are installed and operated (Freeze and Cherry, 1979; El-Hinnawi, 1980; UNEP, 1981).

Groundwater monitoring is often neglected because its importance is not recognized. When this is combined with the complex legal and institutional status of a groundwater body, prudent management becomes difficult. It is still more difficult to see how to integrate groundwater with surface water resources, in spite of the benefits of joint management of two resources with such complementary characteristics. Whereas the problem of achieving acceptable quality of surface water focuses mainly on decreasing the known emissions of pollutants to these systems, the problems facing scientists and engineers involved in the protection of groundwater resources are to identify the areas and the mechanisms by which pollutants can enter groundwater flow systems and to develop reliable predictions of the transport of contaminants within the flow systems. This is necessary as a basis for minimizing the impact of existing or proposed industrial, agricultural or municipal activities on groundwater quality.

Groundwater management should be seen as an integral part of the overall water development plan of a country – or, where the aquifer extends more widely, of several countries. It should focus on the rational exploitation of the resource and on protection of groundwater from pollution. A series of educational, institutional, legal and economic measures may therefore be necessary to improve pollution control and impose standards for effluents and appropriate regulations of their disposal. Groundwater monitoring to obtain an early warning of the depletion of the resource or of its pollution is an important component of sound management.

Agriculture and food production

Agricultural output and food production have increased only slightly since 1980. The total production of cereals in the world increased from 1 568 million tonnes in 1980 to 1 837 million tonnes in 1985; root crops increased from 536 million tonnes to 585 million tonnes; fruits from 290 million tonnes to 300; meat from 132 million tonnes to 148; milk from 466 million tonnes to 508 and fishery products from 72 million tonnes to 84 million tonnes in 1985 (FAO, 1985, 1986). On a per capita production basis, and in spite of some fluctuations, there has been a slight increase in cereals production but a drop in root crops since 1970. The per capita production of fruits, meat, milk and fishery products has remained nearly stable since 1970.

Worldwide, the rate of growth of agricultural output was 3.1% a year in the 1950s, 2.5% in the 1960s and 2.3% a year in the period 1971–84 (World Bank, 1982, 1986). According to the FAO (1986), growth in the world food production slowed in 1985 (2.1%) to less than half the rate achieved in 1984 (4.7%) and less than the average for the period 1980–85 (2.6%). There was a sharp deceleration in growth in developed countries (from 6.5% in 1984 to 0.8% in 1985), while in developing countries growth was maintained at the 1984 rate of increase (3%), but below the average for the period 1980–85 (3.6%). However, substantial regional differences exist (Figure 14). There was an acceleration of growth in agricultural output in South-east Asia from 2.9% per year in the 1960s to 3.8% per year in the 1970s; in Latin America there was a slight increase, from 2.9% to 3%; but in Africa the rate of growth has declined from 3% per year in the 1960s to 1.2% per year since 1971 (World Bank, 1986). Per capita grain production in Africa has dropped markedly (Figure 15) below subsistence level in the last ten years (Brown and Wolf, 1985).

Although the total calorie and protein content of today's food production is more than twice the minimum requirement of the world population, famine and malnutrition remain widespread. The situation has been created and aggravated by a combination of social, economic, environmental and political factors, ranging from the inequitable access to resources and products to the often primitive conditions of production and processing of agricultural output in many areas. Precise estimates of the incidence of chronic malnutrition in developing countries are not possible, but by any account the problem is vast. A recent estimate by the World Bank (1986) puts

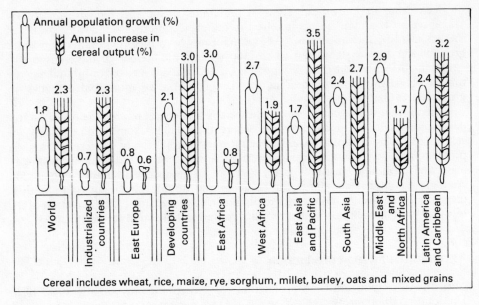

Figure 14 Annual increase in cereal output (%) and annual population growth (%), 1970–82

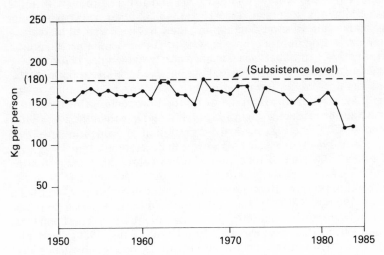

Figure 15 Per capita grain production in Africa
After Brown and Wolf, 1985

the number somewhere between 340 million and 730 million people. If present trends continue, more than 10% of the world population will remain seriously undernourished by the year 2000, unless agricultural output is increased in developing countries. The FAO (1981) has pointed out that a world population of more than 6 billion in the year 2000 will require a level of agricultural output some 50% to 60% higher than in 1980. Demand for food and agricultural products in developing countries will double.

Increasing agricultural output

There are two main approaches to the task of raising agricultural output: increasing the area of cultivated land and increasing the yield per unit of land (Crosson and Frederick, 1977; FAO, 1981; Crosson, 1983; Heady, 1984). In the past two decades, increased acreage has accounted for less than a fifth of the growth in agricultural production in developing countries, and for an even smaller fraction in developed countries (World Bank, 1982). By the year 2000, the greatest contribution to increased crop output – no less than 60% of the total – will come from increases in yields obtained by improved inputs and land management (FAO, 1981).

The total area of potential arable land in the world is about 3 200 million hectares, about 44% of which (1 500 million hectares) is already under cultivation. It has been said that very large areas of new land could be brought under cultivation (Gale Johnson, 1984; Revelle, 1984). But unused arable land is not always available to people who need it most, and opening up new areas remains an expensive means of increasing agricultural production. FAO estimates that about 10% to 15% of unused arable land (170 million to 255 million ha) might be cultivated by the year 2000 (World Bank, 1982). Other estimates are 100 million hectares (Barney, 1980) and 300 million hectares (Buringh, 1981).

Further expansion of agricultural land is constrained in many parts of the world. In tropical Africa, for example, agricultural and livestock development is severely hindered because of such diseases as river blindness (onchocerciasis) and human and animal trypanosomiasis. The latter renders livestock production virtually impossible over some 10 million square kilometres of high rainfall areas – 45% of all the land in sub-Saharan Africa. In arid regions, shortage of water for irrigation constitutes a major constraint on further expansion of the cropland area. On the other hand, increasing pressures to expand the land under cultivation in certain areas have led to serious environmental consequences. Cultivation on steep hillsides and increasing rates of deforestation, especially in the tropics, have led to soil degradation, declines in productivity and desertification (see above). In the tropics, where the areas are biologically richer than in temperate zones, land clearing can cause the destruction – perhaps the extinction – of plant and animal species. The draining of inland wetlands for conversion to agricultural uses can have detrimental effects on fish, wildlife and wetland habitats. Increased agricultural use of estuarine areas, the nurseries for most of the coastal fish stock, may affect bay, river mouth and shallow coastal habitats (NRC, 1982).

The alternative to increasing the area under cultivation is to use existing land more efficiently. Efforts to do so have been successful; productivity gains have been achieved largely by improving the availability and reliability of irrigation and increasing the use of high yielding varieties (HYVs) and fertilizer. In developing countries, cereal yields rose by 2% a year between 1961 and 1980; yields of wheat varieties by 2.7%; yields of sorghum by 2.4%. Although rice yields increased by only 1.6% a year in developing countries as a whole, they rose by more than 3% a year in Indonesia and the Philippines, which were best suited to the new varieties (World Bank, 1982).

The 'green revolution' technological packages require HYVs of seeds and high inputs of water, fertilizers and pesticides. Over the world as a whole, 1 300 billion cubic metres of water are used for irrigation every year, but for this, 3 000 billion cubic metres have to be withdrawn. In other words, 57% of total water withdrawn is lost in the process of storage and transport (Biswas et al, 1983). Increases in the use of water for irrigation have been linked to two factors: growth in the irrigated land area from 163 million hectares in 1968 to 213 million hectares in 1981 (FAO, 1983),[1] and the extent to which techniques of water application and land management have allowed economies in the amount of water used. In some areas, the use of modern irrigation techniques has led to more efficient utilization of water. While irrigation has many advantages, the fact remains that rain fed areas constitute 80% of the developing world's cultivated land and support nearly two-thirds of its farmers (World Bank, 1982).

Water for irrigation is becoming more and more valuable because of the increasing cost of irrigation projects and the limited supply of good quality water. Excessive irrigation wastes large amounts of water, leaches out soil nutrients and micronutrient trace elements and creates problems of secondary salinization and alkalinization, which have damaged millions of hectares of productive lands (see above). It is estimated that the irrigated land area will double by the year 2000 and the problems of salinization and alkalinization are likely to increase. In several regions of the world badly designed irrigation schemes have often created favourable ecological environments for such water borne diseases as schistosomiasis, liver fluke infections, filariasis and malaria. These diseases are not new, but their incidence has markedly increased with the introduction of various water management schemes. In addition to contributing to health hazards, dams built for irrigation and other purposes pose other ecological and environmental problems (El-Hinnawi and Biswas, 1981).

The increased application of chemical fertilizers supplying plant nutrients (nitrogen, phosphorus and potassium) is an essential component of modern agriculture. World consumption of chemical fertilizers rose markedly in the past decade. For nitrogen fertilizers, use increased from 32 million tonnes of nitrogen in 1970 to 61 million tonnes in 1983; for phosphates, from 21 million tonnes of phosphorus pentoxide to 31 million tonnes; and for potash, from 16 million tonnes of potassium oxide to 24 million tonnes (FAO, 1985). The rate of application of fertilizers to land increased markedly with the introduction of HYVs of seeds. For example, in the Philippines the nitrogen input was 17 kg per hectare of paddy before the 'miracle rice' was introduced; after its introduction the nitrogen input increased to 67–80 kg/ha (KiKuchi and Hayama, 1983). The use of fertilizers varies widely from one country to another: in India, the figure is 36 kg/ha; in Egypt, 327 kg/ha, in the USA, 98 kg/ha; in Japan, 412 kg/ha (FAO, 1984b). Worldwide, the consumption of fertilizers increased from 62 kg/ha in 1974–76 to 80 kg/ha in 1981–83 (FAO, 1984b). It has been estimated that the future annual rate of growth of fertilizer use in the world will be about 8%, with agricultural production doubling between 1980 and 2000.

However, it has been estimated that only about 50% of the fertilizer is used by crops; the remainder is lost from the soil system with no benefit to the crop (Engelstad, 1984). Losses occur through leaching, run-off and volatilization. The amount lost varies widely, depending on the crop, the method of application, the type of fertilizer, the soil temperature and other factors. With only about half of the applied fertilizer getting into the crops, there is potential for marked economic loss and for negative environmental impacts.

Chief among the environmental problems of increased fertilizer use are the

---

[1] Various estimates exist for irrigated area in recent years: about 258 million ha in 1984 and 271 million ha in 1985 (WRI/IIED, 1986).

contributions of phosphate and nitrogen fertilizers to eutrophication of surface waters and the excessive concentration of nitrogen compounds in water and the atmosphere. Groundwater in many regions has been contaminated by nitrates; the high nitrate levels (over 40 milligrams per litre) in wells in the Mosel valley in FR Germany have been attributed mainly to the application of nitrogenous fertilizers in vineyards; nitrates have also contaminated groundwater in the Central Sands region of Wisconsin in the USA (McWilliams, 1984). Nitrate levels in many rivers have followed a rising trend over the past two decades (UNEP, 1982a). If present in excessive amounts in drinking water or food, nitrates may pose hazards to health. In some areas where fertilizers are used in excessive amounts, the law of diminishing returns has been found to apply. Although the biological constraints on fertilizer responsiveness can be pushed back with continued plant breeding, further declines seem inevitable. These negative effects of excessive fertilizer use can largely be rectified if fertilizers are applied properly in the correct quantities needed by plants.

Estimates of world crop losses due to insects, pests, disease and weeds vary widely – from as low as 5% to 10% to as high as 30% to 40% (FAO, 1981; World Bank, 1982). The enormity of the problem of pest control is compounded by the vast array of pest species: more than 1 500 diseases are caused by about 50 000 species of fungi; more than 10 000 insect species are pests; more than 1 500 nematode species damage crop plants. In addition, there are about 30 000 weed species, of which more than 1 800 are responsible for major economic losses. The problem of pests can be more serious in developing countries with tropical climates than in countries in temperate zones. For example, the number of diseases reported in rice grown in the tropics is about 500 to 600, as against 54 reported in rice grown in temperate zones. For maize, the values are 125 and 85 respectively (Biswas, 1984).

There are four basic methods of pest control: cultivation methods (ecological means) which discourage the build-up of pest populations; chemical control of pests; selection of crop plants and breeding for resistance; and the deliberate nurture of the natural enemies of pests (biological control). Integrated pest management is a combination of these methods tailored to particular situations (see Chapter 5; see also NRC, 1986b).

Chemical control of pests and diseases is the method widely used in many countries to protect crops. Because different types of pesticides are produced and traded at different costs, the growth of world pesticide use is often measured in terms of world sales rather than in tonnage. World sales of pesticides totalled US$5.5 billion in 1975 and about $28 billion in 1985 (ECE, 1982; OECD, 1985). This represents about an 18% annual increase in sales, in 1977 US$ prices. About 80% of the pesticides used in the world are used in the developed countries. It has been estimated that if agricultural output is to be doubled between 1980 and 2000, the consumption of pesticides in the developed countries will have to grow at a rate of 2–4% per year, with a rate of 7–8% in the developing regions (ECE, 1982). Not all the amounts of pesticides used control pests. The amounts lost vary widely, depending on the pest population and its characteristics, such as its degree of resistance to particular pesticides, the methods of application, and so on (see Chapter 5). Losses of pesticides constitute not only economic losses, but also potential hazards to man and his environment. The continued large scale use of pesticides has led to the appearance and proliferation of resistant strains of pests, as a result of the operation of natural selection. Increasing the dosage of pesticides merely delays the evolution of pests that are immune to a wide array of chemicals (see Chapter 5 for details on resistance to pesticides).

Although agriculture is highly mechanized in developed countries, it is still labour-intensive in developing countries (Figure 16). In 1980, machinery accounted for only 8% of power inputs in agriculture in developing countries. This figure is expected to reach 19% in the year 2000 (FAO, 1981), while the share of draught animals is likely to fall from 25% in 1980 to 18%. The share of labour will fall only slightly, from 67% to 63%; but the fall will be steepest in areas where a high degree of mechanization is introduced, for example in Latin America (FAO, 1981).

Besides its economic and energy costs, increased mechanization accompanying the green revolution has caused a number of environmental impacts, especially in ecologically sensitive areas. Compaction of agricultural and forested soils is a concern throughout the world wherever the level of mechanization is high. It was estimated in 1971 that crop yield reductions due to soil compaction ranged from 1% in the northern USA to 10% in the southern USA, resulting in an annual economic loss in excess of US$1 billion. In 1980, the estimated crop loss was valued at $3 billion (Larson et al, 1984). These losses result from reductions in infiltration of water into and through soils, reduced effectiveness of drainage, reduced plant rooting depth, increased incidence of disease and reduced root efficiency. Farm mechanization in developing countries in which draught animals are replaced by machinery not only involves high capital and operational costs but also leads to loss of animal droppings, which are valuable organic fertilizers.

Almost all of the steps which have led to the enormous increase in agricultural productivity in the last 30 years have a high energy requirement. This is particularly

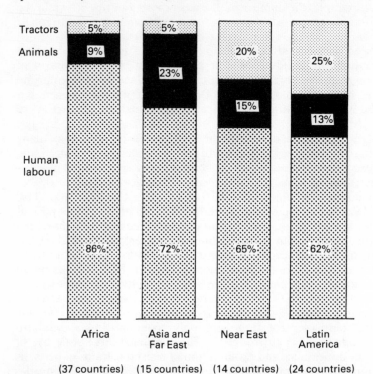

Figure 16 Distribution of human labour, animal power and tractors in agriculture

true of mechanization in agriculture and in fertilizer production. Agricultural production, excluding food processing, storage and transport, accounts for 4.5% of total commercial energy use in the developing countries and 3.5% in the developed countries (FAO, 1981). FAO has estimated that the total commercial energy consumption in agriculture in the developing countries will increase by almost 50% between now and the year 2000. Fertilizer will account for about 60% of this increase, while the rest will be shared by mechanization, irrigation and pesticide use. There is considerable scope for conserving the fossil fuels used in agriculture and increasing the efficiency of energy utilization. One approach is to support and promote the wide use of different renewable sources of energy, especially in the developing countries: organic farming, solar irrigation, wind irrigation, solar drying and so on. Another is to price all inputs in the agricultural system at values based on long-term supply and demand considerations, so that farmers will appreciate their true value and strive to use them in a non-wasteful manner.

The green revolution has come a long way since its beginning. By 1980, some 27% of seed use in the developing countries was estimated to have been from improved varieties; but there were large disparities between countries. In Latin America, 44% of seeds were of improved varieties, whereas in the Near East the share was 32% and in the Far East 23%. In Africa improved varieties made up only 9% of seeds used in 1980 (FAO, 1981).

Plant breeders have helped increase the productivity of many important crops by successfully developing cultivars (cultivated varieties) to fit specific environments and production practices. New and improved cultivars offer practical means of overcoming agricultural production constraints. In germplasm collections around the world the tens of thousands of crop cultivars offer remarkable variability regarding tolerance of adverse water and soil conditions, resistance to or tolerance of major insect pests and diseases, nutritional quality agronomic characteristics such as height, stem strength and growth duration. For example, by using the genetic diversity in the more than 60 000 accessions in the International Rice Research Institute (IRRI) germplasm bank, IRRI scientists have incorporated resistance to six major rice insect pests and diseases, shortened the 150- to 160-day growth duration to 90-110 days and discovered accessions with some tolerance to adverse soil and climatic conditions. Nearly 5 000 crosses are made each year to achieve these results (Brady, 1982; Swaminathan, 1984). Similar outstanding results have been achieved at other national and international research centres.

The extensive use of HYVs of seeds leads to a marked decrease in genetic diversity. This causes two kinds of problems. First, the uniformity of the genetic background of HYVs opens up the possibility that a new disease or pest to which they are not resistant could sweep through an entire area, causing a large crop failure. The second problem is that the reserves of genetic diversity that allow breeders to produce varieties resistant to new diseases and other stresses are being lost as farmers in the developing countries, who grew many varieties and thus were a major source of genetic variability, switch to HYVs (Pray, 1981; Calvin, 1982). Some of the limitations of HYVs that have received increasing attention in recent years stem from their dependence on the presence of a whole package of complementary inputs (water, fertilizer, pesticides etc) which are not always readily available in developing countries. In areas with conditions favourable to the adoption of the new varieties, especially as far as water availability is concerned, the use of the new seeds spread rapidly. In areas with less favourable conditions, the new varieties offer little or no advantage over traditional farming methods (Odhiambo, 1982).

Furthermore, HYVs of grains (eg rice) that have been produced so far have not delivered the range of adaptability to agroclimatic conditions that they promised and they have failed to outperform the traditional varieties in conditions where inputs of water, fertilizer and pesticides have not been optimal. The performance of rice in the best national programmes in rural Asia is still far below what has been achieved in the temperate industrialized regions. Furthermore, the gap between potential and actual production levels is very wide: the potential yield in temperate zones is 15–17 tonnes per hectare, while the actual yield is only 25–40% of that, 4.5–6.0 t/ha; in the humid tropics, the potential yield is 13–15 t/ha, whereas the actual yield is 10–20% of that, ie 1.5–2.5 t/ha (Odhiambo, 1982).

A major socioeconomic impact of the green revolution has been the shift of farmers, in some developing areas, from the cultivation of traditional indigenous crops to the new HYVs to achieve economic gains. This increasing neglect of indigenous crops has caused nutritional problems in some areas and has also led to marked increases in the prices of such crops. In addition, in some developing countries, especially in Africa, societies have been shifting from the native crops like yams, cassava, millet and sorghum to consumption of wheat, which is imported through aid programmes and/or purchased and subsidized by governments. This has greatly increased the dependence of some countries on grain imports. This situation can be rectified only through the introduction of appropriate and environmentally sound technologies to improve the yields of indigenous crops.

Emerging agricultural technologies

Existing agricultural technologies are being improved, or are being applied in new situations, in attempts to increase food production and to reduce both costs and adverse environmental effects. Among the modern and emerging agricultural technologies which have a potential effect on the environment are conventional plant breeding, genetic engineering of plants, biological nitrogen fixation, increased photosynthetic efficiency, increased mechanization, minimum tillage, organic farming, monocultures and polycultures, sequential cropping, expansion of irrigation and improved irrigation technologies.

Many of the current constraints on production cannot be removed by traditional plant breeding techniques. Genetic materials with tolerance to some of the most serious crop pests and diseases and other production constraints have yet to be discovered. The hope for the future is that modern biotechnology (Figure 17) will help provide the cultivars needed to overcome some of the production constraints: excess salt in soil or water, very acid soils, drought, high and low temperatures etc.

Plant genetic engineering, that is to say the manipulation of plant genes, opens up possibilities for extending new genetic information to diverse plant species, overcoming the limits of conventional breeding programmes. However, it should not be considered a technology that will wholly replace plant breeding. Rather, it should be used along with existing methods in an integrated manner, each being used when it will be most effective and economical. If genetic engineering techniques can be mastered, it will be possible to make use of them in the design of plants that are hardier, more nutritious or less expensive to produce or offer high yields. Other possibilities include plants that can thrive in marginal conditions, on soils that are salty, acidic, wet or dry (NRC, 1984b; Collins and Petolino, 1984; Sasson, 1984; Bjurstrom, 1985; Hansen et al, 1986; Dibner, 1986). The successful application of genetic engineering to plants will require fundamental breakthroughs in the

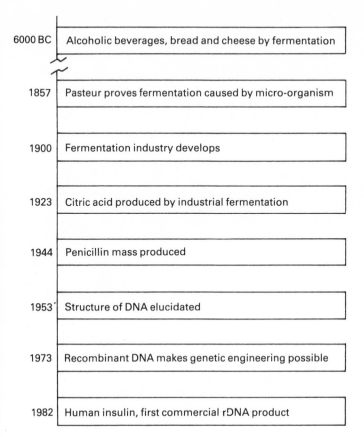

6000 BC	Alcoholic beverages, bread and cheese by fermentation
1857	Pasteur proves fermentation caused by micro-organism
1900	Fermentation industry develops
1923	Citric acid produced by industrial fermentation
1944	Penicillin mass produced
1953	Structure of DNA elucidated
1973	Recombinant DNA makes genetic engineering possible
1982	Human insulin, first commercial rDNA product

Figure 17 Historical evolution of biotechnology
After Bjurstrom, 1985

understanding of gene expression and regulation, as well as increased knowledge of plant physiology, biochemistry, development and metabolism. It is too early to assess with accuracy either the potential or the limitations of genetic engineering as far as crop improvement is concerned. At this stage, gene transfer is not expected to have a significant effect on agricultural production practices until the late 1990s.

Efforts are now under way to apply genetic engineering technologies to specific agricultural problems. For example, the herbicide atrazine is used to kill weeds in maize fields. Maize can tolerate atrazine. However, where maize is planted in rotation with soybeans, the latter are susceptible to residues of atrazine and their yield is affected. An atrazine-resistant soybean would be ideal for growing in rotation with maize. Although some atrazine-resistant strains of plants have been created by classical plant breeding methods, the development of such strains is not feasible with many crops. The most powerful technique will be to transfer the resistant gene into a crop plant using recombinant DNA technology (NRC, 1984b).

Plant tissue culture, the techniques of which have been perfected since 1937, can provide large populations in a relatively short time and in a limited space; mutants can be induced in such populations and the latter can be used for selection purposes. Plant tissue culture also makes it possible to identify plant lines with a greater photosynthetic rate and, therefore, a greater productivity. Efforts made since the mid-1970s to obtain the vegetative multiplication of the oil palm by tissue culture techniques *in vitro* deserve particular mention in view of their economic implications (Sasson, 1984).

Nitrogen is an essential plant nutrient and a key determinant of crop productivity. Most plants are unable to draw the nitrogen they need directly from the air and must therefore obtain it in combined form from the ground. Hence they depend entirely either on fertilizers or on bacteria capable of fixing nitrogen from the atmosphere. These bacteria, which live freely in the soil or are found in the roots of certain plants (mainly legumes), fix considerable amounts of atmospheric nitrogen using energy extracted from organic matter in the soil (free living bacteria) or produced by the host plant (symbiotic bacteria). Biological nitrogen fixation through micro-organisms has traditionally been achieved by introducing legumes into crop rotation. Farmers have long grown the water fern *Azolla* in rice fields; it provides a habitat for blue-green algae that help supply the rice with nitrogen. It is estimated that the fixation of atmospheric nitrogen by well nodulated soybeans can supply between 25% and more than 50% of the total needs of the crop.

Agricultural yields can be sustained at tremendous savings if biological nitrogen fixation can be improved and extended to major crops, such as maize and wheat, that now depend on costly nitrogen fertilizer. Therefore, researchers are looking into the possibility that the genes for nitrogen fixation present in certain bacteria, such as *Klebsiella* and *Rhizobium*, can be transferred to the major crops using genetic engineering techniques. Root organisms such as *Mycorrhizae* can improve the ability of plants to utilize soil phosphorus and other mineral nutrients, and can increase plant resistance to drought and salinity. Improved understanding of the association between micro-organisms and plant roots may allow plants to obtain more of the phosphorus they require from native soil sources rather than fertilizers.

Through photosynthesis, plants are able to produce their own organic matter from carbon dioxide, water and solar energy. Yet the efficiency of photosynthesis, expressed as the ratio between chemical energy fixed by plants and the energy contained in the light rays falling on the plants, is less than 1%. Such a low rate should be capable of improvement. The common limiting factors are light intensities, carbon dioxide concentration, water availability, supply of nutrients, respiration (light and dark) and response of plants to stresses (Hall, 1979). Utilizing available knowledge of the characteristics of plants and of photorespiration may allow the breeding and selection of more efficient photosynthetic plants (Swaminathan, 1984).

Given adequate solar radiation, soil nutrient availability and irrigation, increased atmospheric carbon dioxide should act as a fertilizer for crop plants, raising both photosynthetic production and the efficiency of water use (see Chapter 2). Greenhouse experiments have indicated that a doubling of carbon dioxide under good crop management can increase biomass yield by about 40% (Swaminathan, 1984). Structural adaptations in farming systems will be necessary, both to take advantage of the favourable consequences of increased carbon dioxide and to tackle its negative repercussions.

Genetic engineering can affect not only what crops can be grown, but where and how they are grown. It usually acts in conjunction with other biological and mechanical innovations, whose deployment is governed by social, economic, environmental and political factors. Although our knowledge of the environmental consequences of plant genetic engineering is in its infancy, researchers and the public are becoming increasingly concerned about the safety of the new technology (see, for example, Brill, 1985; Colwell *et al*, 1985; Szybalski, 1985 and OECD, 1986). One cause for such concern is the risk posed by the release of novel organisms into the environment. The introduction of any species into an ecosystem it does not normally inhabit can have unexpected negative results. Guiding or perhaps accelerating the course of evolution can lead to changes which disrupt an ecosystem and, hence, may undermine man's reverence for life.

The introduction of genetically engineered plants, like the introduction of cultivars through normal plant breeding, should have beneficial environmental effects – for example, the reduction of chemical fertilizer and pesticide use, increased tolerance to salt and drought and so on. However, if drought tolerance leads to the expansion of dryland cropping into ever drier regions where rainfall variations from year to year are extreme, increased wind and water erosion could result in severe soil degradation during dry years. The introduction of salt tolerant cultivars could prompt increased use of saline water for irrigation, with the subsequent contamination of shallow groundwater and increased salinization of soils. This in turn would narrow the choice of crops for cultivation in rotation. Increased tolerance to herbicides could make it difficult to eradicate crop plants that have become weeds.

The environmental impacts of improved biological nitrogen fixation should all be beneficial, with perhaps minor exceptions. Yields should rise, thereby increasing crop vegetative growth and providing protection against water and wind erosion in addition to making crop rotations more effective and reducing the need for commercial nitrogen fertilizers. In turn, the reduced fertilizer use should diminish the likelihood of excessive nitrogen applications and of subsequent pollution of ground and surface water supplies. With certain high value crops such as vegetables, biological nitrogen fixation may not lead to any significant reduction in fertilizer use.

The introduction of minimum tillage should generally be highly beneficial in reducing soil erosion. There are, however, two main potentially adverse effects, one arising from greater insect and disease presence in crop residues (which may require greater use of pesticides) and the other from heavy use of herbicides to control weeds. Herbicides are indispensable for minimum tillage to be successful, but they have several adverse impacts on the environment (see Chapter 5).

Although more than 20 000 edible plants are known and perhaps 3 000 have been used by mankind throughout history, a mere handful of crops now dominate the world's food supply. To help feed, clothe, and house an increasing population, to make marginal lands more productive, and to reforest the devastated tropics, we need a revitalized worldwide investigation of little known plant species. Such an effort would expand our agricultural resource base and ease our dangerous dependence on a relative handful of crops (Figure 18).

Fish production

Fish is one of the most widely distributed food commodities in the world. It presently contributes about 6% of the total protein supplies and, taking into account the indirect contribution of fishmeal fed to animals, about 24% of the world's animal protein supplies (FAO, 1985). For many developing countries, fish is an indispensable item of daily diets. About 60% of the population of the developing world derive 40% or more of their total annual protein supplies from fish. Fish and fish products are not only highly nutritious, with protein content varying between 15% and 20% but their biochemistry and amino acid characteristics make them particularly efficient in supplementing the cereal and tuber diets widely consumed in Asia and Africa.

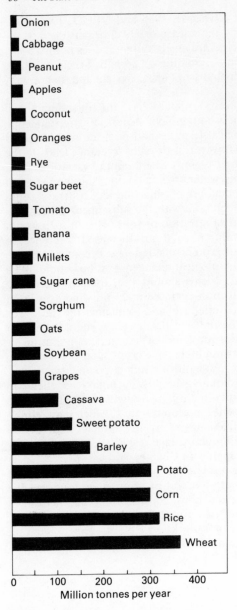

Figure 18 The major crops dominating the world's food supply

The total world fisheries catch has increased during the past few decades. Between 1950 and 1970, it rose steadily and rapidly at annual rates of about 7% (total fishery landings were about 62 million tonnes in 1970). Then between 1971 and 1972 the total catch dropped, largely due to the dramatic fall in the catches of Peruvian anchovy which was then by far the largest fishery in the world. Since 1972 the catch has increased, but only at 1–2% annually. The nominal annual fishery catches in

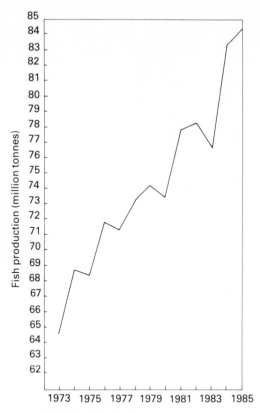

Figure 19 World fishery production
After data by FAO, 1985, 1986

1980 were about 72 million tonnes. From 1980 to 1985, the average annual growth of fish catches reached a high record of 3.2%; world fish production reached about 84 million tonnes in 1985 (FAO, 1986). This increase (Figure 19) was mainly due to substantial rise in catches by South American countries bordering the Pacific Ocean.

Two-thirds of the fish are destined for human consumption while the remainder is used either for the feeding of livestock in the form of fish meal or for the manufacture of fertilizers. The FAO estimates that the world catch ought not to exceed 100 million tonnes per year if the risk of a substantial depletion of fish stocks is to be avoided. However, pressures on stocks in certain areas already amount to overfishing. Overfishing in regions close to the industrial areas of the northern hemisphere, for example, has resulted in a decline in the size and quality of some species of fish and the increasing scarcity of others. Overfishing has led to a sharp drop in catches of cod and herring in particular, the fishing for which in the north-east Atlantic was made subject to quotas in the 1970s and subsequently banned altogether for certain stocks to allow them to recuperate.

The total world aquaculture production has been estimated at about 9 million tonnes (Brown, 1985), consisting mainly of finfish, shellfish and seaweed (Figure 20). Since fish is grown for home consumption in backyard ponds in many developing countries (especially Asian countries), this figure does not include such non-

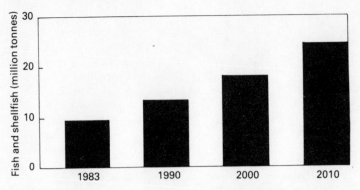

Figure 20 World aquaculture production of fish and shellfish
After Cole, 1984

commercial production which is very difficult to account for. Aquaculture production amounts to about 8–9% of total world fish production, and is developing continuously and at a rapid rate (5–7% per year), principally in South-east Asia, Japan, Europe and North America (Neal, 1984; OECD, 1985).

Aquaculture and environment

Aquaculture is the human controlled cultivation and harvest of both freshwater and marine aquatic species (in the latter case sometimes referred to as mariculture). Although aquaculture has been practised for almost 4 000 years in some Asian countries, it has been brought under systematic research and development planning only in recent times. This has resulted in the introduction of new species of aquatic organisms for cultivation and new techniques for the operation of what has become a growing, extensive industry. Indeed, large scale enterprise, with a comparatively large capital outlay, is already a feature of modern aquaculture. At the other end of the scale is the small operator, ranging from the subsistence level upward. Although the production of food is the most important aspect of aquaculture, cultivation of aquatic plants for feed and other purposes is receiving increased attention in several countries.

Fish farms vary in size from several square metres to hundreds of hectares. The millions of fish farmers in East Asian countries typically have less than one hectare each. Fishponds may be located inland (freshwater ponds) or along coastal zones (brackish or salt water ponds). It has been estimated that the freshwater production is twice that of salt and brackish water (Ackefors and Rosen, 1979). Aquaculture production in freshwater consists mainly of finfish. The corresponding production in brackish and marine water consists mainly of molluscs and seaweed, and to a lesser extent of finfish.

Traditional extensive culture of milkfish, mullets, molluscs and shrimp in Asian and Mediterranean countries accounts for the conversion of moderately large areas of coastal lowlands into ponds or management of shallow water areas as shellfish farms. Countries with coastal areas under extensive pond culture are the Philippines (176 000 ha), Indonesia (192 000 ha), Thailand (25 000 ha) and India (12 000 ha), (Neal, 1984). Recently, some of the traditional ponds have been upgraded for more intensive culture, and large areas of coastal mangroves or marshlands are being converted to ponds.

Mangrove swamps dominate sheltered coastlines throughout the tropics. As a unique protective margin between land and sea, mangrove swamps attract faunal components from adjoining terrestrial and aquatic ecosystems in addition to harbouring many indigenous animal species. Mammals, reptiles and birds exploit the landward mangrove periphery for food and shelter sites, while crabs, prawns and fish migrate into the mangrove zone with the tides for the same purpose. Several countries, for example India, Malaysia and Ecuador, have been planning to develop aquaculture in mangrove lands. In Malaysia, it has been estimated that about 27 000 ha of such land are suitable for brackish water fish culture (Ong, 1982). The evaluation of the losses of mangrove to aquaculture is still in its infancy and much work is needed to develop methodologies for the determination of the environmental costs and benefits of such developments. Essentially all vegetation and wildlife are destroyed in the process of pond construction; water courses and dykes change or restrict the natural movement of water in the areas. On the other hand, mosquito production may be reduced in swampy areas converted to ponds because of consumption of larvae by fish or shrimp.

Freshwater aquaculture has been practised for centuries, especially in Asian countries. From one generation to another, fish farmers have gained considerable exprience in the construction and operation of ponds and in the selection and rearing of different species of fish. In China, pond fish culture accounts today for about two-thirds of the fish produced in the country. Existing annual fish yields from intensively managed ponds average seven tonnes per hectare (Zweig, 1985). One of the keys to this high yield lies in the fish polyculture strategies adopted. Of the 25 fish species cultured in ponds in China, nine predominant species, each with different feeding habits, are most frequently cultured together in a single pond at one time.

Integrated fish farms are quite common in many countries. In China, 90% of the annual yield from aquaculture is produced on integrated farms (Zweig, 1985) where aquaculture is the predominant activity and is combined with agriculture and animal husbandry. The linkages within integrated fish farms are numerous and complex. Livestock manures derived from animals reared within the farm, night soil and agricultural byproducts are used as pond fertilizers for the growth of the microbial food web. In addition, floating aquatic plants – eg water hyacinths, water peanuts and water lettuce – are grown on canals adjacent to ponds and harvested as green fodders for fish and livestock. Anaerobic digesters used in the farm produce methane gas as an energy source from agricultural residues and manures; the nitrogen-rich slurry residues in the digesters are used to fertilize ponds and some crops. On the other hand, the pond bottom humus can be used as a fertilizer for crops grown adjacent to ponds. The integrated fish farms are designed to optimize the use of wastes from each process conducted within them as direct resources for others and to use the available space most efficiently. The intricate, beneficial use of such a wide variety of wastes helps to abate pollution through maximal recycling of many materials that would otherwise need to be discarded. Another form of agricultural/aquacultural integration involves land use rotation between the two activities. In the southern USA, for example, catfish farmers frequently alternate between a crop of catfish and one of soybeans (Brown, 1985). This cuts the production cost of soybeans since the nutrient-rich residue on the land after a year of intensive catfish farming substantially reduces outlays for chemical fertilizer.

Freshwater aquaculture has a number of impacts. Ponds certainly occupy land that could be utilized for other purposes, and aquaculture consumes water by way of evaporation and seepage. Aquaculture is therefore a competitor with agriculture for resources. In some countries, because of the low prices offered for agricultural products, farmers have converted increasing areas of agricultural land into fish ponds to achieve more profit. This has resulted in the loss of agricultural lands in addition to creating hydrogeological problems in adjacent fields due to the increase in the level of groundwater as a result of seepage from the ponds. Some countries, for example Egypt, have prohibited the establishment of fish farms on agricultural lands. On the other hand, small integrated fish farms lend themselves to programmes for rural development.

The quality of water has a substantial bearing on aquaculture. Although some pollutants, if present in the water, can wipe out some fish species, other species (eg shellfish) can tolerate a wide range of chemicals in small doses (eg mercury, cadmium, DDT, PCBs) and microbes (eg hepatitis virus, typhoid bacteria). The continuous presence of such substances in the water, however, leads to a build-up in the soft tissues of such fish species and can cause diseases and epidemics among consumers. In addition, certain marine algae (dinoflagellates) produce toxins which can be concentrated by shellfish. Such toxins have caused a disease termed Paralytic Shellfish Poisoning (PSP) among consumers in several areas of the world (Skulberg et al, 1984; UNEP/ILO/WHO, 1984). Another group of algae, the blue-green algae (cyanobacteria), also contains several toxin forming species. Such toxin producing algae may also cause economic problems for aquaculture, since there are many reports of fish deaths in waters containing blue-green algal blooms (Skulberg et al, 1984).

The use of excreta in aquaculture has been practised in several countries, eg in China, Malaysia, Thailand, Indonesia, and Bangladesh (Edwards, 1985). There are also several examples in the world of commercially viable fish culture systems using sewage. The country with the largest number and largest area of sewage fed fish ponds is India. There is also sewage fish systems in FR Germany (Munich sewage fish pond), Hungary and Israel.

There are potential threats to public health from excreta re-use in aquaculture, which must be avoided. It should be stressed that although there is little danger of disease from eating well cooked fish or vegetables since the heat destroys pathogens, the consumption of raw, partially cooked or improperly preserved products, for example, poorly fermented fish which is widely consumed in parts of Asia, can be a serious health hazard. Although fish do not apparently suffer from infections caused by enteric bacteria and viruses, they may carry pathogens passively. Enteric bacteria and viruses survive for considerably shorter periods in seawater than in freshwater. The coastal water environment may thus cause fewer public health problems in excreta re-use than inland waters. However, edible shellfish such as oysters and mussels concentrate enteric bacteria and viruses in their tissues, and outbreaks of polio, hepatitis A and diarrhoeal disease have all been related to the consumption of shellfish from faecally polluted water. The re-use of sewage containing toxic chemicals such as heavy metals and various organic compounds may lead to their accumulation by cultivated organisms, which may thus constitute a threat to public health (Edwards, 1985).

Aquatic plants include both algae and the higher, flowering forms of vegetation. Among the former are the unicellular forms (phytoplankton), filamentous species and the larger, macroscopic algae or seaweeds that exist almost exclusively in saltwater. The higher forms of plants are more common in freshwater where there are over 150 species, but also occur in brackish and saline waters. All of these forms of aquatic plants have existing or potential uses (NRC, 1978). For example, seaweeds possess substances that can be extracted for use as gelling agents. Water hyacinth, considered a nuisance in some countries, is planted in others (eg in China) for use as feed (UNEP, 1984).

Post-harvest food losses and residues

Food losses

Post-harvest losses are defined as those occurring at any of the stages between harvesting by the farmer and delivery to the consumer, ie losses during harvesting, threshing, cleaning, drying, storage, transport, processing, packaging and distribution of food. Direct losses in quantity occur when grain is left on the field after harvesting, from grain spillage during handling or transport and from grain consumed during storage by rodents or insects. Losses in quantity also arise through inefficient processing, for example in rice mills which give a yield of 60% or less of edible rice from paddy, instead of 65% or more; and in traditional methods of oil extraction from oil seeds, which leave 20–30% of the oil in the presscake. Insects, mites and moulds cause chemical changes in foods which lead to deterioration and hence to losses in quality. Rodents and insects also contaminate food grains with filth and excreta; this material may carry organisms pathogenic to man. Mycotoxins are produced by fungi in insufficiently dried cereals and oil seeds. All these effects are reflected in reduced acceptability of food grains to consumers and, consequently, a reduced market value.

Losses vary by crop, variety, year, pest and pest combination, length of storage, methods of threshing, drying, handling, storage, processing and transportation, rate of consumption and climate. The pattern of losses varies widely from country to country. In developed countries, losses may be high during harvesting because the agricultural machinery used to harvest the crops leaves some of the commodity in the field and mechanically damages some of it. Considerable quantities of foods may be discarded at the point of harvest because they are of the wrong size, shape or colour. These are planned losses. In developing countries, harvest losses are usually lower because most of the crop is hand picked. The amount of material rejected in developing countries is less because the expectation of quality and uniformity is generally lower than for developed countries (FAO/UNEP, 1981).

In developed countries, losses are generally small during processing, storage and handling because of the efficiency of the equipment, good quality storage facilities and close control of critical variables by a highly knowledgeable cadre of managers. In contrast, in developing countries, losses in processing, storage and handling tend to be rather high because of poor facilities and inadequate knowledge of methods to care for the food properly. The estimated annual post-harvest losses in developing countries is about 10% of all durables (cereals and legumes) and about 20% of all perishables (root crops, vegetables, fruits). The total annual cost of such losses amounts to about US$10 billion (NAS, 1978).

In the past decade, technology to reduce post-harvest losses has markedly improved. A variety of traditional, microbiological and other techniques are now available not only to preserve food but to increase its protein and vitamin content. Such technologies need to be transferred and adapted on a wide scale in developing countries.

Agricultural and agroindustrial residues

Residues from agriculture and agroindustries are the non-product outputs from the growing and processing of raw agricultural products such as fruits, vegetables, meat, poultry, fish, milk, grain and trees. While such residues may contain material that can benefit people, their current economic values are less than the apparent cost of collection, transport and processing for beneficial use (UNEP, 1982b). They are therefore discharged as wastes. If residues can be utilized for human benefit, such as to enhance food production, they are no longer wastes but become new resources. Whenever such residues can be utilized, their subsequent gain in economic value may change their status from non-product outputs to products. Such utilization may, however, generate secondary residues which also require careful management.

Residues from agriculture and agroindustries are often more massive than the food itself (Table 3). These residues – in solid, liquid or slurry form – are usually organic and biodegradable, and hence are amenable to conversion by biological, chemical and physical processes, into energy, animal feed, food, organic fertilizers and other beneficial uses as appropriate. Therefore, if such residues, rather than being regarded as wastes, are seen as valuable unused raw materials, it will be possible both to reduce pollution and other undesirable environmental impacts and to increase the base for food production.

Throughout the world, farm crops leave substantial residues, the extent and scale of which is rarely realized. Most cereal crops give between one and three tonnes of straw per tonne of grain (Barnard and Kristoferson, 1985). Modern high yielding varieties (HYVs), as a rule, give a smaller proportion of residues than traditional varieties. This is because plant breeders have deliberately selected strains that concentrate their energy and growth in the marketable portion of the plant, rather than the residue. This does not necessarily mean that HYVs give less residues in total, however. This depends on the growth rate and productivity of the crop, which, in turn, is a function of the agricultural methods used and the amount of inputs supplied. Wheat, with a yearly crop production of 497 million tonnes, rice with 450 million tonnes, corn (maize) with 349 million tonnes, sorghum and millet with 91 million tonnes and several other less widely grown grain crops all contribute more than 2 000 million tonnes of cereal straw.

Agroindustries also produce vast quantities of residues. The sugar cane industry, for example, creates each year 50 million tonnes of sugar cane tops and 67 million

TABLE 3. Crop-to-residue ratios for selected crops

Crop	Residue	Tonnes residue/t crop
Rice	Straw	1.1–2.9
Wheat	Straw	0.7–1.8
Maize	Stalk	1.5–2.5
Sorghum	Stalk	0.9–4.6
Millet	Stalk	2.0–3.7
Barley	Straw	0.6–1.8
Rye	Straw	1.1–2.0
Oats	Straw	0.9–1.8
Cotton	Stalks	3.5–5.0
Jute	Sticks	2.0
Coconut (copra)	Shell	0.7–1.1
	Husk	1.6–4.5

Source: Barnard and Kristoferson (1985)

tonnes of bagasse, as well as molasses and press mud (UNEP, 1982b). Although molasses waste water is used in some countries to fertilize rice paddies, the press mud is widely used as a soil conditioner and as a component of animal feed and the bagasse is often burned as a low grade fuel in the sugar mills themselves, the sugar cane residues are generally greatly underutilized. Pineapple is typical of many fruits for which much of the crop is wasted. Where pineapples are canned, less than 20% of the whole fruit is used; the remainder, often in the form of a highly polluting liquid, can cause considerable disposal problems. In Mexico, for example, 980 000 tonnes of pineapples are processed annually creating 490 000 tonnes of waste (Gonzalez et al, 1985). Annual whey production in the world (whey is the watery portion that separates from the curds during the manufacture of cheese or casein) is estimated to be about 72 million tonnes (Kosaric and Asher, 1982). Currently, only about 50% of the whey is utilized for human food and animal feeds, while the rest is wasted. This waste amounts to about 250 million kg of nutritionally high quality whey proteins, 87 million kg of milk fat, 1 552 kg lactose, 160 million kg minerals and 16 million kg lactic acid. This amount is approximately equivalent to the yearly caloric requirements of about nine million people (Kosaric and Asher, 1982).

There are many other examples of underutilized agricultural and agroindustrial residues. Dicharged in excess into the environment, these residues can poison the soil, kill fish, cause artificial enrichment (eutrophication) of lakes, pollute rivers and streams, create unpleasant smells and cause air pollution harmful to human health. Symptoms of this pollution are especially evident near high density animal stocking areas. For example, lakes and inland waterways have been subject to large scale eutrophication caused by animal manure trickling from the land which has been biologically and physically overloaded. The byproducts from cereal production also cause pollution problems. For instance, the straw stem left after removal of the grain must be lifted from the ground in order to control pests and diseases and to prevent fouling of the soil for the next crop. In some countries, most of the straw produced is burnt in the field, causing smoke and fire hazards and other ecological problems. The same considerations apply to agroindustrial residues. In liquid form these residues are often extremely polluting. For instance, the waste waters created when starch is extracted from tapioca are up to 20 times more polluting, those from palm oil production up to 200 times more polluting and those from whey up to 300 times more polluting, than municipal sewage (UNEP/FAO, 1977).

Agricultural residues have been used as fuel in developing countries, especially in rural areas, since ancient times. They still constitute a considerable share of the fuel used in such areas (Barnard and Kristoferson, 1985). The fuel properties of agricultural residues vary widely. Woody crop residues make the best cooking fuels. Coconut shells, jute sticks, millet stalks and pigeon pea stems, for example all burn well. Most other crop residues make poorer fuels. Cereal straw and lightweight crop stalks burn too quickly. Rice husks are even worse, and without treatment – such as briquetting into fuel pellets – they usually need special stoves if they are to be used at all. Several technologies have been developed to use agricultural residues more efficiently as fuel. Such technologies include gasification, pyrolysis into liquid fuels, preparation of charcoal, production of biogas, etc (see El-Hinnawi and Biswas, 1981). There are several advantages for the conversion of residues into biogas. In addition to the gas produced, the slurry formed in the biogas plants is rich in nutrients and can be used as organic fertilizer and/or for feeding fish ponds.

Several opportunities exist for the recycling of agroindustrial residues. In meat production, for example, the edible and non-edible residues can often be utilized and converted into useful products. For example, fats can be converted into tallow and grease, meat scraps and blood into animal feed, bone into bone meal, glands into pharmaceutical products. New mechanical deboning processes can increase the amount of available red meat by 3–4%, thus reducing residue production. Again, the total recovery of blood, which contains about 17% protein, from animal slaughterhouses could result in the production of over 180 000 tonnes of protein in the USA alone (see also, Zaleski et al, 1985; Carter et al, 1985; Fallows and Wheelock, 1982a).

The uses to which agroindustrial residues may be put are many and varied. Rice bran, for example, contains about 15–20% oil. It also contains vitamin B, amino acids and other nutrients. The oil in the rice bran can be extracted and utilized for cooking, and de-oiled bran can be used as animal feed. Rice straw can be utilized as the raw material for paper, board and animal feeds. When cheese is produced from milk, half the nutrients are left in whey. Several uses of whey have been developed, which include production of softer cheeses, dairy spreads, whipping creams, enrichment of infant foods, etc (Kosaric and Asher, 1982; Fallows and Wheelock, 1982b). Corn (maize) cobs from which the grain has been removed can be processed into lubricating oil, acetic acid and formic acid. The residue can be used as bulk filler for animal feeds and as fuel (see also, Fallows and Wheelock, 1982c). Several technologies exist for the recycling of potato processing industries which include starch recovery, alcohol production and single cell protein production (Fallows and Wheelock, 1982d). Using biotechnological techniques it has been found that some 79.4 kg of high quality protein can be recovered from every 500 kg of fermented pineapple residues instead of the 12.5 kg of crude protein recovered from the same amount using conventional techniques (Gonzalez et al, 1985).

Opportunities to recycle and use the agricultural and agroindustrial residues are thus enormous and limited only by lack of incentives and of appropriate research and development. As residues come to be recognized as potentially valuable resources, pressures will mount to ensure that they are adequately utilized and thus contribute to national development. Towards this end research is needed to develop appropriate and environmentally sound technologies for residue utilization and to establish social costs and benefits of residue utilization. Until recently, little attention was given to the social cost of the discharge of residues into the environment and the elimination or dispersal of the residues themselves was seen as the solution to the problem. However, in many cases this has proved to be a costly process and recycling and utilization of residues have been recently considered a problem of public utility and interest. The utilization of agricultural and agroindustrial residues offers considerable promise. But this optimism must be tempered with the recognition that the result must be a usable product at an economical cost and that the procedures used must not cause greater environmental or social problems than the original method of residue disposal. This is pre-eminently a field where generalizations are dangerous and where the full range of ecodevelopment impacts must be carefully considered.

References

ACKEFORS, H. and ROSEN, C.G. (1979). Farming aquatic animals, *Ambio*, **8**, 132

BARNARD, G. and KRISTOFERSON, L. (1985). *Agricultural Residues as Fuel in the Third World*, Technical Report No 4, Earthscan, International Institute for Environment and Development, London

BARNEY, G.O. (1980). *The Global 2000 Report to the President of the USA*, Pergamon Press, New York

BAUMGARTNER, A. and REICHEL, E. (1975). *The World Water Balance*, Oldenburg Verlag, Munich

BISWAS, A.K. (1984). *Climate and Development*, Tycooly International, Dublin

BISWAS, A.K. *et al* (1983). *Long Distance Water Transfer*, Tycooly International, Dublin

BJURSTROM, E. (1985). Biotechnology, *Chemical Engineering*, 18 February, 126

BOUWER, H. (1977). Land subsidence and cracking due to ground water depletion, *Ground Water*, **15**, 358

BRADY, N.C. (1982). Chemistry and the world food supply, *Science*, **218**, No 4575

BRILL, W.J. (1985). Safety concerns and genetic engineering in agriculture, *Science*, **227**, 381

BROWN, L.R. (1985). Maintaining world fisheries, in BROWN, L.R. *et al*, eds, *State of the World, 1985*, W.W. Norton, New York

BROWN, L.R. and WOLF, E.C. (1984). *Soil Erosion: Quiet Crisis*, Worldwatch Paper No 60, Worldwatch Institute, Washington, DC

BROWN, L. R. and WOLF, E. C. (1985). *Reversing Africa's Decline*, Worldwatch Paper No 65, Worldwatch Institute, Washington, DC

BURINGH, P. (1981). *An Assessment of Losses and Degradation of Productive Land in the World*, Food and Agriculture Organization of the United Nations, Rome

BURMASTER, D.E. (1986). Ground water: saving the unseen resource, *Environment*, **28**, 25

CALVIN, M. (1982). Basic chemical research and future food supplies, in BIXTER, G. and SHEMILT, L.W., eds, *Chemistry and World Food Supplies – CHEMRAWN II*, International Rice Research Institute, Los Banos, Philippines

CARTER, P.M. *et al* (1985). Recent development in the utilization of meat and fish wastes in the tropics, *Industry and Environment*, **8**, 15

COLE, M. (1984). Aquaculture: a growing industry, *Economic Impact*, **48**, 70

COLLINS, G.B. and PETOLINO, J.G. (1984). *Applications of Genetic Engineering to Crop Improvement*, Martinus Nijhoff/W.Junk, Dordrecht

COLWELL, R.K. *et al* (1985). Genetic engineering in agriculture, *Science*, **229**, 111

CROSSON, P. (1983). A schematic view of resources, technology and environment in agricultural development, *Agriculture, Ecosystems and Environment*, **9**, 4

CROSSON, P. and FREDERICK, K.D. (1977). *The World Food Situation*, Research Paper No 6, Resources for the Future, Washington, DC

DECK, F.L.O. (1986). Community water supply and sanitation in developing countries, 1970-1990, *World Health Statistics Quarterly*, **39**, 2

DIBNER, M.D. (1986). Biotechnology in Europe, *Science*, **232**, 1365

DREGNE, H.E. (1984). *Desertification of Arid Lands*, Hardwood Academic, New York

DUYVENBOODEN, W.V. and LOCH, J.P. (1983). Nitrate in the Netherlands – a serious threat to ground water, *Aqua*, **2**, 59

ECE (1982). *Market Trends for Chemical Products, 1975-1980 and Prospects to 1990*, Report ECE/CHEM/40, Vol 1, Economic Commission for Europe, Geneva

ECKHOLM, E.P. (1976). *Losing Ground*, W.W. Norton, New York

EDWARDS, P. (1985). *Aquaculture: A Component of Low Cost Sanitation Technology*, World Bank Technical Paper No 36, World Bank, Washington, DC

EL-HINNAWI, E. (1980). *Nuclear Energy and the Environment*, Pergamon Press, Oxford

EL-HINNAWI, E. (1985). *Environmental Refugees*, United Nations Environment Programme, Nairobi

EL-HINNAWI, E. and ABDEL MOGHEETH, S. (1972). Geochemistry of ground water from Burg El-Arab, Egypt, *Neues Jarbuch für Geologie und Palaeontologie Abhandlungen*, **140**, 185

EL-HINNAWI, E. and ATWA, S.M. (1973). Geochemistry of ground water from some localities west of the Nile delta, *Geolgische Rundschau*, **62**, 225

EL-HINNAWI, E. and BISWAS, A.K. (1981). *Renewable Sources of Energy and the Environment*, Tycooly International, Dublin

ENGELSTAD, O.P. (1984). Crop nutrition technology, in ENGLISH B.C. *et al*, eds, *Future Agricultural Technology and Resource Conservation*, Iowa State University Press, Ames, IA

FALLOWS, S.J. and WHEELOCK, J.V. (1982a). Byproducts from the UK food systems. 2. The meat industry, *Conservation and Recycling*, **5**, 173

FALLOWS, S.J. and WHEELOCK, J.V. (1982b). Byproducts from the UK food system. 3. The dairy industry, *Conservation and Recycling*, **5**, 183

FALLOWS, S.J. and WHEELOCK, J.V. (1982c). Byproducts from the UK food system. 4. The cereals industries, *Conservation and Recycling*, **5**, 191

FALLOWS, S.J. and WHEELOCK, J.V. (1982d). Byproducts from the UK food system. 5. The potato processing industry, *Conservation and Recycling*, **5**, 163

FAO (1979). *Ground Water Pollution: Technology, Economics and Management*, FAO Irrigation and Drainage Paper No 31, Food and Agriculture Organization of the United Nations, Rome

FAO (1981). *Agriculture – Toward 2000*, Food and Agriculture Organization of the United Nations, Rome

FAO (1983). *Production Yearbook*, Vol 36, FAO Statistics Series No 47, Food and Agriculture Organization of the United Nations, Rome

FAO (1984a). *Land, Food and People*, Food and Agriculture Organization of the United Nations, Rome

FAO (1984b). *Fertilizer Yearbook*, Vol 34, Food and Agriculture Organization of the United Nations, Rome

FAO (1985). *The State of Food and Agriculture – 1984*, Agriculture Series No 18, Food and Agriculture Organization of the United Nations, Rome

FAO (1986). *The State of Food and Agriculture – 1986,* Document CL 90/2, FAO, Rome

FAO/UNEP (1981). *Food Loss Prevention in Perishable Crops*, FAO Agriculture Series, Bulletin 43, Food and Agriculture Organization of the United Nations, Rome

FARVAR, T.(1973). *The Careless Technology,* Stacey, London

FOEGEN, J.H. (1986). Contaminated water, *The Futurist*, March/April, 22

FORSLUND, J. (1986). Ground water quality today and tomorrow, *World Health Statistics Quarterly*, **39**, 81

FREEZE, R.A. and CHERRY, J.A. (1979). *Ground Water*, Prentice-Hall, NJ

GALE JOHNSON, D. (1984). World food and agriculture, in SIMON, J.L. and KHAN, H. eds, *The Resourceful Earth*, Blackwell Scientific, Oxford

GONZALEZ, E.E. *et al* (1985). Biotechnology for the processing of pineapple waste, *Industry and Environment*, **8**, 19

HALL, D.O. (1979). Solar energy use through biology – past, present and future, *Solar Energy*, **22**, 4

HANSEN, M. *et al* (1986). Plant breeding and biotechnology, *BioScience*, **36**, 29

HEADY, E.O. (1984). The setting for agricultural production and resource use in the future, in ENGLISH B.C. *et al*, eds, *Future Agricultural Technology and Resource Conservation*, Iowa State University Press, Ames, IA

HOLDEN, P.W. (1986). *Pesticides and Ground Water Quality*, National Academy Press, Washington, DC

JALEES, K. (1985). Loss of productive soil in India, *International Journal of Environmental Studies,* **24**, 245

KIKUCHI, M. and HAYAMA, Y. (1983). New rice technology, intrarural migration and institutional innovation in the Philippines, *Population and Development Review,* **9**, 2

KOSARIC, N. and ASHER, Y. (1982). Cheese whey and its utilization, *Conservation and Recycling*, **5**, 23

KSH (1986). *State and Protection of the Environment,* Központi Statisztikai Hivatal, Budapest

LARSON, W.E. *et al* (1984). Our agricultural resources: management for conservation, in ENGLISH, B.C. *et al,* eds, *Future Agricultural Technology and Resource Conservation*, Iowa State University Press, Ames, IA

MABBUTT, J.A. (1984). A new global assessment of the status and trends of desertification, *Environmental Conservation*, **11**, 103

McWILLIAMS, L. (1984). Gound water pollution in Wisconsin: a bumper crop yields growing problems, *Environment*, **26**, 4

NAS (1978). *Post-harvest Food Losses in Developing Countries*, National Academy of Sciences, Washington, DC

NEAL, R.A. (1984). Agriculture expansion and environmental considerations, *Mazingira*, July, 24

NRC (1978). *Agriculture in the United States: Constraints and Opportunities*, National Academy of Sciences, Washington, DC

NRC (1982). *Impacts of Emerging Agricultural Trends on Fish and Wildlife Habitat*, National Research Council, National Academy Press, Washington, DC

NRC (1984a). *Ground water contamination*, Studies in Geophysics, National Research Council, National Academy Press, Washington, DC

NRC (1984b). *Genetic Engineering of Plants,* National Research Council, National Academy Press, Washington, DC

NRC (1986a). *Ground Water Quality Protection*, National Research Council, National Academy Press, Washington, DC

NRC (1986b). *Pesticide Resistance*, National Research Council, National Academy Press, Washington, DC

ODHIAMBO, T.R. (1982). Biological constraints on food production and on the level and efficient use of chemical inputs, in BIXTER, G. and SHEMILT, L.W., eds, *Chemistry and World Food Supplies – CHEMRAWN II*, International Rice Research Institute, Los Banos, Philippines

OECD (1985). *The State of the Environment – 1985*, Organization for Economic Cooperation and Development, Paris

OECD (1986). *Recombinant DNA Safety Considerations*, Organization for Economic Cooperation and Development, Paris

ONG, J.E. (1982). Mangroves and aquaculture in Malaysia, *Ambio*, **11**, 252

PAVLOV, G. (1982). *The Protection and Improvement of the Environment in Bulgaria*, CMEA, Committee for Scientific and Technological Cooperation, Moscow

PIMENTEL, D. *et al* (1976). *Science*, **194**, 149

PRAY, C.E. (1981). The Green Revolution as a case study in transfer of technology, *Annals of the American Academy of Political and Social Sciences,* No 458

REVELLE, R. (1984). The world supply of agricultural land, in SIMON, J.L. and KAHN, H. eds, *The Resourceful Earth*, Blackwell Scientific, Oxford

SASSON, A. (1984). Biotechnologies: challenges and promises, *Sextant*, No 2, UNESCO, Paris

SKULBERG, O.M. *et al* (1984). Toxic blue-green algal blooms in Europe, *Ambio*, **13**, 144

SWAMINATHAN, M.S. (1984). Climate and agriculture, in BISWAS, A.K. *et al,* eds, *Climate and Development*, Tycooly International, Dublin

SZYBALSKI, W. (1985). Comments on Brill's article, *Science*, **229**, 112

TOLBA, M.K. (1984). A harvest of dust?, *Environmental Conservation,* **11**, 1

UNEP (1981). *Environmental Impacts of Production and Use of Energy*, Tycooly International, Dublin

UNEP (1982a). *The World Environment, 1972-1982*, Tycooly International, Dublin

UNEP (1982b). *Guidelines on Management of Agricultural and Agro-Industrial Residue Utilization*, Industry and Environment Guidelines Series, United Nations Environment Programme, Nairobi

UNEP (1984). *Water Hyacinth*, UNEP Reports and Proceeding Series No 7, United Nations Environment Programme, Nairobi

UNEP/FAO (1977). *Residue Utilization – Management of Agricultural and Agro-Industrial Wastes*, UNEP/FAO/ISS Seminar, Food and Agriculture Organization of the United Nations, Rome

UNEP/FAO (1983). *Guidelines for the Control of Soil Degradation*, Food and Agriculture Organization of the United Nations, Rome

UNEP/ILO/WHO (1984). *Aquatic Biotoxins*, Environmental Health Criteria No 37, World Health Organization, Geneva

VAN DAM, A. (1978). Water management in the 1980s, *Water Supply and Management*, **1**, 349

WHITE, R.J. (1983). Nitrate in British waters, *Aqua*, **2**, 51

WORLD BANK (1982). *World Development Report 1982*, World Bank, Washington, DC

WORLD BANK (1986). *World Development Report 1986*, World Bank, Washington, DC

WRI/IIED (1986). *World Resources 1986*, Basic Books, New York

YATES, M.V. (1985). Septic tank density and ground water contamination, *Ground Water*, September/October, 586

ZALESKI, S.J. *et al* (1985). New technology for processing animal blood and its fractions, *Industry and Environment*, **8**, 13

ZWEIG, R.D. (1985). Freshwater aquaculture in China, *Ambio*, **14**, 66

Chapter 4

Energy and transport

Energy production and consumption

World commercial energy consumption has increased more than threefold over the past three decades but has recently slowed down (Figure 21). It has generally been assumed that there is a consistent positive relationship between Gross National Product (GNP) and energy consumption. Thus, as a country's GNP in real terms rises over time, its energy consumption goes up as well. However, the degree of dependence, economy versus energy, can be influenced by a variety of factors. For example, the structure of the economy will affect the correlation between GNP and energy consumption; the rate of increase of GNP and energy use is somewhat similar for energy-intensive exports, but for non-energy-intensive exports, GNP increases at a much faster rate than energy use. Gradual and steady improvements in the efficiencies of energy conversion and utilization have shown up as historical trends indicating decreasing ratios between per capita energy consumption and per capita real GNP. The lifestyle preferred by a given society will also enter into the equation. The level of comfort in terms of temperatures maintained during summer and winter plus the levels of illumination in residential, commercial and industrial structures is but one example. The preference for suburban living, mobility and decreased reliance on mass transit systems furnish another, and both examples, in their own way, can lead to increases in per capita energy consumption without a compensating increase in economic productivity. There are far too many other potential factors that could be listed here – the growing energy intensiveness of agriculture and the food industry and the displacement of natural products by synthetics, are again only two examples.

The increase in energy consumption in the past fifty years or so was accompanied by a major change in primary energy sources. In the 1920s coal accounted for about 80% of the world's total commercial energy consumption; its share in later years was greatly reduced due to the increase in oil discoveries. Numerous technological changes took place to give impetus to this shift from coal to oil. A whole set of new technologies were developed not only to improve methods of oil supply but also to expand the range of its end-uses. Advances in oil exploration and production technology improved the supply capacity of the oil industry; improvements in transport of oil by pipelines and tanker technology added to the advantage of oil as easily transportable fuel; and the development of refining technology contributed greatly to improving efficiency in its end-uses. All these factors worked to strengthen the competitiveness of oil as an alternative fuel to coal. As regards end-uses, the

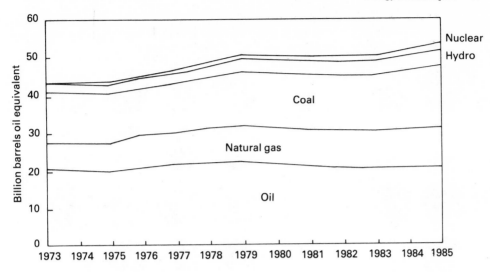

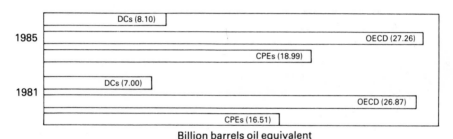

Figure 21 World consumption of commercial energy sources
After OPEC, 1986

widespread use of internal combustion engines, particularly in transport and in power generation, greatly increased the demand for oil. The result of this shift to oil was a drop of coal's share in the world's commercial energy consumption to 61% in 1960 and to 35% in 1970; in 1984, the percentage was 30. The major transition to oil and natural gas took place in the early 1960s (El-Hinnawi, 1981).

The consequences of the shift to cheap oil (in 1950, the posted price of a barrel of oil in the Middle East was about $2; it dropped to $1.8 until 1970) were far reaching. The shift implied not only the creation of physical and economic structures based on the use of oil but also the spread of particular social institutions and cultural values that made life dependent on its ready availability. Obviously it is in the developed countries, where most of the above mentioned technological changes and new patterns of energy consumption took place, that the shift from coal to oil and its consequences have been most visible. The considerable amounts of oil thus consumed in these countries is a clear reflection not only of their dependence on oil but of a wasteful use of a low priced resource. In developing countries, however, dependence on oil is even more complete, since these countries started industrialization and development efforts after the shift from coal to oil had been well established. Not only were oil dependent structures built up in these countries

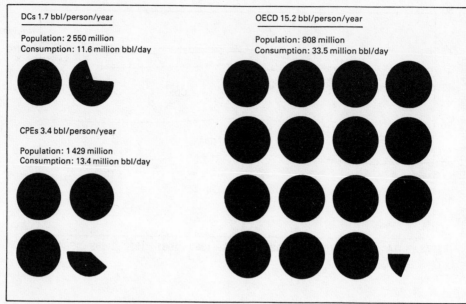

DCs 1.7 bbl/person/year

Population: 2 550 million
Consumption: 11.6 million bbl/day

CPEs 3.4 bbl/person/year

Population: 1 429 million
Consumption: 13.4 million bbl/day

OECD 15.2 bbl/person/year

Population: 808 million
Consumption: 33.5 million bbl/day

Figure 22 Per capita oil consumption
After OPEC, 1986

through imports of oil geared capital goods from developed countries, but the latter's oil based pattern of life was also taken over to a significant degree.

Consumption of the world's commercial energy resources is heavily concentrated in the developed regions – the industrial market economies and the centrally planned economies (Figure 21). These regions, with about 30% of the total world population, account for about 85% of the total world consumption of commercial energy; the other 70% of world population, living in the developing countries, consume about 15%. The per capita commercial energy consumption in the OECD countries is about nine times that in the developing countries (Figure 22). This heavy concentration in the developed regions is a reflection of the more advanced level of development already achieved. Their industries are characterized by energy-intensive processes; extensive coverage of communities and individual households by power grid systems provides ready access to energy for the daily life of people for heating, cooking, lighting and domestic work; and mechanization has reached not only farming and factory work but also commercial facilities. As a result, per capita commercial energy consumption is about nine times that of the developing countries.

Several studies have been made to estimate future energy demand in the world (see El-Hinnawi, 1981 and WRI/IIED, 1986 for a summary of these forecasts). Estimates vary from 9 500 million tonnes of oil equivalent (mtoe) to 12 000 mtoe by the year 2000; wider variations exist in estimates of demand by the year 2050 (the maximum estimate reaches 39 000 mtoe in the year 2050). It should be noted, however, that these and other energy forecasts depend on a number of different assumptions and different aggregating procedures that make them *roughly indicative* and subject to a wide range of error and changes. The main elements affecting these forecasts are:

1. world and regional scenarios of economic development;
2. correlation of economic growth with energy consumption;

3. physical, economic, environmental and geopolitical constraints applying to energy production and consumption;
4. future prices of different sources of energy;
5. future availability of different sources of energy and the development of appropriate technologies to harness them; and
6. public acceptance of energy sources and conservation measures.

In addition, an inherent deficiency in all these forecasts is that they neglect non-commercial sources of energy which constitute a major source of energy in developing countries. Even by concentrating only on commercial sources of energy a wide range of error is encountered in assumptions pertaining to developing countries, especially in relation to the rate of substitution of non-commercial sources of energy by commercial ones (El-Hinnawi, 1981).

The 1970s brought into focus the general realization that fossil fuel resources, especially oil and natural gas, are finite in nature and that countries should explore the possibilities of using other sources of energy as well, establishing thereby an appropriate energy mix to meet their demands for sustainable development. Several scenarios have been proposed: expanded utilization of coal resources which are more abundant than those of oil and natural gas; development of non-conventional fossil fuels like oil shales and tar sands; further development of nuclear power; and development of different renewable sources of energy, etc (El-Hinnawi, 1981; El-Hinnawi et al, 1983). However, the development of an appropriate energy mix depends on a number of economic, environmental and geopolitical factors.

Of the many environmental impacts associated with any energy technology, some are substantial and others small; some are important and others have long-term effects; some might be adverse and others beneficial and they might occur in different geographic areas and might affect different communities in different ways (see, El-Hinnawi, 1980; UNEP, 1981a; El-Hinnawi and Biswas, 1981; El-Hinnawi and Hashmi, 1982; UNEP, 1982; El-Hinnawi et al, 1983 for details on the environmental impacts of production and use of different energy sources). A distinction should be made between the assessment of the nature, scale and geographic distribution of the impact and the evaluation which is concerned with its value or importance. For many environmental changes which are identified as impacts, the state of knowledge and technology will often permit only a qualitative assessment. Only in a few cases it is possible to evaluate an impact quantitatively. Decisions must ultimately be made on the bases of combination of cost–benefit analysis, other quantifiable inputs and qualitative information.

The 1970s brought into focus some important issues: the further development of nuclear power, the scarcity of fuelwood and the importance of increasing the efficiency of energy utilization. These issues are dealt with in the following sections.

Nuclear power

Electricity was first generated from nuclear reactors in 1954. The growth in capacity was slow until the early 1960s, but the number of new reactors ordered per year then rose dramatically to a peak in 1973 (about 75 reactors with capacities greater than 150 MWe were ordered in that year), after which it fell equally dramatically for economic, environmental and social reasons (UNEP, 1982). By March 1979, 186 nuclear reactors with a total capacity of 112 GWe were in operation in 20 countries.

The accident at Three Mile Island that occurred in 1979 has had its effect in slowing down nuclear programmes in several countries (especially in the USA). As a matter of fact the accident has augmented public concern about safety and the environmental impacts of nuclear power. The estimates that were originally made for nuclear power growth by the turn of the century had to be scaled down (El-Hinnawi, 1980). In 1975, the IAEA estimated that by the year 2000 nuclear power would contribute 2 600 GWe. Two years later, this figure was reduced to 2 000 GWe and in 1981 it was further reduced to 1 075 GWe. The latest forecast by IAEA projects a worldwide capacity for the year 2000 of between 720 and 950 GWe. This would constitute 15–18% of the total world electrical generating capacity. These figures are likely to change after the serious accident that occurred in 1986 at Chernobyl, USSR.

At the end of 1985 there were 374 nuclear power plants, with a total capacity of about 250 GWe (Figure 23), in operation in the world (Bennett and Skjoeldebrand, 1986). In energy terms, nuclear power plants generated about 1 400 terawatt-hours of electricity during 1985 and accounted for about 15% of the world's electricity generation during that year. The nuclear share in electricity generation varies greatly from country to country and also from region to region in some countries (for example, in the USA). If present growth in nuclear power remains unaffected by the recent accident at Chernobyl, the worldwide nuclear generating capacity may reach 370 GWe by 1990.

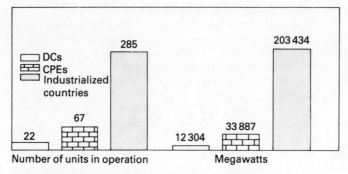

Figure 23 Nuclear power in the world at the end of 1985
After OPEC, 1986

The uncertainty of the future of nuclear power has been compounded by many issues which include, *inter alia:*

1. economic recession;
2. changing scenarios of correlation between economic growth and energy consumption;
3. instability of oil prices (there was a marked decrease in oil prices in 1986 and although prices increased by the end of the year, they may not reach the pre-1985 levels for some years;
4. physical, economic, environmental and political constraints applying to nuclear energy development; and
5. public reaction and concern about nuclear power.

Many of these issues still remain without satisfactory solutions (for a review of the environmental impacts of nuclear energy see, El-Hinnawi, 1980 and UNEP, 1981a).

The fuelwood problem

Wood has been the primary source of energy for cooking, heating and other basic needs for almost all man's history since prehistoric times. It remains so in developing countries, in many urban areas as well as in the countryside (Figure 24). Well over two billion people, about half the population of the world, use it for cooking, their most important use of energy (World Bank, 1980). People in developing countries on average each use between 1.3 and 2.5 cubic metres of it a year (El-Hinnawi and Biswas, 1981; Goodman, 1985). Until recently the sheer weight of fuelwood burned in the world was not realized – and neither was the effect of gathering it on the environment.

Worldwide, about 2.8 billion hectares (or 69% of the forested areas) are covered with closed forests and 1.3 billion hectares (Figure 25) are less densely wooded open forests (WRI/IIED, 1986). Natural shrublands and degraded forests in developing countries cover 675 million hectares. When these categories of wooded land are added to open and closed forests, the total (4.7 billion hectares) represents about 32% of the world's total land area.

The total volume of wood (stock) contained in forests has been estimated at 340 to 360 billion m³. This is the *resource base* and only the annual increment from this capital can be used without destroying the resource base. Such annual increment has been estimated to be 6 610 million m³ (Openshaw, 1978, 1980). Official statistics (FAO, 1985) indicate that the total world consumption of roundwood in 1983

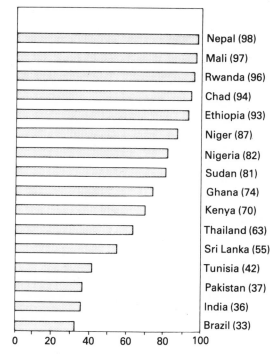

Figure 24 Estimate of fuelwood and charcoal as percentage of total energy consumption in selected developing countries
After Hall *et al*, 1982

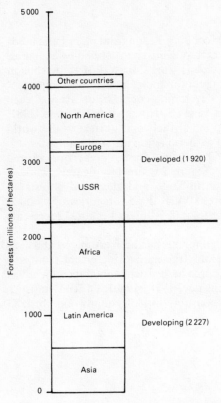

Figure 25 Distribution of forest areas in 1985
Drawn from data given by WRI/IIED, 1986

(Figure 26) was about 3 000 million m³ (about 54% of which was used as fuelwood and charcoal). It should be noted that these figures may be considerably under-estimated. No accurate records are kept by many countries of self-collected or self-produced products such as fuelwood and charcoal and these are not accounted for in official statistics. The figures given above indicate that the annual increment of the forest resource base would meet the world demand for wood. However, on a worldwide basis, all the increment is not being removed, and much of this unremoved increment is in the inaccessible northern coniferous forests of Alaska, Canada and the USSR. This has led to overexploitation of the forest resources in certain regions, thereby destroying the resource base.

Different assessments of the rate of deforestation have been made in the last few years (see, Melillo et al, 1985; WRI/IIED, 1986). The average annual rate of total deforestation in tropical countries has been estimated at 11 million hectares (UNEP, 1982; WRI/IIED, 1986). Over the past ten years, 1.3 million hectares of closed broadleaved forests have been cleared annually in Africa. Another 2.3 million hectares of open woodlands have also been deforested each year in Africa between 1980 and 1985 (FAO, 1985). Much larger areas were degraded through harvesting for fuelwood and construction wood, cutting for fodder, grazing, fire and by drought. Conversion and degradation have been particularly severe in semiarid West and East Africa, where supplies of the fuelwood, poles, forage and other secondary

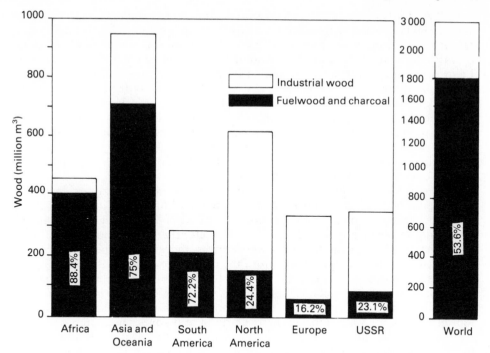

Figure 26 Production of industrial and fuelwood (including charcoal) in different regions, 1981–83
After FAO, 1985

forest products that rural households need have dwindled. In all, African countries account for 62% of the deforestation of the world's open tropical forests and woodlands (WRI/IIED, 1986). Over half of the forest loss occurred in the West African countries. Each year, 290 000 hectares of closed forest in the Ivory Coast and 300 000 hectares in Nigeria are deforested. Most of the forest loss in East Africa is occurring in Madagascar and in Ethiopia. In the latter, the forested area has shrunk from 16% of the land area in the 1950s to 4% in the 1970s, leaving the country increasingly vulnerable to droughts and floods.

In tropical Asia, 1.8 million hectares of closed forest were deforested every year between 1976 and 1980. Especially large areas have been deforested in Indonesia, Thailand, Malaysia, the Philippines, India, Burma and Laos. Asia's highest rates of deforestation are in Nepal and Thailand, where the population is large relative to the size of remaining closed forest areas. The forest area of the Himalayan watershed has declined by 40% over the past 30 years, contributing to shortages of food, fuel and wood in the uplands and to floods and siltation in the lowlands.

With the present rate of deforestation in the developing countries, where fuelwood is most needed (the demand will increase by the year 2000), situations have evolved where fuelwood has become quite scarce. By 1980, 96 million people in the countryside of developing countries were acutely short of fuelwood and could not meet their needs (FAO, 1983). They lived on the dry land south of the Sahara, in East and South-east Africa, and in mountainous parts of the continent; in the Himalayas and the hills of South Asia; on the Andean plateau and the arid lands on the Pacific coast of South America. Another 150 million lived in cities surrounded by countryside with not enough firewood.

In 1980, too, another 1 283 million people (about 1 050 million country dwellers and 233 million urban people) lived in areas where they could still get enough wood, but only by cutting down trees faster than they grow. Seventy million lived in the countryside of North Africa and the Middle East, and 143 million in dry parts of the Latin American countryside; 131 million lived in rural Africa south of the Sahara, mainly in savannah areas in the west, centre and south-east of the continent; and no fewer than 710 million lived in the countryside and small towns of Asia, mainly in the great plains of the Indus and Ganges rivers and in South-east Asia. As long as this situation continues, trees will steadily disappear, until the people of these areas become acutely short of firewood around the year 2000. By then, of course, populations will have grown and in all, about three billion people will be facing acute scarcity or cutting down trees faster than they grow.

Fuelwood scarcity has several harmful consequences. It causes increasing hardship to the rural poor, due to the large amount of time spent in collecting fuel. Thus, fuel gathering joins water collection as a source of daily drudgery, cutting into potentially productive time, especially for women. The urban poor, on the other hand, may be faced with rising fuelwood prices and even if other fuels become competitive, the poor often cannot afford the initial investment in the necessary gas or kerosene stoves. The destruction of the tree cover can also have detrimental environmental consequences. Trees play a vital role in restoring soil fertility and maintaining soil structure, so their removal tends to be followed by loss of topsoil by wind or water erosion, particularly in arid zones, mountains and other fragile ecological areas. In certain circumstances, the switch from fuelwood to crop and animal residues can exacerbate the ecological damage arising from the loss of tree cover, leading to reductions in crop yields (Barnard and Kristoferson, 1985).

In the mid-1970s, as awareness of fuelwood problems increased, there was a great deal of interest in wood conservation through the development of more efficient stoves. The commonly used cooking stoves in the developing countries have efficiencies of between 6% and 10% (ie from 90–94% of the total heat value of the fuelwood is wasted). Several attempts have been made to increase the efficiency of wood stoves. In Indonesia, the Singer type stove with an efficiency of 27% has led to substantial savings in wood consumption. Other types of efficient stoves include the Indian Junagadh stove (30% efficiency), the Guatemala Lorena type (15–20% efficiency) and the New Nepali Chulo (about 20% efficiency). However, the dissemination of such efficient stoves has been slow and has encountered a number of economic, social and cultural problems. In view of the limited scope for improving the efficiency with which fuelwood is used in the home, new sources of fuelwood (to replace those being depleted) or substitute fuels are essential in alleviating the problems of fuelwood scarcity.

Energy farms

The logical, immediate response to the growing crisis of fuelwood is to manage forests better and to plant more trees in energy farms. There are three main types of fuelwood plantations: large scale forest usually planted on publicly owned land; smaller village woodlots, meeting the needs of rural communities; and even smaller, scattered plantings, including house gardens, fences and groups of trees to provide shade, protection, fruit or fodder for livestock. In some places, rural communities traditionally grow fuelwood integrated closely with food crops. Even in such crowded areas as Java or the Mekong Delta traditional farming systems set aside between 2% and 5% of the agricultural land for tree planting, with great effect.

Many countries have recently been paying a good deal of attention to wood plantations. The Repulic of Korea's New Community movement, which began in 1971, planted 40 000 hectares of trees by 1976. An estimated 30 million hectares of land was under plantation in China by 1970. A recent assessment by FAO and UNEP shows that plantations of wood for industry, fuelwood, charcoal, other products and soil protection, cover about 2.7 million hectares in Indonesia, 2.6 million in India, 400 000 in Bangladesh, 300 000 in the Philippines and over 200 000 in Thailand. Plantations were also under way in Sri Lanka, Pakistan, Malaysia, Nepal, Burma and Brunei (UNEP, 1981b).

In energy farms, specially selected fast growing trees should be planted in closely spaced rows and harvested every four to seven years. They will need fertilizers, weed and pest controls and, possibly, irrigation – more intensive cultivation than is normal in forestry. If this is done, yields should be well above those obtained from present practices, which allow trees to grow longer and harvest them less intensively. Productivity will also depend on how well trees suit local conditions. They should be chosen to grow quickly even on poor soil, need as little care as possible, resist pests and diseases, and be able to survive droughts and similar crises. They should also be suitable for coppicing – sprouting anew from their stumps after they have been cut close to the ground, so that they produce crop after crop from the same roots. Their wood should, naturally, have a high heating value. And they should be suitable for as many uses as possible so that their trunks and branches could be exploited for firewood, or charcoal, while their leaves are used for cattle food or fertilizer or turned into energy in biogas plants (Moss and Morgan, 1981; Bungay, 1981; Hall *et al*, 1982).

Some suitable species have already been identified. One important group are the tropical legumes, which automatically provide their own fertilizer by fixing nitrogen from the air. As they grow they therefore actually improve the soil. *Leucaena leucocephala* – the giant ipil ipil is one variety – is the best known member of the family. It is particularly bountiful, for it also produces high protein seeds and foliage which makes an excellent animal feed supplement and green fertilizer. Other tropical legume trees, such as various *Acacia, Calliandra* and *Sesbania* species, also grow fast. So do some trees from other families: *Eucalyptus* and *Casuarina* trees are among the most promising (NAS, 1980).

Fast growing trees like these are enormously productive if they are well matched to local conditions. Many species will produce more than 20 cubic metres of wood per hectare every year when grown on reasonably good soil. In exceptional cases *Leucaena, Eucalyptus* and several other species are reported to have produced as much as 50 m^3/ha/year (Benemann, 1978).

Once the wood is harvested it can be used to generate heat, steam or electricity. Ipil ipil plantations have already been established in the Philippines to produce electric power. They are intended to fuel several stations with a total capacity of 200 megawatts by 1987 – and by the year 2000, 700 000 hectares of wood plantations and 2 000 megawatts of electricity are planned (Harlow and Adriano, 1980). In Tamil Nadu, India, 11 500 hectares of *Casuarina* trees will provide fuel for a power plant generating 100 megawatts (Revelle, 1979).

Alternatively, wood can be turned into charcoal, gas or liquid fuel. None of these uses is new. Charcoal has been produced since the dawn of civilization; some say that making it was the first chemical process ever discovered by man. Relatively large

Eucalyptus energy farms (8 000 hectares), dedicated to charcoal production for steel mills, have been in operation since the early 1950s in Argentina and Brazil (NAS, 1980). Wood alcohol was used as a liquid fuel for most of the 18th and part of the 19th centuries. Kerosene and other fuels took its place; but now there is new interest in mixing it with gasoline for motor fuel.

Making gas from wood and charcoal is another old technology that is being revived. Several European countries and Japan had projects for fuelling engines with the gas before World War II. By late 1941, 70 000 cars in Sweden alone used it, as did 55% of the trucks and 70% of the buses (Bungay, 1981). Farm equipment also made good use of it. After the war most vehicles switched to gasoline because it was a better and more convenient fuel. Now the gas is coming into its own again in several countries, particularly in the countryside. In the Philippines, for example, the process is used to run fishing boats, water pumps and some public service vehicles, and to produce electricity (Harlow and Adriano, 1980).

Even when all the conditions are right for new fuelwood plantations, they are often never established. This is because some governments do not give enough support to tree growing in the countryside. They are not aware enough either of the effort that will be needed to meet their countries' energy needs in future or of the opportunities for tree planting. At the same time, some local peoples often show just as little interest, for they see firewood as something that has traditionally been free for the taking. This apathy is reinforced by incapacity. Some nations just do not have the institutional framework to implement major fuelwood programmes and have only a limited capacity to organize and support tree growing by local villages and farms.

Countries that overcome these problems of attitude and structure face a new set of practical difficulties in setting up large scale and extensive plantations. Allocating the land for the new trees is the first problem. The countries' best and most accessible land will usually already be used for agriculture. So the main areas that are readily available for trees will either be remote or on poor or impoverished land. Both pose problems. Producing fuelwood in distant parts of a country is only economically feasible if it can be transported cheaply, which is most unlikely, or turned into charcoal before transport, a process that requires capital and skill unlikely to be present in such remote areas. Developing poor land requires careful choice of species and sometimes special techniques in establishing plantations. Even when good or moderate land is available for plantation development it would seem, on economic and natural resource grounds, that such areas should be developed to produce timber and pulpwood, rather than fuel, because these will attract more revenue. Lastly, it is hard to get enough skilled and semiskilled labour to implement the kind of planting programmes necessary to meet fuelwood requirements from large scale plantations.

Agroforestry has much to offer when land is scarce. It involves intercropping trees and field crops, so that both food and fuel can be produced from the same land. Naturally, the crops must be chosen carefully so that they complement rather than compete with each other. *Eucalyptus*, for example, is not a good choice for agroforestry because it soaks up a lot of moisture and tends to produce toxic substances. *Leucaena*, on the other hand, helps to fertilize the whole area around it because it is a legume. It also has an open leaf structure which does not shade out ground crops as much as some other trees (Hall *et al*, 1982). Many of the tree planting schemes based on fast growing trees have several complementary objectives and are aimed at providing jobs, improving the environment and bringing social benefits to the local people as well as growing renewable energy. The Philippines Dendrothermal Programme illustrates this well (Harlow and Adriano, 1980). The programme, which includes fuelling a series of small (three megawatt) power plants with ipil ipil trees, aims in the long term to provide rural development and to settle shifting cultivators.

Environmental protection is an important part of any successful plan for energy, because, despite appearances, growing trees is not always benign. The whole process of producing wood for fuel can cause environmental problems, from preparing the sites and planting the trees to managing the forests with fertilizers and pest controls, from cutting the wood and converting it to energy to burning the fuel and disposing of its wastes.

Intensive tree farming might impoverish the soil in the long term by removing nutrients and organic matter from it. This process, which, it is feared could be caused by the shorter growing times and more thorough harvesting of modern methods, would, of course, cause productivity to decline as the soil grew poorer. Intensive harvesting will remove many times more nutrients than conventional methods (Van Hook *et al*, 1980). Several studies of whole tree harvesting (which removes the complete tree, twigs and all, leaving little debris behind) have noted that nutrients in the soil have declined (Plotkin, 1980). Fertilizers can alleviate nutrient depletion, but they may not work well unless those who use them fully understand what is going wrong. In some cases using fertilizer to increase growth will actually make the problem worse; the fertilizer will cause chemical reactions in the soil which decrease its supply of other nutrients (Plotkin, 1980). And inorganic fertilizers cannot replace any loss of organic matter, which is often identified as critically important in maintaining the productive potential of forest soil.

Soil erosion and leaching can also follow felling, with far reaching consequences. The result, again, is that the soil becomes poorer as it loses nutrients, and productivity eventually declines. Once good, nourishing soil is lost, natural processes can take several thousands of years to replace it. Wildlife habitats can also be changed. Usually there is merely a temporary shift after felling when species that like open areas replace their neighbours from the forest until new planted trees grow up. The effects are much more severe when the habitats of endangered species are totally eliminated, so that they can never return (Van Hook *et al*, 1980).

Other energy plantations

Wood may be the most obvious and widely used form of green energy, but it is far from being the only one. Some plants, for example, produce materials like hydrocarbons, some of which are the main constituents of oil and natural gas. Once again, this has been known for centuries – pre-Colombian civilizations in Latin America systematically cultivated trees which produced liquid that could be made into rubber. Even today the natural rubber tree, *Hevea braziliensis*, is much the best known of these plants. Its latex is no use for energy farming, since it is made up of hydrocarbons of a very heavy molecular weight; hydrocarbons of lower molecular weight are needed for fuel. Some studies have shown, however, that many species of plants may produce just what is required. Bushes of the *Euphorbia* group seem to be particularly promising. Experiments with two species (*Euphorbia lathyris* and *Euphorbia tirucalli*) have shown that they can yield between 17 and 36 barrels per hectare a year. Better still, many of the 8 000 or so known species in the family will grow on semiarid land, which means that they can be cultivated where many other plants will not flourish and can be particularly useful in developing countries that are prone to droughts (Calvin, 1979; Bungay, 1981).

Other plants, including soybeans, sunflowers and groundnuts, also produce oils. Most of them can be used to fuel diesel engines without further processing, either by themselves or blended with diesel fuel. Most of them, too, can grow in a wide range of soils, provided that they get the right amount of water and the right temperature, though their ability to tolerate different climatic conditions varies significantly between species. But such peanut power or beanzol is unlikely to do much to replace diesel, because the oils cost much more and are, of course, wanted for food.

Some crops contain sugars and starches that can be turned into fuel by fermentation. Sugar cane and sweet sorghum are the main sugar crops and both grow fast in good conditions when farmed by modern agricultural methods. Fifty tons of sugar cane will grow each year per hectare in Brazil and yields may go up to as much as 120 tons per hectare per year as they do in Hawaii. Sweet sorghum will produce an annual crop of about 45 tons per hectare. Both their sugars can be directly fermented to produce ethanol, a form of alcohol. Sugar cane will produce about 3 600 litres of alcohol per hectare and sweet sorghum about 3 500 (Brown, 1980; El-Hinnawi and Biswas, 1981).

Cassava (mandioca) – a subsistence crop in many developing countries – is the primary starch crop of interest. It has many advantages. It tolerates poor soil and adverse weather conditions much better than the sugar crops mentioned above and unlike them, it does not need high levels of fertilizer or pesticides to give good yields. About 10 to 12 tons of cassava are produced per hectare each year – and this can be turned into about 2 160 litres of alcohol (Brown, 1980; Hall *et al*, 1982).

Other plants, like corn, rice and other cereals, can also be turned into ethanol. Corn is indeed used to produce alcohol, particularly in the USA (about six tons of corn are produced annually per hectare, yielding about 2 200 litres of alcohol). But, of course, these cereals are more valuable for food than for fuel.

Ethanol can either be used as a fuel on its own or blended with gasoline 'gasohol'. Gasohol is now used on wide scale in automobiles in some countries, eg in Brazil, Kenya, the Philippines and the USA. Internal combustion engines need no modification if up to 20% of ethanol is mixed with gasoline. Although ethanol has a lower calorific value than gasoline, it has a higher density and a motor running on ethanol is 18% more powerful than one running on gasoline. When added to gasoline, alcohol increases the octane rating of the fuel and so eliminates the use of lead additives. In addition, vehicles running on gasohol emit less hydrocarbons and carbon monoxide than those running on gasoline. However, they emit more nitrogen oxides and aldehydes. The environmental impacts of such changes in emissions have not yet been studied in detail.

Brazil has the largest programme for making alcohol from biomass. Its National Alcohol Programme, PROALCOOL, aims at producing about 10.7 million cubic metres per year. Nearly all the county's cars already run on gasohol and more than a million run on pure alcohol. However, not every country in the world can resort to producing ethanol for fuel. Only those that produce enough food, but too little energy, for their needs, may embark on a programme of making alcohol fuel from biomass, and then only if their climate, soil, water supplies and other environmental conditions are favourable. Ethanol production can be a very polluting industry if adequate measures are not taken to treat the voluminous liquid effluents produced. There is also the question of the energy balance in producing ethanol. The energy required to produce ethyl alcohol (energy used in crop plantations and the industrial production process) should be less than the energy of the alcohol produced (ie there should be a net energy gain). This energy balance varies from site to site and depends on the agricultural and industrial technologies applied.

Energy conservation

More than one-half of the energy put into daily use – in transport, industry, agriculture, households and other consumer sectors – is wasted due to losses induced by technology and by man. In the ECE region, for example, the average efficiency (useful output as percentage of input) of energy utilization was estimated at 42% (ECE, 1976). In other regions, lower or higher efficiencies depend on the socioeconomic conditions and on the technologies of energy utilization.

Energy conservation has been defined as the strategy of adjusting and optimizing energy using systems and procedures so as to reduce energy requirements per unit of output (or well being) without affecting socioeconomic development or causing disruption in lifestyles (Schipper, 1976). The principal effort should be directed at obtaining more work from the fuel already being consumed. Energy conservation does not mean going without; it means going further with what is available. The question, 'How much fuel do we have?' must be joined by the question, 'How well are we using it?'.

Energy consumption is the product of innumerable decisions made by countless energy users, large and small. Such decisions depend on a host of economic factors such as incomes, costs, investments and taxes. Energy consumption also depends on technologies and on efficiencies of energy use, on climate and geography, on social patterns and norms, on government regulations, on environmental priorities and requirements and on perceptions of the role that energy plays in human affairs. These factors interact differently, and have different implications for different nations, and among different users (Wilson, 1977). The main sectors of energy use are residential and commercial, transport, industry and agriculture. Increasing the efficiency of energy utilization in these sectors can result in very substantial and worthwhile energy savings.

Buildings consume energy in three main phases. First, energy is used to manufacture materials for construction. More energy is used directly in the construction process. Finally, daily and seasonal operation requires additional energy throughout the building's lifetime. The amounts of energy consumed in these phases vary considerably from one country to another and are higher in developed than in developing countries. Substantial savings in energy consumption in the residential and commercial sector can be achieved through the application of appropriate building technologies (building material, design, insulation etc) and the use of energy efficient equipment (heating, air-conditioning, lighting etc). In Sweden, for example, space heating requirements are 30–40% lower per square metre of space in homes and commercial buildings than in the USA, the difference being ascribed to generally more energy efficient structures in Sweden (Schipper and Lichtenberg, 1975). One-half of the direct energy now spent on lighting is superfluous and most lights operate inefficiently. Currently, incandescent bulbs convert only one-twentieth of the energy in electricity into light; fluorescent bulbs convert over one-fifth. There is no fundamental theoretical reason why a much higher conversion efficiency of electricity into light should not be obtained. Research and development have increased the efficiency of many household technologies in recent years (Flavin, 1986 a, b). In 1985, a US study found that in the past decade the efficiency of new refrigerators had increased 52% and that of room air-conditioners 76%. New Japanese and European fluorescent lights use one-third as much power as systems now in use. Schipper and Ketoff (1985) pointed out that for seven countries (Denmark, France, FR Germany, Sweden, Norway, USA and Canada), residential oil use decreased by 40% between 1972 and 1984, for a saving of about 59 million tonnes of oil equivalent per year. One-third of this resulted from reductions in the number of homes heated with oil, the rest from reductions in oil use per oil heated home. Of the total oil savings, at least 46% are of a permanent nature, while the rest could be reversed with a continued slide in oil prices, although it seems likely that most of the savings will be maintained and may even increase.

In the transport sector, the efficiency of energy utilization varies considerably. Railroads and waterways, for example, are more efficient than aircraft or auto-mobiles. The latter are the least efficient, and they account for the bulk of energy consumption in the transport sector. Private cars consume about 7% of the world's commercial energy, or 17% of the oil used each year (Chandler, 1985). The USA, in fact, uses 10% of the world's oil output as gasoline for motor cars and light trucks. Substantial energy savings can be made in the transport system by improving engineering, by improving load factors on existing modes and, more important, by changing habits of transport. Fuel economy around the world averages about 21 miles per gallon (8.9 km per litre), though it varies widely (the US automobile fleet is the world's least efficient). New cars have a fuel economy of up to 32 miles per gallon and several manufacturers have produced prototype cars that obtain up to 93 miles per gallon (Chandler, 1985). The predominant use of light automobiles in some countries and the switch to buses and fixed rail transport systems in intracity travel has led to considerable energy savings (Schipper and Lichtenberg, 1975; IEA, 1984; Chandler, 1985). Conservation efforts in the transport sector often bring unexpected secondary benefits. For example, the reduction of highway speed limits in the USA (which was intended to increase fuel efficiency), had the additional benefit of increasing automobile tyre life and, more important, reducing highway accidents and deaths.

Industrial processes consume more of the world's commercial energy than either transport or housing. In some countries, particularly the centrally planned economies of the USSR and Eastern Europe, the share allocated to industry approaches two-thirds of all energy consumed. Of the world's 250 major industrial products that consume significant amounts of energy in production, 12 together consume more than 70% of the energy used by the entire industrial sector. These products are petroleum fuels, petrochemicals, steel, aluminium, fertilizers, cement, glass, bricks and ceramics, pulp and paper, sugar and finished textiles (Gamba et al, 1986).

Substantial savings of energy in industry could be achieved through good housekeeping and technological innovations. The conversion from steam engines to diesel electric, the introduction of more energy efficient components into existing processes, more energy conscious maintenance and operation of equipment, replacement of existing facilities by more energy efficient ones, introduction of energy efficient innovations in industrial processes, multipurpose use of energy, for example, for electricity and steam generation in industry, are examples of the many ways and means that could lead to more efficient use of energy in the industrial sector. The steel industry, for example, contains several typical opportunities for conservation. Hot coke is usually quenched with water in the USA, thus dissipating its heat while producing air and water pollution. In Europe and the USSR, coke is cooled with a recycled inert gas and much of its heat is recaptured to perform useful work (Hayes, 1976). Aluminium refining is an exceedingly energy-intensive operation and the industry has therefore situated its major installations near sources of cheap energy, for example near large hydroelectric facilities. Technical advances in the traditional refining process can reduce energy requirements by more than one-fifth. It should be noted that a reduction of industrial energy use does not demand a reduction in economic production. Rather, it requires industry to use the fuel it consumes more efficiently.

Japan provides a model of industrial energy efficiency and has made major gains since the early 1970s. The energy intensities of chemical and steel production have dropped by 38% and 16% respectively since 1973 and energy use per unit of output has fallen in every major industry since 1975 (Chandler, 1985). The French industrial sector also ranks among the most energy efficient, and, like Japan, made large improvements after 1973. Energy intensity in textile, building materials, rubber and plastics and mechanical construction fell by more than 30%, an annual rate of improvement of more than 3.5%. In the USA, the energy intensity of the production of paper, aluminium, steel and cement fell by 17% between 1972 and 1981 (Chandler, 1985).

No short list can exhaust the possibilities for substantial conservation of energy. Most goods could be both manufactured and made to work more efficiently. A variety of energy saving measures have been recently adopted by various countries, including fiscal measures, regulations and standards, encouragement of action by common means (public transport, total energy systems), public education and research and development. Energy policies designed to encourage efficient use of energy will probably have to incorporate many of these measures. Even before considering the question of what sources of energy to develop tomorrow, one must confront energy conservation today; inefficient energy use means inefficient and costly malfunctions in the economy.

Energy efficiency has been far and away the largest contributor to the improved world oil situation during the past decade. Indeed, statistics show that greater efficiency accounts for over half the 36% decline in the energy/GNP ratio of industrial countries since 1973 (Figure 27). Between 1973 and 1984, US energy efficiency rose 23%. Western Europe realized a 16% decline in its energy intensity between 1973 and 1984. Japan led the world with a remarkable 29% decline in its energy/GNP ratio (Flavin, 1986a). Yet there remains an enormous potential to improve further the energy efficiency of the world's economies.

Developing countries face enormous obstacles in attempting to improve energy efficiency. Third World factories often consume two to five times as much fuel for a given process, due to decades old industrial equipment and a frequent shortage of trained personnel to perform simple maintenance and retrofits (Flavin, 1986a). Because factories are often required to produce a fixed quota of goods at a fixed price, there is little incentive to lower energy costs. Third World buildings and transport systems are also inefficient.

In many developing countries much of the energy consumed is from resources that have not so far been accounted for in most international statistics, such as firewood, cowdung and agricultural residues. The commonly held axiom that 'only the affluent can afford conservation' is thoroughly discredited by the fuelwood crisis. Proper management of energy resources is essential in the poor countries because of energy's importance in domestic life, agriculture, the creation of productive jobs and the balancing of trade with other nations. Just as in the industrialized countries,

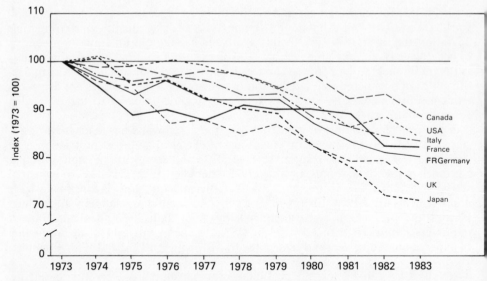

Figure 27 Change in total energy required per unit of GDP in some OECD countries
After OECD, 1985

there are significant environmental benefits associated with energy conservation, as well as economic benefits; the additional benefits of preserving social options by reducing dependence on certain sources of energy cannot be minimized.

Energy conservation has, undoubtedly, several beneficial economic and environmental consequences. Energy conservation today will allow the earth's limited resource base of high quality fuels to be stretched further. It will enable future generations to share in the earth's finite stock of fossil fuels. Energy conservation will allow a portion of these fuels to be reserved for non-energy purposes: to make drugs, lubricants, and other compounds. It will help reduce environmental degradation associated with all current energy production technologies. Energy conservation will permit the avoidance of, or minimal reliance on, doubtful energy sources while the search for safe, sustainable sources continues. Conservation also decreases the likelihood that the climatological threshold (for example, with carbon dioxide production, or with regional heat generation) will be crossed, triggering consequences that may be devastating.

Transport and environment

From the earliest times, transport has been a vital influence in the evolution of civilizations. Today, more people travel over greater distances and more fuels, raw materials and products are transported around the world than ever before. Transport industries make a major contribution to national economies. But like many other activities, transport has some undesirable impacts on the environment.

Most cities were built long before the development of the automobile. Their narrow streets were designed for pedestrians and animal drawn wagons. Today, they are being overwhelmed by motor cars, lorries and buses and are finding this increase in motorized traffic increasingly difficult to accommodate. Congestion, reducing average road speeds to below 15 km/h (especially in developing countries), neutralizes the benefits of the motor vehicle and leads to pressure for more urban roads and/or flyovers.

On the road, the number of motor vehicles in the world increased from about 246 million in 1970 to about 427 million in 1980 and reached 467 million in 1983 (OECD, 1985). Most motor vehicles have been in OECD countries, accounting for 86.2% of all vehicles in 1970 and for 76.2% in 1983. The number of motor vehicles is rapidly increasing in the developing countries : it doubled from about 53 million in 1975 to about 111 million in 1983. The number of motor vehicles increased, however, at a much slower rate in OECD countries; the rate of increase from 1975 to 1983 was 29%. Passenger cars constituted the bulk of motor vehicles on the road. It has been estimated that the average level of motorization is now about 75 cars per 1000 inhabitants worldwide but reaches 540 in the USA, over 400 in Canada, Australia and New Zealand, 220 in Japan and ranges from 200 to 400 in Europe (OECD, 1985). It has also been estimated that the world fleet of passenger cars will increase to about 700 million by the year 2000, reaching one car for every eight people (Brown, 1984). Road freight has also increased in scale and efficiency. Modern diesel-powered lorries, commonly with trailers, are providing a dramatically increased level of community service, especially over short distances. The number of goods vehicles in the world increased from about 68 million in 1975 to about 99 million in 1983 (about 68% in OECD countries).

Other kinds of transport also grew over the past decade. The total volume of international seaborne trade reached 3 320 million tonnes in 1984, an increase of 6.7% over 1983. Tanker cargoes in 1984 (1 427 million tonnes) showed a slight increase over 1983, but were still 23.7% less than in 1980. Dry cargo, however, reached record volumes in 1984 (1 893 million tonnes) with both main bulk commodities and other dry cargo increasing by more than 10.6% over 1983 (UNCTAD, 1985). Over the past decade there have also been increases in air traffic and rail transport, and pipelines are now transporting coal, gas, oil and other bulk materials over longer distances.

The expansion of transport in the world, especially in developing countries, has obviously consumed much land. Motorways in the OECD countries increased from 73 000 km in 1970 to 108 000 km in 1980 (an increase of 48%), and reached 114 000 km in 1983. All roads in OECD countries increased from 11.7 million km in 1970 to 12.5 million km in 1983 (OECD, 1985). Road development programmes have been scaled down and the increase in roads has been much slower than in the past. This has been attributed to economic and, in part, environmental reasons. The slow rate of road construction in OECD countries is also due to the fact that most of these countries have already established most of the necessary infrastructure and have reached the level of saturation. The situation is different in developing countries. In these countries there is need for additional roads of all kinds – the pace of construction has been slow for economic reasons; existing roads are not adequately maintained and in most countries the condition of roads is deteriorating.

The ever increasing number of motor vehicles on the roads since the 1950s has resulted in an upsurge of traffic accidents in both developed and developing countries that has taken on the characteristic of an epidemic. It has been estimated that about 300 000 people are killed each year in traffic accidents and that several millions are injured (Bayliss, 1983). While fatality rates probably exceed 50 per 100 million vehicle-kilometres in some developing countries (eg Lesotho and Sierra Leone) they have reduced to fewer than 5 per 100 million vehicle-kilometres in developed countries. Subsequent to road safety measures introduced in most

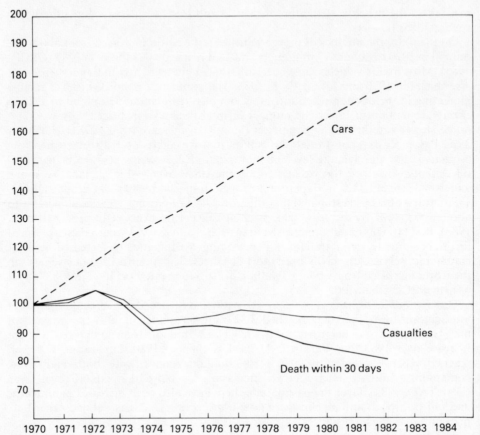

Figure 28 The drop in casualties in Europe despite the increase in number of cars in use due to enforcement of road safety measures, 1970 index = 100
After ECMT/OECD, 1985

European countries since 1973 (speed limits, compulsory seat belts, crash helmets etc) the numbers of killed and casualties dropped sharply (Figure 28) despite the increase in the number of cars in use (ECMT/OECD, 1985). In many cities in the developing countries (eg Caracas, Bangkok, Cairo), with congested streets, pressure for road space (for driving and/or parking) has meant such encroachment on the pavements that space for pedestrians barely exists and walking and cycling have become dangerous and unpleasant.

Transport is a great consumer of energy. The efficiency of energy utilization varies considerably. Railroads and waterways, for example, are more efficient than aircraft or automobiles. The latter are the least efficient, and they account for the bulk of energy consumption in the transport sector.

The most familiar environmental impacts of road transport are those from air pollution. Petrol burning vehicles emit carbon monoxide, hydrocarbons, oxides of nitrogen, particulates and trace compounds. In confined spaces (like tunnels or narrow streets) carbon monoxide concentrations can rise to levels hazardous to health, especially to people with heart or lung weakness. Oxides of nitrogen and hydrocarbons, on the other hand, are not directly toxic, but interact in the presence of sunlight to produce an oxidant smog which irritates the eyes and lungs and damages sensitive plants. Most OECD countries have implemented emission standards for new motor vehicles (especially for carbon monoxide, hydrocarbons and nitrogen oxides). In most European countries, the lead content of petrol has been reduced to levels between 0.15 and 0.40 grams per litre and steps are being taken to introduce unleaded petrol (OECD, 1985). Studies carried out near highways have shown that trace metals such as cadmium, lead, nickel, zinc, copper and chromium are more highly concentrated on vegetation and soil near highways than on crops from sites farther away (Ndiokwere, 1984; Falahi-Ardakani, 1984). The discharge of used motor oils in the environment poses public health problems because such oils contain high quantities of polycyclic aromatic hydrocarbons which are known to be carcinogenic (Pasquini and Monarca, 1983).

Increasing numbers of automobiles and light duty trucks are likely to be equipped with diesel engines in the future because they have higher fuel efficiencies than gasoline engines and because diesel fuel has traditionally cost less than gasoline. Diesel powered vehicles now achieve 20–40% more distance per unit volume of fuel than gasoline powered vehicles because of their higher fuel efficiencies and because diesel fuel contains about 15% more energy than an equal volume of gasoline (DOE, 1982).

Current diesel powered vehicles emit more visible smoke and odours than gasoline powered vehicles and this has led to conern about their possible effect on human health and the environment. Diesel vehicles emit 30 to 50 times more particulate matter than a comparable gasoline vehicle (Choudhury and Bush, 1981; Cuddihy et al, 1984). Diesel exhaust particles consist of chain aggregates of carbon microspheres coated with a variety of organic compounds that comprise 15–65% of the total particle mass. Several hundred organic compounds have been identified in solvent extracts of diesel exhaust particles (Menster and Sharkey, 1977), several of which (eg polynuclear aromatic hydrocarbons) are known to be carcinogenic.

Diesel exhaust particles are small and they readily deposit in the respiratory tract when inhaled. There are two concerns related to inhaling high concentrations of particles. First, they may cause respiratory functional changes and increased susceptibility to infections because of their toxic properties. Second, they may increase the risk of developing respiratory tract cancers because they contain mutagenic and carcinogenic compounds (see Pepelko, 1981).

Aircraft and railway locomotives together emit a far smaller volume of air pollutants than road vehicles do. However, high flying aircraft release oxides of nitrogen directly into the lower stratosphere where they may become involved in chemical reactions which could affect the ozone layer (see Chapter 2). Aircraft emissions contribute up to 3% of the total annual emissions in urban areas surrounding airports, but in rural areas an airport may represent the largest single contributor of total emissions in its area of air quality influence. The major pollutants from airport related services are carbon monoxide, hydrocarbons, particulates and nitrogen oxides (Clark et al, 1985).

Noise

Of all present day sources of noise, the noise from transport – above all that from road vehicles – is the most diffused. In many countries it is the source that creates the greatest problems. Everywhere it is growing in intensity, spreading to areas until now unaffected, reaching ever further into the night hours and creating as much concern as any other type of pollution. Recent data show that about 110 million people are exposed to road traffic noise levels in excess of 65 dBA in the OECD countries (OECD, 1985). For aircraft noise, about 0.5% of the population in the European countries and Japan are exposed to noise levels in excess of 65 dBA, whereas the proportion of the population affected in the USA is 2%, or some five million people. Overall, about 16% of the population of the OECD countries – approximately 130 million people – are exposed to noise levels in excess of 65 dBA. It is recognized in many countries that the percentage of population living in grey areas, that is those exposed to noise levels between 55 and 65 dBA, is increasing and therefore that noise has become a more significant problem than it was thought to be a few years ago.

Noise disrupts activity, disturbs sleep and hinders people carrying out their work. Noise also generates stress. Quite apart from the permanent damage it causes to hearing, it also has a very considerable impact on how an individual functions physiologically, psychologically and socially, both because of the effort required to acclimatize to noise and because of the frustration resulting from the deterioration in the quality of life and sleep.

Many countries have adopted regulations to control maximum permissible noise levels for the different categories of motor vehicles. However, the problem still remains (even increasing in magnitude in several urban centres in developing countries), and more efforts are required to reduce the exposure to noise from traffic. This can be achieved only by an integrated approach, using adequate urban planning and road design, including use of sound screens or barriers, soundproofing of buildings and traffic control as well as legislation.

Annoyance to people living near airports caused by the noise of jet take-offs and landings has become a psychophysiological and economic problem of enormous magnitude and complexity. As a result of the expansion of air traffic, airports tend to occupy large land areas, with multiple runways and large air spaces for landing and take-off procedures. At the same time, under the pressure of population, communities tend to expand towards airports and thus to enter zones of higher noise. At present, aircraft noise affects people near airports, but an increase in the use of vertical and short take-off and landing aircraft and of supersonic transport is likely to affect a much wider population. It can be said, however, that the existing problems with aircraft noise are much less serious now than they would have been, had they not been recognized early and serious steps taken to reduce their impact. Aircraft noise has been curbed in many places by a combination of operational controls and new technology. Many airports have banned night flights. They often require aircraft to reduce their thrust soon after take-off and climb more slowly and to approach and leave along corridors that avoid residential areas. At the same time, aircraft engines are becoming quieter.

References

BARNARD, G. and KRISTOFERSON, L. (1985). *Agricultural Residues as Fuel in the Third World*, Earthscan, International Institute for Environment and Development, London

BAYLISS, D. (1983). *Automobile Traffic in Developing Countries: Environmental and Health Issues*, Who Report EFP/EC/WP/83.4, World Health Organization, Geneva

BENEMANN, J.R. (1978). *Biofuels: A Survey*, Electric Power Research Institute, Palo Alto, CA

BENNETT, L.L. and SKJOELDEBRAND, R. (1986). Worldwide nuclear power status and trends, *IAEA Bulletin*, **28**, 40

BROWN, L.R. (1980). *Food or Fuel*, Worldwatch Paper No 35, Worldwatch Institute, Washington, DC

BROWN, L.R. (1984). Reconsidering the automobile's future, in BROWN, L.R. *et al*, eds, *State of the World – 1984*, W.W. Norton, New York

BUNGAY, H.R. (1981). *Energy: The Biomass Option*, John Wiley, New York

CALVIN, M. (1979). Petroleum plantations and synthetic chloroplasts, *Energy*, **4**, 851

CHANDLER, W.V. (1985). Increasing energy efficiency, in BROWN, L.R. *et al*, eds, *State of the World – 1985*, W.W. Norton, New York

CHOUDHURY, D.R. and BUSH, B. (1981). Polynuclear aromatic hydrocarbons in diesel emission particulates, *Environment International*, **5**, 229

CLARKE, A.I. *et al* (1985). Air quality impact assessment at an airport, *Environmental Pollution*, (Series B), **9**, 1

CUDDIHY, R.G. *et al* (1984). Health risks from light-duty diesel vehicles, *Environmental Science and Technology*, **18**, 14A

DOE (1982). *1983 Gas Mileage Guide*, DOE/CE-0019/2, US Department of Energy, Washington, DC

ECE (1976). *Increased Energy Economy and Efficiency in the ECE Region*, Report E/ECE/883/Rev.1, Economic Commission for Europe, Geneva

ECMT/OECD (1985). *Statistical Report on Road Accidents in 1983*, European Conference of Ministers of Transport, Organization for Economic Cooperation and Development, Paris

EL-HINNAWI, E. (1980). *Nuclear Energy and the Environment*, Pergamon Press, Oxford

EL-HINNAWI, E. (1981). The promise of renewable sources of energy, in EL-HINNAWI, E. and BISWAS, A.K., eds, *Renewable Sources of Energy and the Environment*, Tycooly International, Dublin

EL-HINNAWI, E. and BISWAS, A.K. (1981). *Renewable Sources of Energy and the Environment*, Tycooly International, Dublin

EL-HINNAWI, E. and HASHMI, M. (1982). *Global Environmental Issues*, Tycooly International, Dublin

EL-HINNAWI, E. *et al* (1983). *New and Renewable Sources of Energy*, Tycooly International, Dublin

FALAHI-ARDAKANI, A. (1984). Contamination of environment with heavy metals emitted from automobiles, *Ecotoxicology and Environmental Safety*, **8**, 152

FAO (1983). *Fuelwood Supplies in Developing Countries*, Food and Agriculture Organization of the United Nations, Rome

FAO (1985). *Yearbook of Forest Products 1972-1983*, Food and Agriculture Organization of the United Nations, Rome

FLAVIN, C. (1986a). Moving beyond oil, in BROWN L.R. *et al*, eds, *State of the World – 1986*, W.W. Norton, New York

FLAVIN, C. (1986b). *Electricity for a Developing World: New Directions*, Worldwatch Paper No 70, Worldwatch Institute, Washington, DC

GAMBA, J.R. *et al* (1986). *Industrial Energy Rationalization in Developing Countries*, Johns Hopkins University Press, Baltimore, MD

GOODMAN, G.T. (1985). Energy and development: where do we go from here?, *Ambio*, **14**, 186

HALL, D.O. *et al* (1982). *Biomass for Energy in the Developing Countries*, Pergamon Press, Oxford

HARLOW, C.S. and ADRIANO, A.S. (1980). The Philippine dendrothermal power programme, in the *Proceedings of the BioEnergy '80 Congress*, BioEnergy Council, Washington, DC

HAYES, D. (1976). *Energy: the Case for Conservation*, Worldwatch Paper No 4, Worldwatch Institute, Washington, DC

IEA (1984). *Fuel Efficiency of Passenger Cars*, International Energy Agency, Organization for Economic Cooperation and Development, Paris

MELILLO, J. *et al* (1985). Comparison of two recent estimates of disturbances in tropical forests, *Environmental Conservation*, **12**, 37

MENSTER, M. and SHARKEY, A.G. (1977). *Chemical Characterization of Diesel Exhaust Particles*, PERC/RI-77/5, Pittsburgh Energy Research Centre, Pittsburgh, PA

MOSS, R.P. and MORGAN, W.B. (1981). *Fuelwood and Rural Energy*, Tycooly International, Dublin

NAS (1980). *Firewood Crops*, National Academy of Sciences, Washington, DC

NDIOKWERE, C.L. (1984). A study of heavy metal pollution from motor vehicle emissions and its effects on roadside soil, vegetation and crops in Nigeria, *Environmental Pollution* (Series B), 7, 35

OECD (1985). *The State of the Environment – 1985*, Organization for Economic Cooperation and Development, Paris

OPEC (1986). *Facts and Figures*, OPEC, Vienna

OPENSHAW, K. (1978). Woodfuel – a time for re-assessment, *Natural Resources Forum*, 3, 35

OPENSHAW, K. (1980). Energy requirements for household cooking in Africa with existing and improved cooking stoves, in the *Proceedings of the BioEnergy '80 Congress*, BioEnergy Council, Washington, DC

PASQUINI, R. and MONARCA, S. (1983). Detection of mutagenic carcinogenic compounds in unused and used motor oils, *The Science of the Total Environment*, 32, 55

PEPELKO, W.E. (1981). Health effect of diesel engine emissions, *Environment International*, Special issue, 5, Nos 4-6

PLOTKIN, S.E. (1980). Energy from biomass, *Environment*, 22, 6

REVELLE, R. (1979). Energy sources for rural development, *Energy*, 4, 969

SCHIPPER, L. (1976). Raising the productivity of energy utilization, *Annual Review of Energy*, 1, 445

SCHIPPER, L. and KETOFF, A.N. (1985). The international decline in household oil use, *Science*, 230, 1118

SCHIPPER, L. and LICHTENBERG, A. (1975). *Efficient Energy Use: The Swedish Example*, Rept No ERG-75-09, Energy and Resources Group, University of California, CA

UNCTAD (1985). *Review of Maritime Transport – 1984*, United Nations Conference on Trade and Development, Geneva

UNEP (1981a). *The Environmental Impacts of Production and Use of Energy*, Tycooly International, Dublin

UNEP (1981b). *Asia-Pacific Report: The Resources of Development*, United Nations Environment Programme, Nairobi

UNEP (1982). *The World Environment, 1972-1982*, Tycooly International, Dublin

VAN HOOK, R.I. *et al* (1980). Environmental effects of harvesting forests for energy, in the *Proceedings of the BioEnergy '80 Congress*, Bioenergy Council, Washington, DC

WILSON, C. (1977). *Energy Global Prospects, 1985-2000*, McGraw Hill, New York

WORLD BANK (1980). *World Development Report 1980*, World Bank, Washington, DC

WRI/IIED (1986). *World Resources – 1986*, Basic Books, New York

Chapter 5

Chemicals and hazardous waste

At home, in industry, in agriculture and in the control of disease, man uses a great number of different chemical substances. According to recent estimates, about nine million chemicals are known (Dowling, 1985); some 70 000 chemical products are on the market today and approximately 1 000 new chemicals enter commercial use each year. There can be no question that many chemical products have brought beneficial effects to man and his environment; others, however, have brought unprecedented harm.

Chemical substances enter the environment – and people – through complex and interrelated paths. Some of them, such as fertilizers and pesticides, enter the environment as a result of direct application; others, for example, sulphur oxides, nitrogen oxides, polycyclic aromatic hydrocarbons and trace metals, result from combustion processes. A third source of chemical substances is to be found in waste effluent flows from the manufacture, transport and consumption of almost all products used by modern society. Many manufacturing processes generate unwanted byproducts and air and water borne wastes which are sometimes more toxic than the raw materials. Once chemical substances have entered the environment, they undergo physical and chemical changes, including combination with other chemicals, that affect their toxicity. Through such chemical transformation a relatively harmless chemical may become a toxic byproduct in the environment. It may further enter the food chain and accumulate in living organisms.

A vast amount of scientific information is available on the short-term effects of well known chemicals hazardous to human health or to animal species, especially domestic animals. If man is exposed to enough arsenic to cause death or illness, for example, the effects are immediate and obvious. But it is still not known what happens if man is exposed to this or other chemicals at very low concentrations over a period of 20 or 30 years. Effects may appear a long time after exposure to either a large dose over a short period or a relatively small dose over an extended period. The consequences can be measured in terms of mortality and morbidity and of physiological changes which are the precursors of morbidity. Genetic mutations (production of new, mostly detrimental, hereditary traits) may be induced in proto-plasm by chemical mutagenesis and they can be permanent. Other hazards to health resulting from long-term exposure to toxic substances include the possibilities of carcinogenicity (cancer) and teratogenicity (birth defects).

Man is exposed to chemicals in three main ways – by inhalation, by ingestion and through contact with the body surface. As far as the general population is concerned, food (including drinking water) is the major source of exposure to most toxic chemicals. These substances reach human food by many routes. Some contaminate it directly in preparation or processing. Others pass from soil to plants, and thence via herbivorous animals to meat or milk. Strictly speaking, a food chain is a sequence of the latter kind.

Hazardous chemicals present in food and water comprise a wide range of both inorganic and organic substances. Such substances can be derived from a variety of sources, of which the most important are air pollutants deposited directly on to the aerial parts of food plants; pollutants taken up from the soil or irrigation water via the roots of food plants; pollutants taken up from the aquatic environment by fish and other aquatic organisms; residues of bioactive substances used in animal husbandry and their metabolites; substances produced by the growth of bacteria or moulds in or on foods; residues and breakdown products of pesticides; substances produced during food manufacture or preparation; substances migrating from food packaging material or leached from ceramic and enamelled foodware; contaminants present in drinking water, eg those resulting from chlorination or contact with lead or copper pipes; and intentional food additives.

National authorities have the responsibility and obligation to ensure that toxic chemicals are not present in food at levels that may adversely affect the health of consumers. Countries may set legal limits for food contaminants and monitor compliance with such limits. To ascertain whether a consumer is at risk or not, it is necessary to estimate the actual dietary intake of a contaminant for comparison with acceptable daily intakes (ADIs) or provisional tolerable weekly intakes (PTWIs). Obtaining such an estimate is also important in determining whether there is a relationship between any observed effects in humans and the intake of a particular contaminant. The estimation of the actual dietary intake of contaminants as a measure of exposure is thus indispensable for risk assessment. Under the GEMS, UNEP, FAO and WHO have prepared guidelines for the study of dietary intakes of chemical contaminants (WHO, 1985). The Joint FAO/WHO Food Contamination Monitoring Programme was initiated in 1976 and is one of the major health related activities of GEMS. It aims to collect and assess data on levels of certain chemicals in individual foods and in total diet samples.

The immediate impacts on human health and the environment resulting from an accident in a chemical plant, including long-term effects, are a matter of concern. The release of dioxin after an explosion at a chemical plant in Seveso, Italy, in 1976, the explosion of a huge natural liquefied gas tank in Mexico in 1984, the major accident at a chemical plant in Bhopal, India, in December 1984, and the recent accident at the Sandoz Chemical plant in Switzerland that occurred in November 1986 and has led to the contamination of the waters of the Rhine over long distances with poisonous chemicals are examples of serious incidents that can occur and that cause genuine concern for the safety of man and the environment. A number of administrative and technical steps have recently been taken to prevent such accidents and mitigate their consequences. A recent example is the European Economic Community's directive on the major hazards of certain industrial activities (the 'Seveso' directive). The directive obliges manufacturers within the Community to identify potential danger areas in the manufacturing process and to take all necessary measures to prevent major accidents as well as to limit their consequences, should they occur, for man and the environment. A major recommendation of the World Industry Conference on Environmental Management (Versailles, November 1984) was that, in order to strengthen the anticipatory and preventive approach to environmental management within industry, each line manager from the chief executive down should also think of himself or herself as an environmental manager. Clear accountability for environmental performance should accompany managerial responsibility in each case.

Less attention has, however, hitherto been paid to routine emissions of small amounts of toxic chemicals as part of normal plant operations or as a result of minor accidents. To illustrate the magnitude of these releases, the US National Response Centre received in the period between January 1983 and March 1985 more than 24 000 notifications of accidental releases. These included releases from both stationary sources such as chemical plants and mobile sources such as trucks. The US Environmental Protection Agency estimates that approximately 2 000 potentially cancer causing or toxic chemicals are likely to get into the air as a result of such releases (Kean, 1986).

A number of industrialized countries have enacted legislation in attempts to 'control' industrial chemicals prior to marketing, in order to protect man and the environment by ensuring their proper handling and use. However, the task has been complex and slow because the tools necessary to evaluate chemical effects, especially long-term toxicology and ecotoxicology, are not sufficiently developed for the task. Assessment of risk to human populations based on data from laboratory animals remains a controversial issue and many uncertainties remain regarding the methods used to determine the potential threat to the environment from chemicals.

Unlike developed countries, most developing countries have no toxic chemical control laws, nor the technical or institutional capability for implementing such laws. During recent years, several cases have come to light where products banned or severely restricted in the industrialized countries have been sold to, or 'dumped' on, the developing countries. Developing countries have been very concerned over this situation. In 1984, the UNEP Governing Council adopted a Provisional Notification Scheme for banned and severely restricted chemicals. Under this scheme, to which 34 governments had adhered by December 1984, the competent national authorities of exporting countries will inform importing countries of national bans or restrictions on chemicals which are internationally traded. In addition, the UN has issued a list of products whose consumption and/or sale have been banned, withdrawn, severely restricted, or in the case of pharmaceuticals, not approved by governments. Some 500 products are already included in this list.

The most effective way to control the flow of harmful chemicals throughout the environment is naturally to minimize or prevent their production and release. As the type and quantity of toxic emissions and byproducts are largely determined by the technology used, improvement of the equipment and development of alternative technologies is a key element in controlling the occurrence of hazardous substances. Many chemcials that are intentionally applied to the environment because of their toxic properties may be a threat to human health and cause harm to living organisms other than the target populations. Although the real risks of several families of chemicals have not yet been fully documented, evidence gathered so far clearly indicates that efforts should be made to develop non-toxic alternatives.

Pesticides

The control of plant pests and vectors of human and livestock diseases has been based on the extensive use of chemical pesticides. The use of these chemicals for pest and vector control has dramatically reduced morbidity and mortality due to vector

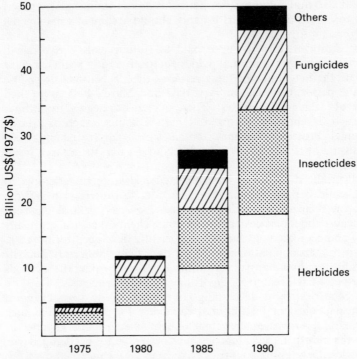

Figure 29 Sales and consumption of pesticides in the world
Drawn from data given by ECE, 1982 and OECD, 1985

borne diseases and has been a principal factor in boosting agricultural productivity in many parts of the world. In addition, pesticides have played a major role in reducing pre- and post-harvest food losses. In general, pesticides have been one of the major weapons in the struggle against food shortages.

The production of pesticides, concentrated in a limited number of countries (15 industrial producers in 5 countries account for more than 90% of world production), has increased at the rate of 4–5% a year over the past decade or so (ECE, 1982) and their consumption has risen apace, first in developed and now in developing countries (Figure 29; Table 4). Of pesticide production, 90% is used for agricultural purposes (primarily on maize, cotton and rice) and most of the rest in the health protection field.

The success of pesticides, however, has exacted a price in terms of side effects, some of them involving human health. Many pesticides are broad spectrum biocides, not only toxic to target arthropods but also to vertebrates and man. Unless applied

TABLE 4. Distribution of consumption of pesticides (%)

	Developed countries	Developing countries
Herbicides	90	10
Insecticides	55	45
Fungicides	88	12

Source: ECE (1982); OECD (1985)

carefully, some of them can kill or seriously affect people, useful animals, fish and birds. Even when properly used, chemical pesticides have a number of unavoidable side effects. Their persistence and ubiquity, coupled with a tendency for some compounds to concentrate in organisms as they move up the food chain, may increase their toxicity to fish, birds and other forms of life, including man and cause other harmful effects to man's health and well being.

The most recent estimates suggest that the number of unintentional acute pesticide poisonings in the world is of the order of one million cases per year with an overall percentage of fatality cases ranging from 0.5 to 2.0. While the figures represent only 4% of fatalities due to all types of unintentional acute poisonings worldwide, it must be emphasized that most of them are avoidable and that their geographical distribution is likely to be non-uniform, with the greatest number of cases in developing countries making intensive use of the products on cash crops without observing the necessary safety precautions. Gupta (1986) pointed out that of the pesticide poisoning cases estimated in the developing countries, India accounts for one-third. Farm labourers employed for spraying operations are the worst affected and most of them are exposed for long periods through working continuously with pesticides. Cases of blindness, cancer, deformities, diseases of the liver and the nervous system from pesticide poisoning have been identified in the cotton growing districts of two Indian states.

The amount of pesticide impinging on target pests is generally an extremely small percentage of the amount applied. Often less than 0.1% of pesticides applied to crops actually reaches target pests (Pimentel and Levitan, 1986). Thus, over 99% moves into ecosystems to contaminate land, water and air. Pesticide residues are a common cause of poisoning both in the field and in the home and a widespread but largely unassessed source of chronic professional exposure. They can also contaminate people at low levels through their ingestion of food containing concentrations far below those giving rise to overt toxic symptoms. Concentrations of persistent organochlorine compounds in food and dietary intakes of contaminants are measured in a number of countries. At the international level, the ongoing FAO/WHO/UNEP Joint Food Contamination Monitoring Programme receives data on contaminants in the food and diet from 22 participating countries. Organochlorine residue concentrations in terrestrial, freshwater and marine wildlife have been available through some national monitoring programmes, especially in OECD countries. DDT complex levels in the fat of cow's milk showed a marked decline in Japan and the Netherlands during the 1970s and a similar trend is observed in Japanese and US finfish. Those of aldrin and dieldrin have been falling consistently in both cow's and human milk in Japan, the Netherlands and Switzerland. Figure 30 shows the results of a recent study by GEMS (Slorach and Vaz, 1983) on the distribution of DDT and DDE in human milk in some developed and developing countries.

Residues of pesticides applied directly to the aerial parts of plants close to the time of harvest or used post-harvest will be present to some extent in the food when it is consumed. The use of ethylene oxide for the fumigation of spices results in the presence of residues of this mutagen and certain of its biologically active reaction products in the fumigated products. The ingestion of contaminated bread prepared from wheat and other cereals treated with alkylmercury fungicides has resulted in a number of epidemics of poisoning in a number of countries. The largest recorded epidemic, in Iraq in 1971–72, resulted in the admission of over 6 000 patients to hospital and over 500 deaths in hospital (WHO, 1976a).

Within the framework of the International Programme on Chemical Safety

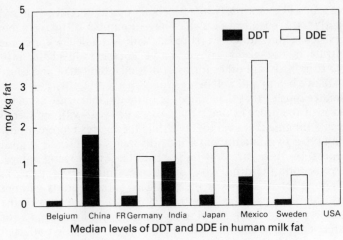

Median levels of DDT and DDE in human milk fat

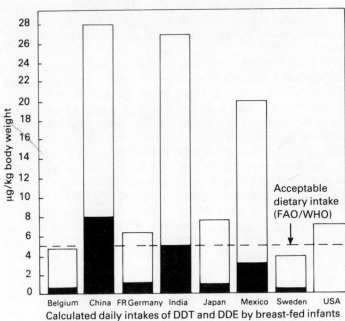

Calculated daily intakes of DDT and DDE by breast-fed infants

Figure 30 The distribution of DDT and DDE in human milk in some developed and developing countries
After data given by Slorach and Vaz, 1983

(IPCS), the United Nations Environment Programme, the International Labour Organization and the World Health Organization have published a series of environmental health criteria for a number of pesticides. So far, health critieria have been published for DDT, heptachlor, paraquat, diquat, endosulfan, quintozene, tecnazene, chlordecone and mirex.

Despite the great variety of existing weed killers (there are more than 180 basic types of herbicides), atrazine and alachlor constitute about half of the herbicides used. Large amounts of 2,4-D (2,4-dichlorophenoxy acetic acid) and 2,4,5-T (2,4,5-

trichlorophenoxy acetic acid) are also used. About 90% of all herbicides are used in developed countries. Because most herbicides must be released into the environment in order to perform their function, it is inevitable that some portion, however small, of these chemicals will reach the general population via the diet and other routes. For example, from 1965 to 1970, the average daily intake of 2,4-D from food bought in five major US cities varied between 0.005 and 0.001 mg (Hileman, 1982). 2,4,5-T and 2,4-D, and chemically related silvex have aroused the most concern because of their possible toxic effects on humans and other animals. Both 2,4,5-T and silvex contain dioxin (2,3,7,8-tetrachlorodibenzo-p-dioxin) as a contaminant. This is one of the most powerful poisons known and was also present in Agent Orange (a mixture of 2,4,5-T and 2,4-D), the herbicide used in war in Vietnam (see Chapter 7). Producers of 2,4,5-T claim, however, that Agent Orange contained much higher levels of dioxin – 1.91 ppm compared to the 0.01-0.02 ppm level of dioxin in the 2,4,5-T sold today.

There is laboratory evidence that the dioxin contaminant of 2,4,5-T and silvex shows embryo toxicity, reproductive effects, teratogenic effects and carcinogenic effects in animals. There is also epidemiologic evidence that 2,4,5-T caused spontaneous abortions on Oregon women living near forests that had been sprayed with 2,4,5-T to control weeds. The degree of concern about 2,4,5-T has been so great that all uses of this herbicide have been banned in the USA except to control weeds on rice and rangeland (Hileman, 1982).

Resistance to pesticides

Pests tend to live in balance with their natural enemies and be kept at least partially in check. It has been a common experience that, when pest control by chemicals is introduced to a new crop and/or area, spectacular increases in yield are often obtained for several seasons. Gradually, these increases become harder to maintain even when new pesticides are used. This is because few pesticides are relatively specific to pests and not only the pest is killed but also its natural enemies. This increases the need for further chemical control. Additionally, an insect species which may have caused no damage because it was kept completely in check by predators and parasites, can become a serious new pest. The best examples of this are with cotton, where numbers of pest species in developing countries have increased from 3–4 to as many as 10. Thus, a dependence on continued pesticides use has been created.

The repeated application of pesticides to a pest population can result in the selection of individuals which can tolerate doses of the pesticide higher than that required to kill the majority. The individual members of resistant strains can breed and thus produce resistant populations. Pesticide resistance is a dynamic, multi-dimensional phenomenon, dependent on biochemical, physiological, genetic and ecological factors. All of these vary with species, population and geographic location. Resistant strains develop through the survival and reproduction of individuals carrying a genome altered by one or more of many possible mechanisms that allow survival after exposure to a pesticide (Brattsten et al, 1986). The selective pressure exerted by the pesticide sharply increases the frequency of the genetic condition expressed as resistance within the exposed population. Although these resistant strains can be killed by increasing the dosage of the pesticide, the intensity of resistance can vary over a very wide range, so that while some resistant strains can be killed by a small increase in dosage, some remain virtually unaffected. Although resistance to pesticides has been known since 1911, it has occurred at a greatly accelerated pace since 1947 (Table 5; Figure 31) as a result of the large scale

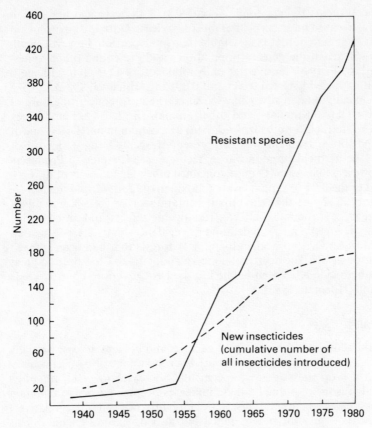

Figure 31 Resistant species of arthropods and new insecticides introduced
1938–40
After Bull, 1982 with modification

TABLE 5. Increases in arthropod resistance, 1970–80

	Number of resistant species	
	1970	*1980*
Number of species (irrespective of number of chemicals resisted)	224	428
Number of species resisting:		
DDT	98	229
Cyclodienes	140	269
Organophosphates	54	200
Carbamates	3	51
Pyrethroids	3	22
Fumigants	3	17
Others	12	41
Total for all groups	313	829

Source: Georghiou and Mellon (1983)

introduction and application of synthetic pesticides (Bull, 1982; Georghiou and Mellon, 1983; Dover and Croft, 1984, 1986). Resistance to pesticides has been reported for such diverse groups as insects, mites, ticks, fungi and rodents. The danger of the situation is that there is reason to suppose that all pests are likely to be able to develop resistance to all types of chemical pesticide in time, given appropriate selection pressure. This could seriously and adversely affect the efficiency and economy of pest control operations on a global scale, with corresponding grave effects on both world health and world food production.

Several factors influence the development of resistance in a population, but the main ones are the presence and frequency of resistant genes in the original pest population; the selection pressure, involving the proportion of the population exposed to selection and the proportion killed; the number of generations per year of the pest; and the isolation of the population affected. Of these, the second is by far the most important, as is borne out by the fact that resistance has appeared mainly in pests of major economic importance which have been subjected to pesticide application of long duration over wide areas. Thus large scale campaigns may be expected to cause development of resistance; a good example of this is the correlation between the reported increase in resistance to dieldrin over the period 1955–60, which coincided with the global WHO malaria eradication programme (Busvine, 1976; see also Chapter 6).

Although annual or more frequent use of the same type of herbicides may quickly alter the weed spectrum in a given location, no evidence has yet come to light that indicates the development of genetic resistance in susceptible biotypes similar to that occurring amongst insects (FAO, 1977).

The background to the appearance of plant pathogens resistant to the newer fungicides illustrates another aspect of the resistance problem. Up to 1965–70, very few reports of resistant pathogens were received by FAO; after this date, however, and concurrent with the introduction of new systemic fungicides, the problem increased, and now about a hundred species of plant pathogens have been reported as resistant (Dover and Croft, 1984).

The discovery of pesticides with novel or unconventional modes of action, such as chemosterilants, hormones and growth inhibitors, was hailed as important, because it was thought to be less likely that pests could develop resistance to them. This was particularly the case with the hormone pesticides, but resistance to these has already appeared. Chemosterilants are so toxic that they cannot be used except in the laboratory; but even here, artificial selection has shown that it is possible to induce resistance. New compounds such as growth regulators and microbial pesticides have not been in use long enough or on a wide enough scale to show perceptible resistance, but here again, as with chemosterilants, it has been possible in the laboratory to develop resistance by artificial selection. In addition, and more worrying, is the fact that it has been found that certain insects like the flour beetle, *Tribolium*, which has developed multiple resistance to conventional pesticides, have acquired significant cross-resistance to the growth inhibitor methoprene. As regards microbial pesticides, it has already been shown that house flies can become resistant both to the spores of *Bacillus thuringiensis* and to its toxin. The general picture at present, therefore, is that it seems probable that most types of pesticides are capable of exerting selection pressure on target pest populations leading to resistance.

This situation therefore requires the development of alternative strategies and fortunately several components of such an approach are now available. The classical alternative approach is to change the pesticide (Mulla, 1977). In the short term and in the case of pest control programmes already in progress, this is probably the practical solution. However, the situation is complicated by the existence of multiple resistance, which often limits the number of substitute pesticides which can be used; in some cases cross-resistance has even been found to compounds which have never been used on a large scale against the particular pest in question. Another limiting factor is price; the use of an alternative compound satisfactory from the point of view of resistance may not be practicable because of the increased cost. Substitution may also be limited by environmental considerations; compounds acceptable from the resistance and financial points of view may have unacceptable environmental effects.

Alternatives to chemical pest control

The best alternative approach, especially in the long term, would be one that altogether obviates, or reduces the need for, the use of pesticides. There are five alternative approaches to chemical pest control:

1. environmental control;
2. genetic and sterile male technique;
3. biological control;
4. behavioural control; and
5. resistance breeding.

Environmental control measures comprise all man-made alterations to the micro- or macroenvironment of the pest–host contact. Techniques can vary from simple cultural practices like digging up egg pods of pests, or planting trap crops, through provision of services like piped water supplies and sewage disposal facilities, to major environmental modifications such as altering river or lake levels. All these methods hold considerable promise for the future, but they need to be developed in relation to the particular ecosystem in which they are to be applied and they may develop secondary environmental problems. Thus, their costs and benefits must be assessed carefully.

Field experience with genetic and sterile male control techniques suggest that the practical problems are great. Here again, there is evidence that pest populations can evolve biological strategies which nullify, in part or in whole, the effects of control.

Biological control is the use of living organisms as pest control agents. The most widely used and successful method, the introduction and establishment of appropriate organisms, aims at providing permanent control of a particular pest. Biological control by inoculation, augmentation or inundation is also practised, but this requires continuous or periodic mass rearing of control agents for release. Beneficial organisms already present in the crop may also be conserved to enhance their impact on the pest with temporary or permanent results. Introduction, which produces long-term results, is preferred as no further input is required, biological or chemical, once control has been established. Across the spectrum of agricultural pests, biological control has been applied more often and consequently has been more successful in the control of insect pests and weeds (Greathead and Waage, 1983). However, biological control needs to be developed in relation to the requirements of the pest–host ecosystem, which takes time. Also, care has to be taken not to produce unwanted environmental effects by import of esoteric predators/parasites. Again, there is the likelihood that pest populations could in the long run evolve behavioural strategies which could limit the effectiveness of biological control.

Behavioural control of pests by use of sex pheromones and related compounds and by attractant and repellent chemicals is also in its infancy. Although some field experiments have been successful, many practical problems have yet to be over-come, and the cost and cost–benefit economics need to be clarified. As with biological control, there is no inherent reason, given sufficient selection pressure, why pest populations could not evolve mechanisms to minimize the effect of behavioural chemicals.

Resistance breeding, the development of varieties of plant and animal species with built-in genetic characteristics which confer resistance in the genotype to a particular pest or pest complex, is a most elegant method of pest control. In crop breeding, this technique has been practised for centuries with great success; it is less developed as regards animal production. However, it is already known that pest populations can and do develop strains which overcome the plant resistance; this is because the nature of the relationship between pest and host is one of biological coevolution. This being so, any change in the host will eventually evoke, if selection pressure is sufficient, a change in the pest.

Faced with these difficulties, increased attention focuses on the concept of 'integrated pest management', which seeks to develop an approach to pest control based on the integration of all control techniques to the specific pest–host complex under consideration. While this system has been considerably developed, both in theory and in practice, as regards agricultural pest control, there are difficulties in its application to public health vector control. The common subsidies of pesticides in the developing countries (total subsidies ranges from 15% of what the total retail cost would be without subsidy to a high of 80–90%) undermine efforts to promote the most cost effective methods of integrated pest management (Repetto, 1985).

Although various ecologically sound alternatives hold great potential for future pest control strategies, no method used singly will be effective for the total control of pests. Pesticides should always be used in combination with other feasible control measures. Improved housing, sewage systems and better general drainage and refuse disposal can largely banish some insect disease vectors from human dwellings. Control of these diseases can be supplemented by prophylactic drugs or immunization. Various agricultural practices, such as crop rotation, changes of sowing, harvest or irrigation times and the use of immune varieties, are employed for pests affecting crops and domestic animals. Better control and supervision of the distribution and application of pesticides where their use cannot be avoided is also required. However, there is no single solution to the problem of resistance; each case must be considered from many angles. An important prerequisite for the success of pest management is the dissemination of adequate information, public awareness and the training of non-professionals.

Heavy metals

Heavy metals are arbitrarily defined as those metals having a density at least five times greater than that of water. Such metals occur naturally in the earth's crust in different concentrations and in some locations in highly concentrated form constituting ore deposits. Although metals have many physical properties in common, their chemical reactivity is quite different and their toxic effect on biological systems is even more diverse.

Many heavy metals are essential to life, even though they occur only in trace amounts in the body tissues (Mertz, 1981; Rainbow, 1985). But heavy metals can be toxic. A metal can be regarded as toxic if it injures the growth or metabolism of cells when it is present above a given concentration. Almost all metals are toxic at high concentrations and some are severe poisons even at very low concentrations. Copper, for example, is a micronutrient, a necessary constituent of all organisms; but if the copper intake is increased above the proper level, it becomes highly toxic. Like copper, each metal has an optimum range of concentration, in excess of which the element is toxic. The toxicity of a metal depends on its route of administration and the chemical compound with which it is bound. The combining of a metal with an organic compound may either increase or decrease its toxic effects on cells. On the other hand, the combination of a metal with sulphur to form a sulphide results in a less toxic compound than the corresponding hydroxide or oxide because the sulphide is less soluble in body fluids than the oxide. Toxicity generally results

1. when an excessive concentration is presented to an organism over a prolonged period of time;
2. when the metal is presented in an unusual biochemical form; or
3. when the metal is presented to an organism by way of an unusual route of intake.

Less well understood, but perhaps of equal significance, are the carcinogenic and teratogenic properties of some metals.

Man has been exposed more and more widely to metallic contaminants in his environment, resulting from the products of industry. Smelting of ores and refining of metals has been going on for a long time, introducing metals into air and water, but human exposures were usually local; during the past 50 years they have become fairly general. Exposures to lead have occurred in circumscribed areas of the world for 3 000 years or more and were high among the Roman upper classes; the use of lead pipes in soft water areas has led to sporadic episodes of lead poisoning in persons drinking these waters, but not until 1924, when alkyl lead was put into gasoline as an antiknock agent, were whole populations exposed to lead at an annually increasing rate. Cadmium was an industrial curiosity in 1900, but today its use is sharply increasing, with resultant contamination of air, water and food. Mercury has been widely used for amalgamation of gold from crushed ore, but discovery of its catalytic and fungicidal properties has resulted in considerable local contamination from seeds and from the dumping of effluents into stagnant lakes. Nowadays, man is exposed to metals in amounts exceeding those to which his forebears were exposed. The earth is rapidly becoming a place where few human beings can be found who are exposed only to background environmental levels. As a result, the human body burden of many metals has considerably increased over that of primitive man. The question naturally arises whether any of these metals exhibit recondite toxicity, expressed as metabolic breakdown resulting in disease or as slow metabolic deterioration resulting in decreased longevity. Suspicion falls on any metal which accumulates in human tissues with age. Of the trace metals essential to life, health and optimal function, none accumulates under present exposures, except in unusual and individual exposure situations.

Sources, pathways and effects

There are three main kinds of sources of metals in the environment. The most obvious is the process of extraction and purification: mining, smelting and refining. The second, and less familiar, is the release of metals from fossil fuels such as coal or oil when these are burned. Cadmium, lead, mercury, nickel, vanadium, chromium and copper are all present in these fuels, and considerable amounts enter the air, or are deposited in ash, from them. The third and most diverse source is production and use of industrial products containing metals, which is increasing as new applications are continuously being found. Modern chemical industry, for example, uses many metals or metal compounds as catalysts. Production of many plastics use metal compounds as stabilizers. Metals are added to lubricants and so find their way into the environment. The relative role of these various activities as sources (and their significance in relation to the natural background in various areas) needs careful assessment if potential hazards are to be evaluated.

Metals follow many pathways and cycles in the environment, and some of them undergo transformations in the process – like the conversion of inorganic mercury to the more toxic methyl form and the subsequent accumulation of the latter by fish. Some plants and invertebrate animals also accumulate metals to potentially toxic levels. The possibility of such accumulation and transformation must be considered when judgements are made about the safety of a particular metal-laden discharge to the environment. This is especially so because once toxic concentrations have been reached, it may take a long time to reduce them to non-toxic levels.

Pathways within man and other targets are also crucially important. The rates and mechanisms of absorption and excretion and the extent to which metals are deposited in such tissues as bone or the kidney cortex and then only slowly removed, need to be known if risks are to be assessed. The biological half-life of methyl mercury in man, for example, is about 70 days, that of cadmium around 20 years and that of lead only a few weeks in blood and soft tissue, but at least ten years in bone.

The effects of metals on ecosystems are very inadequately known. Some appear to affect the rate of basic processes: molybdenum deficiency, for example, may inhibit bacteria responsible for the fixation of nitrogen, while small amounts of copper may slow the decomposition of forest litter. Small amounts of copper and zinc are, however, essential nutrients for most organisms. There are also wide variations in the uptake of metals from the soil by different plants. Some plant species tolerate high lead levels and absorb little of the metal, whereas mercury and cadmium in the soil are toxic to most organisms. Some crops, including wheat and rice, can, however, take up so much cadmium from the soil that they become hazardous to consumers. Cadmium accumulates in the organs of grazing animals and lead levels in the kidneys and livers of sheep grazing near major roads, and mercury in the feathers of birds in areas where alkylmercury fungicides were used have likewise been shown to be raised. Where metal-rich mine drainage enters fresh waters there are often obvious ecological effects, including a great reduction in the invertebrate fauna and the absence of fish.

Heavy metals are toxic to marine organisms above a threshold availability; yet many are essential to metabolism at lower concentrations. Heavy metal concentrations are raised locally in coastal waters but levels in open oceans have stabilized during the earth's history and oceanic dissolved concentrations are typically controlled not by the rate of entry of metals from land but by the rate of their removal from solution via geochemical and more usually biological processes, the metals being accumulated by marine organisms (Rainbow, 1985).

Attention to the effects of metals on man focused first on acute poisoning following industrial exposure or through diet. Many metals have been known to be toxic for centuries. Inhalation of mercury vapour in both the mining and felthat industries used to cause many cases of damage to the central nervous system. Lead poisoning was for decades a well known hazard to smelters and later to those engaged in storage battery production. Inhalation of manganese has been known for many years to cause irreversible damage to the central nervous system. Cadmium, mercury, tin, lead, vanadium, chromium, molybdenum, manganese, cobalt and nickel are all known to pose hazards to those working with them.

Today, increasing emphasis is being placed on the carcinogenic effects of metals. Chromium, nickel, lead and cadmium are all proven or suspected causes of certain cancers associated with industrial processes. Large doses of cadmium and nickel are teratogenic in animals, but this effect is not well established in man.

It should be noted that no pollutant acts on a target in isolation. Other variables – such as the presence of other substances, age and the nutritional or reproductive state of the subject – have a major influence. The availability of metals to plants is affected by acidity, organic content and other features of the soil. Lead absorption and toxicity appear higher in children than in adults. Copper and molybdenum modify one another's effects. Iron deficiency increases the absorption of cadmium. Insufficient emphasis has been placed in many analyses on the need to look at susceptibility to metals in the overall context of the physiology of the whole target organism and to search for the environmental and other variables that can accentuate – or reduce – an impact.

Since the 1960s, attention has focused especially on lead, cadmium and mercury, because they have been shown to cause more general environmental hazards, in each case mainly through the ingestion of excessive quantities. These three metals and others are discussed in detail in the following sections.

Lead

Lead occurs naturally in the earth's crust in the concentration of about 13 mg/kg (Taylor, 1964). As with many other metals, there are some areas with much higher concentrations, including the lead ore deposits scattered throughout the world. Lead is a widely used metal; it has been mined and used for several thousand years. Emissions of lead by man significantly increased about 250 years ago at the beginning of the Industrial Revolution and again after 1925 with the use of lead in gasoline. Estimates of current worldwide emissions of lead from anthropogenic sources amount to 450 million kg per year, as compared to about 25 million kg from

TABLE 6. Maximum permitted lead content of gasoline in different countries (1983)

	Lead content g/l
Belgium	0.4
Denmark	0.4
France	0.4
FR Germany	0.15
Italy	0.4
Netherlands	0.4 (0.15 from 1986)
UK	0.4 (0.15 from 1986)
Sweden	0.15
Switzerland	0.15
Canada	0.77
Japan	0.31
USA	0.29

Source: Royal Commission on Environmental Pollution (1983)

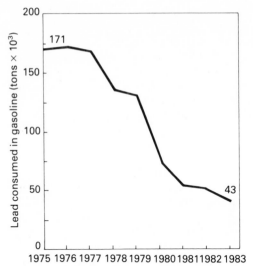

Figure 32 Decrease in lead consumed in gasoline
in the USA
After CEQ, 1984

natural sources (Bennett, 1981). About 60% of anthropogenic emissions result from gasoline combustion. Lead is added to gasoline in the form of tetra–alkyl lead compounds (mostly tetra–methyl lead and tetra–ethyl lead), but exhaust gases contain predominantly inorganic lead aerosol. The degree of pollution from the combustion of alkyl lead differs from country to country, depending on car densities. Because of current legislative actions (especially in developed countries) with respect to the maximum permissible concentration of lead in gasoline (Table 6), the consumption of lead for the production of alkyl lead additives decreased in the 1970s (Figure 32); a further decline is expected as more cars equipped with catalysts which require lead free gasoline will be used.

From a geochemical point of view, the transport and distribution of lead from stationary or mobile sources is mainly via air. Although large amounts are probably also discharged into soil and water, lead tends to localize near the points of such discharge. Lead that is discharged into the air over areas of high traffic density falls out mainly within the immediate metropolitan zone. The fraction that remains air borne is widely dispersed. Residence time for these small particles is of the order of days and is influenced by rainfall. In spite of widespread dispersion, with consequent dilution, there is evidence of lead accumulation at points extremely remote from human activity, for example, in glacial strata in Greenland (WHO, 1977).

The levels of lead in agricultural soils are typically about 40–50 mg/kg (Bennett, 1981). Lead concentrations in the soil are raised by deposition of air borne lead, especially near to industries using the metal. In turn, concentrations in plants, including vegetables, may be raised (although only a small proportion of the lead in the soil is generaly taken up by plant roots). Drinking water generally contains less than 10 μg lead/l, but in some areas where lead water pipes and tanks are used and the water is chemically able to attack them, the concentration may reach 2 000–3 000 μg/l (WHO, 1977). Lead concentration in surface ocean water is about 0.3 μg/l (Bennett, 1981). However, surface waters in the Mediterranean generally contain up to 7.2 μg/l and sediments 9–300 μg/g lead, while concentrations in organisms range from 1.5 μg/g in fish to 480 $\mu g/g$ (dry weight) in mussels. The latter, like other filter feeding aquatic organisms, accumulate lead and other metals in their tissues (IRPTC/UNEP, 1978).

There is a good deal of information about the toxicity of lead to non-human target species. Most plants and micro-organisms appear tolerant of quite high concentrations (EPA, 1977). Among aquatic species the most sensitive fish (such as trout) show symptoms if exposed to around 100 $\mu g/l$ over long periods, although rainbow trout display some effects at concentrations down to $6-16\mu g/l$ and reproduction of the crustacean *Daphnia magna* stops at lead concentrations around $30\mu g/l$ (EPA, 1973). There is least information about effects on birds and mammals, but poisoning of domestic livestock has been reported in areas near lead smelters.

The concentration of lead in urban air ranges in general from 0.5 to $5\mu g/m^3$, depending on the density of automobile traffic (Bennett, 1981). In suburban and rural areas, the lead concentration is generally less than 0.5 $\mu g/m^3$. Some reductions in lead concentration in air have been noted resulting from restricted use of lead in gasoline, such as from 2.8 $\mu g/m^3$ to 1.1 $\mu g/m^3$ in cities of FR Germany and from $3\mu g/m^3$ to 1.5 $\mu g/m^3$ in New York City (Bennett, 1981).

The presence of lead in the air is an increasing hazard to the health of urban dwellers. The metal's effects include damage to the liver, kidney, brain and central nervous and reproductive systems. Children are especially susceptible to lead poisoning (NAS, 1979; Boeckx, 1986). Alkyl lead is more toxic than inorganic lead (Schroeder, 1971; WHO, 1977). At 20 m^3 of air inhaled per day, the bodily intake of lead in cities would be 40–80 μg per day. About 35% of this inhaled lead is absorbed by the lungs (WHO, 1977).

About 90% of the lead swallowed by human adults passes through the gut to the faeces. Once absorbed into the body, lead is distributed to all the tissues. Concentration in the blood and soft tissues fluctuates rapidly according to uptake and excretion rates, but lead is only slowly exchanged between these tissues and the bones, where the half-life of the metal is 10 years or more. Average blood lead concentrations of 40–60 $\mu g/100$ ml are found in lead industries where exposure is minimal (WHO, 1977). Lead in blood of individuals with only normal background exposure is 10–20 $\mu g/100$ ml on average (Bennett, 1981). Geometric means for lead in blood range from about 6 $\mu g/100$ ml in Beijing and Tokyo to 22.5 $\mu g/100$ ml in Mexico City. In Baltimore, Lima, Stockholm and Zagreb values below 10 $\mu g/100$ ml are encountered (Friberg and Vahter, 1983). The mean blood lead concentration in US cities is about 14 $\mu g/100$ ml (Boeckx, 1986). In Bangkok, on the other hand, values as high 34 $\mu g/100$ ml were reported (Nay Htun and Ramachandran, 1977). At concentrations in blood only above those commonly found in urban populations, biochemical changes can be produced. At higher but still moderate levels of exposure, there may be some signs of impairment to the central nervous system, especially in children and certain haematological effects (anaemia may be apparent at 70–80 $\mu g/100$ ml). Severe lead poisoning can cause major damage to the brain and is also associated with gastric and kidney disorders. Kidney failure can occur slowly, appearing long after exposure. Some effects on human reproduction have also been reported (WHO, 1977).

Cadmium

Cadmium is present in the earth's crust at an average concentration of 0.2 mg/kg (Taylor, 1964). Much higher concentrations occur in zinc–lead–copper ores. Zinc ores constitute the main industrial source of cadmium and the metal is fractionated during the smelting or electrolytic processes employed for the refining of zinc. There is, therefore, the possibility of a considerable release of cadmium into the environment during zinc refining operations and, to a lesser extent, during lead and copper smelting.

Cadmium is widely used in industrial processes. Typical uses are electroplating, plasticizers, pigment production, nickel cadmium batteries, etc. Cadmium is present as a trace element in phosphate fertilizers, sewage sludge and fossil fuels. Estimates of the global emission of cadmium to the atmosphere are about 0.8 million kg per year from natural sources and 7.3 million kg per year from anthropogenic sources (Nriagu, 1979). Anthropogenic emissions increased from 3.4 million kg per year in the 1950s to 7.3 million kg per year in the 1970s (Nriagu, 1979).

Cadmium is released into the air as a result of incineration or disposal of cadmium containing products (for example, rubber tyres and plastic containers) and as a byproduct in the refining of other metals, primarily zinc. Near smelters, atmospheric cadmium concentration can be as high as 0.5 μg/m^3. High concentrations have also been encountered in some working environments, although more typical values are now around 0.05–0.02 μg/m^3 (ILO, 1977). One study showed that of 58 cities in the USA, cadmium was found in the air of 36, in concentrations ranging between 0.002 and 0.370 μg/m^3 (Schroeder, 1971). Of 29 non-urban areas, 17 showed cadmium levels of 0.004 to 0.026 μg/m^3. In nearly all cases cadmium was associated with zinc. Annual averages of 0.006 to 0.021 μg/m^3 were reported from three Belgian cities during 1972–77 (Bennett, 1981).

Cadmium concentrations in soil are generally less than 1 mg/kg in non-polluted areas. However, concentrations are much higher in soil and fresh water around smelters and industries processing materials that contain the metal. The amount of water borne cadmium is affected by acidity, but concentrations up to 10 μg/l are found in some mining areas, while in neutral or alkaline waters suspended particulate matter can contain as much as 700 μg/l of cadmium. Concentrations in sediments can exceed 100 mg/kg (Fleischer et al, 1974).

Plants vary in their ability to take up cadmium from soil, but some grasses, wheat and lettuce do so fairly readily and plant/soil ratios for most crops range between 0.5:1 and 2:1 (Fulkerson et al, 1973). When rice is grown in an environment highly contaminated by cadmium, concentrations can reach 0.5–1 mg/kg, which is 10 to 15 times higher than in non-contaminated areas. The sensitivity of plants to cadmium also varies; spinach, lettuce and soybean being affected when levels reach 3–4 mg/kg, while other species may tolerate concentrations ten or a hundred times greater. Aquatic organisms vary more widely in their sensitivity.

The main impact of prolonged human exposure to cadmium is on the kidney, although obstructive lung disorders can also result from respiratory exposure (WHO, 1979b). The effect on the kidney is due to accumulation of cadmium in the renal cortex, leading to tubular protein urea. Renal tubular dysfunction may occur when the concentration is around 200 mg/kg in the renal cortex (WHO, 1979b). Cadmium absorbed by the body is only slowly excreted; as a consequence, cadmium toxicity is markedly cumulative, so that there is the possibility of chronic cadmium poisoning among industrial workers regularly exposed to this metal or its compounds. An epidemiological survey of workers exposed to cadmium dust found excessive proteinuria due to kidney damage in 68% of a group of male workers with over 20 years exposure (Lauwerys et al, 1974).

Probably the most notorious case of cadmium toxicity was the disorder known as Itai-Itai disease which occurred in Japan in the late 1940s. The disease arose from increased uptake of cadmium in locally consumed rice grown in paddy fields irrigated with cadmium contaminated river water. The disorder involved was essentially an osteomalacia, associated with kidney damage and proteinuria (WHO, 1979b), affecting villagers who were dependent on the rice crop as a main source of food. It is now established that Itai-Itai disease is caused by chronic cadmium poisoning, although there are a number of predisposing factors – sex, age, nutrition – which have an effect on susceptibility. Cômparable environmental contamination has been reported from other countries; but the main difference between these and those in Japan is that the daily diet of the population is more varied as compared with the nearly regular daily rice diet at the affected site in Japan (Friberg, 1979).

Mercury

Mercury is less abundant in the earth's crust than lead or cadmium; the abundance of mercury is about 0.8 mg/kg (Taylor, 1964). Mercury is concentrated in certain sulphide ores and in mercury deposits. Mercury has a wide range of industrial uses. The chloralkali, electrical equipment and paint industries are large consumers. Losses occur from direct uses of mercury and also from energy production, mining and related activities, particularly copper smelting and fossil fuel burning. The major source of mercury in the environment, however, is from natural degassing of the earth's crust. Natural sources contribute about 27 million kg of mercury to the atmosphere each year, while anthropogenic sources contribute about 10 million kg per year (NAS, 1978).

The concentration of mercury in the atmosphere is usually below 0.05 $\mu g/m^3$ and averages approximately 0.02 $\mu g/m^3$. The concentrations of mercury in soil are variable but usually rather low. The range is about 0.010 to 0.300 $\mu g/g$; however, the levels can exceed 0.500 $\mu g/g$ in mineralized areas (NAS, 1978). Bodies of freshwater for which there is no independent evidence of contamination contain mercury at less than 0.2 $\mu g/l$. Oceanic mercury is usually less than 0.3 $\mu g/l$ (WHO, 1976a). Industrially polluted river water commonly contains about 5 $\mu g/l$ and the level can reach 50 $\mu g/l$ near points of discharge.

The discharge of mercury in liquid effluents is of particular concern as in freshwater and marine sediments inorganic mercury compounds can be methylated by bacteria to produce methylmercury. Methylmercury can bioaccumulate to a considerable extent in fish and so result in dietary exposure for man. Fish consumption is the primary source of dietary mercury in the general population, whose range of daily intake of mercury is from 1–20 μg (WHO, 1976a). The provisional tolerable weekly intake of total mercury is 300 μg of which no more than 200 μg should be methylmercury (WHO, 1972).

Historically, the problem of mercury poisoning has been associated either with consumption of treated seed grain or with consumption of fish from a locally highly polluted environment. The latter pollution has typically arisen from pulp and paper mills, where organomercurials have been used as slimicides or in chloralkali plants, where mercury metal is used as an electrode.

Significant differences are observed in the metabolism of mercury depending on its chemical form. Inorganic and elemental mercury accumulate mainly in the kidneys and to a lesser extent in the brain. Methylmercury can penetrate the blood–brain barrier and both man and other primates concentrate methylmercury in the brain with exceptional efficiency (WHO, 1976). Elemental and organic mercury easily cross the placental barrier and also enter maternal milk, contributing to the exposure of breast fed infants. Ultimately, central nervous system dysfunction results, although the actual biochemical mechanism of toxicity is uncertain. The damage persists even after exposure ceases and no curative treatment is known.

Mass intoxications caused by alkylmercury compounds have taken place in the general population on several occasions. These epidemics are of two main types: the first is typified by the Iraqi outbreak (1971–72) where the exposure was by consumption of bread prepared from seed grain dressed with methyl or ethylmercury fungicides. Similar outbreaks are known to have occurred in Pakistan, Guatemala and Ghana. The other type of intoxication is that characterized by Minamata disease (first outbreak in 1953) caused by long-term consumption of fish highly contaminated with methylmercury. The first cases of Minamata disease were reported in 1956 in Minamata Bay area, Japan. At the end of March 1980 there were 1 294 persons certified as having Minamata disease. In the Agno River Basin, Japan, the Minamata disease was first reported in 1965; at the end of March, 1980, 602 persons had been certified as victims of the disease (El-Hinnawi and Hashmi, 1982).

Other metals

In addition to lead, cadmium and mercury several trace metals are known to constitute some hazards to man and environment. Manganese poisoning, especially as result of high-speed drilling of alloys, which produces large amounts of manganese dioxide dust, is a potential industrial hazard. Over 400 cases of chronic manganese poisoning have been reported (WHO, 1979a). Excessive inhalation has caused pneumonia among workers and inhalation and ingestion of heavily contaminated water has also been reported as associated with chronic and irreversible brain disorders resembling Parkinson's disease. There is less information about possible hazards to the general population. The daily exposure to air borne manganese of people living outside industrial areas is estimated at 2–10 μg, whereas adults are likely to take in 2 000–8 000 μg/day from food.

Tin is another element which might be of concern in certain localities. Except near some industrial sites, tin is either undetectable in the air or present at concentrations below 0.01 μg/m^3. In soil, where detected, concentration ranges from 2 to 200 ppm, the metal being strongly absorbed by humus. It has only been found occasionally in fresh- and seawater. The inorganic and organic tin compounds are generally not highly toxic to man and animals. Gastrointestinal symptoms (nausea, diarrhoea) may be caused by the consumption of 50 to 100 mg of tin in foods (Piscator, 1979). Several outbreaks of food tin poisoning have been reported, with concentrations in the food of 250 to 500 μg/g (Piscator, 1979). Pneumoconiosis may be caused by long-term inhalation of tin oxide dusts and fumes. Systemic effects of tin exposure observed in animals include neurological damage and renal lesions.

Copper is essential to all living organisms, has a wide range of effects depending on concentration and chemical formulation and is widely used by man in the electrical industry in such alloys as brass, in chemical catalysts and in algicides, wood preservatives and antifouling paints. The worldwide anthropogenic emission of copper to the atmosphere has been estimated at about 56 million kg per year; emission from natural sources amounts to about 18 million kg per year (Davies and Bennett, 1983). The average atmospheric concentration of copper in urban areas ranges from 0.030 to 0.200 μg/m^3. In soils, the median concentration of copper is about 30 μg/g, but higher concentrations are encountered, especially near industries or copper smelters. Copper levels in surface waters vary considerably, ranging from 0.5 to 1 000 μg/l (Davies and Bennett, 1983). Copper fumes and fine dust, such as may be encountered in industrial settings, sometimes give rise to an influenza-like syndrome known as 'metal-fume fever'. This can occur after exposure to about 0.1 mg/m^3 of fine copper dust although symptoms usually disappear within 24 hours. Industrial exposure to copper dust or fumes does not appear to result in chronic disease. However, workers involved with spraying vineyards with a fungicide containing a 1–2% solution of copper sulphate have developed a respiratory disorder known as 'vineyard sprayer's lung'. These workers developed interstitial pulmonary lesions, including histiocytic granulomas and associated nodular fibrohyaline scars which contained abundant deposits of copper. It has also been reported that the pulmonary lesions may regress, remain stationary or progress towards a diffuse pulmonary fibrosis. During the course of the disease, lung cancer may develop (Davies and Bennett, 1983).

Nickel is widely distributed throughout the earth's crust and is a relatively abundant element. It occurs in marine organisms, is present in the oceans, and is a common microconstituent of plant and animal tissues. Foods can be contaminated with nickel during handling, processing and cooking by utensils containing large quantities of nickel. Excessive exposure to nickel compounds may cause a variety of local effects, but only nickel carbonyl is associated with systemic effects. Exposure to nickel-containing mists and dusts may cause asthma, pneumoconiosis and irritation of nasal membranes. Nickel metal and compounds can have strong sensitizing effects on skin leading to dermatitis. Initial symptoms of nickel carbonyl exposures are mild nausea, headache, dyspnoea and chest pain. These symptoms may disappear, but following a latency period of 0.5 to 5 days, severe pulmonary insufficiency may occur.

Intermediate chemical compounds

Not all the chemicals produced by industry reach the general public. Many of these are intermediate products used in processing or manufacturing an end product for public consumption. Polychlorinated biphenyls (PCBs), acrylonitrile and vinyl chloride are examples of these intermediate products, some of which are potentially hazardous to man and environment. Vinyl chloride, for example, has been identified as a powerful carcinogen for humans when present in the atmosphere (IARC, 1976). PCBs and several other compounds are highly toxic, carcinogenic, teratogenic or mutagenic.

The accidental release into the environment of these chemicals has led to various detrimental impacts. The commercial production of PCBs began in 1930; in the same year cases of poisoning were reported among workers engaged in their manufacture (WHO, 1976b). The nature of this occupational disease was characterized by a skin affliction with acne-like eruptions; occasionally the liver was involved, in some cases with fatal consequences. Subsequent safety precautions largely appear to have prevented further outbreaks of this disease in connection with the manufacture of PCBs. The distribution of PCBs in the environment was not recognized until 1966 (WHO, 1976b). The serious outbreaks of poisoning in man and in domestic animals from the ingestion of food accidentally contaminated with PCBs have stimulated investigation into the toxic effects of PCBs on animals and on nutritional food chains. This has resulted in limitation of the commercial exploitation of PCBs and in regulations to limit the residues in human and animal food. However, accidental discharges of PCBs in the environment have caused severe impacts. In a large scale leakage accident in Japan, with contamination of rice oil by PCBs from leaking heat exchangers, there was evidence among human consumers of serious illness, leading to death in severe cases. PCBs have also been found to be highly toxic to marine crustaceans; a large accidental discharge of this material in Escambia Bay, Florida, led to widespread mortality of shrimps.

Accidents in the chemical industry have occurred and will continue to occur with expansion in the industry, especially in developing countries. Such accidents resulted in the release into the environment of hazardous intermediate chemical compounds. In 1976, an explosion at a chemical factory in the North Italian town of Seveso released a cloud of vapour which contaminated the surrounding area. The vapour, a mixture consisting primarily of trichlorophenol, also contained dioxin. Several thousands of people were evacuated after the explosion; the most obvious effect on those exposed to the cloud of vapour, especially the children, was the eruption of chloracne, a skin disease with disfiguring sores. The leak of toxic vapour (methyl isocyanate, which is a basic compound for the manufacture of the pesticide carbaryl) in December, 1984 at the Union Carbide pesticide plant on the outskirts of the town of Bhopal, India, is considered to be the worst industrial accident on record. More than 2 500 were killed as a result of the accident; some 150 000 people were treated at hospitals and at least 200 000 people fled Bhopal.

Hazardous waste

Virtually all industrial activity generates some materials that are considered waste and are discarded because they are perceived to have no further economic use. The term waste can be defined as a 'non-product material or energy output, the value of which is less than the costs of collecting, processing and transporting for use'. According to this definition, materials that have economic potential for re-use, recovery or recycling are not truly waste (these are called residues such as, eg agricultural and agroindustrial residues; see Chapter 3).

Certain wastes are defined as hazardous. The term 'hazardous' has been used differently in different countries. In the USA, wastes are defined as hazardous because they may :

1. cause or significantly contribute to an increase in mortality or an increase in serious irreversible, or incapacitating reversible, illness; or
2. pose a substantial present or potential hazard to human health or the environment when improperly treated, stored, transported, disposed of, or otherwise managed (NRC, 1985).

In the FR Germany, the term 'special waste' is used instead of 'hazardous waste'. The technical definition for such wastes is that 'because of their nature, composition, or quantity they are especially dangerous to health, air, or water quality, are explosive, flammable, or could promote infectious diseases, and therefore special requirements for their control are necessary' (Dowling, 1985). The WHO has defined hazardous waste as a waste that 'has physical, chemical or biological characteristics which require special handling and disposal procedures to avoid risk to health and/or other adverse environmental effects' (WHO, 1983).

One approach to the problem of adequately defining what constitutes a hazardous waste is to draw up a list of known wastes that present no significant short-term

**TABLE 7. List of toxic or dangerous substances
and materials selected as requiring priority
consideration**

---

 1 Arsenic and compounds
 2 Mercury and compounds
 3 Cadmium and compounds
 4 Thallium and compounds
 5 Beryllium and compounds
 6 Chromium(VI) compounds
 7 Lead and compounds
 8 Antimony and compounds
 9 Phenolic compounds
10 Cyanide compounds
11 Isocyanates
12 Organohalogenated compounds
13 Chlorinated solvents
14 Organic solvents
15 Biocides and phytopharmaceutical substances
16 Tarry materials from refining and tar residues
17 Pharmaceutical compounds
18 Peroxides, chlorates, perchlorates and azides
19 Ethers
20 Asbestos
21 Selenium and compounds
22 Tellurium and compounds
23 Polycyclic aromatic hydrocarbons
24 Metal carbonyls
25 Soluble copper compounds

Source: WHO (1983)

handling or long-term environmental hazards, and to define hazardous waste by exclusion, ie as any wastes not listed. This 'exclusive list' (Table 7) approach has been used successfully in some countries, eg in the UK (WHO, 1983). However, more widely employed for regulatory purposes are listings of hazardous waste, either with or without accompanying criteria. This 'inclusive list' approach is currently employed in Belgium, Denmark, France, FR Germany, the Netherlands, Sweden, the UK and the USA. The lists comprise wastes from certain industries, wastes containing specific components or specific waste streams identified by the processes from which they originate. The inclusive list offers a greater degree of certainty but suffers from the disadvantage that omissions may well be significantly hazardous. Because cross-border transport of wastes has recently become an important issue, pressure has been increasing for international harmonization of the definition and classification of hazardous wastes.

Estimates of the quantities of hazardous waste generated by industry vary widely, depending on the definition of hazardous waste used. It is estimated that OECD countries generate about 300 million tonnes of hazardous wastes annually (Table 8), of which 264 million tonnes are by the USA (OECD, 1985). More than 10% of the waste generated in OECD countries is transported across national frontiers for disposal. For OECD Europe in 1983 about 2.2 million tonnes of hazardous waste crossed national frontiers on the way to treatment, storage and/or disposal. Cross-frontier traffic in such wastes in OECD Europe is likely to involve between 20 000 and 30 000 border crossing events annually. For North America, available data suggest about 5 000 border crossings of all hazardous wastes annually (OECD,

TABLE 8. Production and movement of hazardous waste in 1983 in the OECD countries

	Hazardous waste produced (in 000 tonnes)	Number of border crossings per year
North America	268 000	5 000
OECD Pacific	8 000	
OECD Europe	24 000	100 000
OECD total	300 000	105 000

Source: OECD (1985)

1985). This international transport of hazardous waste reflects the absence of disposal or treatment facilities in the countries of origin and economies of scale in disposal or treatment facilities.

The disposal of hazardous waste has become a difficult and controversial problem in waste management. In many cases the present methods for the disposal of hazardous waste are not so reliable as to preclude any risk to man and the environment. In many countries no data, or only incomplete data, are available at the national level on amounts of hazardous wastes generated or on the techniques used by the producers to dispose of these wastes. Over 75% of hazardous waste generated by industries in OECD countries is disposed of on land, including landfills, deep well injection and underground disposal (Figure 33). Wastes may be disposed of in bulk or stored in drums, barrels or tanks.

Undisciplined disposal of hazardous wastes can cause fires, explosions, air, water and land pollution, contamination of food and drinking water, damage to people

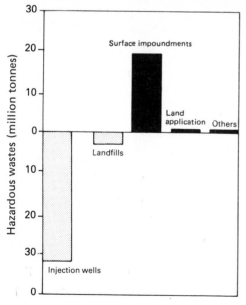

Figure 33 Disposal of hazardous wastes in 1981 in the USA by disposal process type; total quantity disposed was about 55 million tonnes
After CEQ, 1984 with modification

who get them on their skins or inhale their vapours and harm to plants and animals. It is an alarming list and in practice most of the things that could go wrong have indeed occurred. In fact the incidents that have hit the headlines are probably only a few of those that have actually taken place; many more are likely to have gone unreported. Even those incidents which have become internationally famous have not always been critically studied and analysed.

Perhaps the most notorious incident of all was the outbreak of Minamata disease in Japan. Methylmercury discharged from a chemical factory into the sea, or produced in the sea from inorganic mercury discharges, contaminated the fish eaten by local people at the town of Minamata on Kyushu island, Japan. As a result of this and a similar incident at Niigata on the east coast of Honshu, nearly two thousand people have so far suffered neurological disorders; about four hundred have died (El-Hinnawi and Hashmi, 1982). There have also been episodes of mercury poisoning in Puerto Rico and Brazil (Szekely, 1977). Disposing of liquid waste from mines has also long been a problem. Chronic poisoning of humans (Itai-Itai disease) ascribed to consumption of locally grown rice contaminated with cadmium from zinc mine drainage has been reported from Toyama Prefecture, Japan (Friberg *et al*, 1976). More contamination of rice fields, this time from copper mining, is known to have occurred in Malaysia (Sardar, 1980).

The Rhine and the Mississippi are classic examples of rivers continually polluted by industrial waste. Both are used for drinking water. The Netherlands draws water from the Rhine, downstream of many industrial waste discharges and the Mississippi supplies New Orleans. Both rivers are so polluted by organochlorine and other compounds that it is doubtful whether they are suitable sources of drinking water. Studies have suggested that their contamination could be linked to the fact that the people who have to use these waters suffer slightly higher cancer rates than expected (Kool *et al*, 1982).

There have been several hundred cases of contamination of water wells by poisons from hazardous wastes – the most common of all the dangers to arise from improper waste disposal. These have often occurred because the wastes were put into sand or gravel pits or old mine workings in fractured strata. Places like these attract people disposing of liquid waste and slurry because they are cheap and the liquid disappears quickly, flowing out into the subsoil and into groundwater; but this is part of the problem because the soils contain little clay and other absorbent substances. As a result they do not filter the waste, trapping the dangerous chemicals and so protecting the groundwater from contamination. To make things worse, the wells are usually shallow and privately owned and the water receives no treatment that could remove the pollution. Among the main poisons that have turned up in such water supplies are arsenic, pesticides, gasoline, phenols, chromate and chlorinated hydrocarbons (Brown, 1979; Pettijohn, 1979).

Several serious incidents have been reported from the USA (Brown, 1979). Wastes from the manufacture of defoliants, pesticides and chemical warfare agents were stored in unlined canals and ponds at the Rocky Mountain Arsenal near Denver, Colorado, in alluvial deposits which allowed dangerous chemicals to get through to the groundwater. An area of at least 40 km^2 was poisoned. From 1951 crops irrigated from shallow wells turned brown and died and sheep and other livestock drinking from the wells perished. Even though over a million dollars was spent in trying to put the problem right, it has still not been permanently solved. At Toone-Teague Road, Medon, Tennessee, people suffered respiratory disease, dizziness and fatigue because private wells were contaminated by pesticides (heptachlor, endrin, dieldrin) dumped in an old river bed. At Perham, Minnesota, in 1972, 11 people were poisoned by arsenic from a well recently drilled near a disused village rubbish tip. Just over 20 kg of grasshopper bait had been buried 40 years before (Brown, 1979).

Other dumping has exposed people to poisonous vapours from organic compounds at concentrations that would not be permitted even in factories (industries expose their workers under controlled conditions to higher levels than would be tolerated for the general public). The victims have suffered headaches, nausea, dizziness and discomfort when breathing – and, after prolonged exposure, skin rash, sores, pimples and numbness of the limbs. At Love Canal, near the Niagara Falls, USA, homes were built on a former dump containing pesticides, chemicals used in making plastics and the sludge from the bottom of stills. The dump was sealed with clay and sold to the local community. At Lekkerkerk, near Rotterdam, in the Netherlands, drums of paint solvents (aromatic hydrocarbons) were included in rubble used to reclaim land. Houses were then built on it. In both cases several hundred families had to be evacuated and decontamination measures costing tens of millions of dollars had to be undertaken (El-Hinnawi and Hashmi, 1982).

A very severe problem in many countries is that of waste that was disposed of in thousands of more or less satisfactory pre-existing landfill sites. Many such sites have been discovered during the last few years. For example, in Denmark 3 200 abandoned sites have been found, 500 of them containing chemical waste; in the Netherlands there are 4 000 abandoned sites and 350 require immediate remedial action (OECD, 1985). In the USA concern has focused on the health effects of chemical waste in over 20 000 uncontrolled sites – many of which are abandoned, covered over or even forgotten – that contain chemicals with enormous diversity of physical and chemical characteristics. The Comprehensive Environmental Response, Compensation and Liability Act – the Superfund Act – was passed in December 1980 to address these sites. As of March 1986, the US Environmental Protection Agency had designated 842 sites on its National Priority List for remedial attention. Under the Superfund, 1.6 billion US dollars have been earmarked for the remedial operations (CEQ, 1984; OECD, 1985).

Hazardous waste can be treated by a variety of physical, chemical and biological methods to reduce its bulk or toxicity. Incineration, which destroys waste by subjecting it to very high temperatures in a controlled manner for a specific length of time, can also be considered a form of waste treatment. Physical treatments include methods such as settlement, evaporation, air flotation and various filtration and centrifuge techniques. Other techniques such as absorption/desorption, extraction under vacuum and azeotropic distillation are also employed. Chemical treatments are used to achieve the complete breakdown of hazardous waste into non-toxic substances, and more usually to modify the chemical properties of the waste; for example, to reduce the water solubility or to neutralize the acidity or alkalinity.

Environmentally acceptable disposal of certain hazardous waste may be too expensive in landfill sites or in chemical or thermal treatment plants. In such cases deep underground disposal may provide an environmentally and economically acceptable alternative, if done in inactive mines which meet specific geological and technical criteria. Only one such deep mine disposal facility is currently in operation, in FR Germany (OECD, 1985). Another method of disposing of hazardous waste is in deep wells. At present approximately 140 deep injection wells are in operation in the USA. There are also injection plants in Canada, FR Germany and Spain. Deep well injection is not permitted in the Netherlands or Japan (OECD, 1985).

Laws controlling the disposal of hazardous wastes are now in effect in most developed countries. The immediate need is to make sure that they are enforced in a cost effective and environmentally sound way. Some developed countries have still to create an effective enforcement system staffed with adequately trained people. Developing countries following the same legislative path may have greater problems in recruiting the right staff.

As the controls have tightened in many developed countries, chemical industries have had to pay more for getting rid of their wastes. Some have been tempted to avoid these extra costs by moving their operations or exporting their wastes to countries where the laws are less strict, or less strictly enforced. These countries could well become international dustbins and end up with the same sort of problems that brought the strict legislation in the first place. There have even been a few cases where companies have shipped waste to another country, ostensibly for storage, and then abandoned it. Waste from the Netherlands ended up in the UK in this way and wastes from the USA have been stored in a warehouse in Mexico. Recently, dioxin containing waste from Seveso, Italy, disappeared during transfrontier transport and was finally found to be inadequately stored in an abandoned slaughterhouse in France. Developing countries are particularly vulnerable to such pollution exports.

Companies setting up in developing countries often stipulate that their processes must remain secret. If they insist that the composition of their wastes should also be cloaked in secrecy the host countries may never know exactly what hazardous substances, in what quantities, have been put into their disposal sites – and will find it almost impossible to control the situation. In fact, so much secrecy can rarely be necessary, and, if companies do insist on it, countries should require them to give assurances about the hazards posed by their wastes and to accept financial liability for any problems caused.

Naturally, national laws and codes of practice do not necessarily provide a reliable guide to what actually goes on in a country. That depends on how rigorously the regulations are enforced and on whether codes are merely seen as targets or used as manuals of working practice. It does seem, though, that there are significant differences among developed countries. This reflects variations in national aims and practices and results in different costs. The US legislation aims, among other things, at outlawing unlined lagoons and a containment philosophy is now in force. The high water table of the Netherlands has strictly limited disposal in the ground. Disused salt mines in very stable strata in the FR Germany make particularly good disposal sites and supplement special local treatment facilities. The UK and the CMEA member states share a preference for mixing hazardous and other wastes, including household garbage, and disposing of it in the ground in carefully selected sites. This practice protects water supplies by relying on the hazardous wastes being degraded and fixed in the site and undergoing chemical changes in unsaturated and impermeable strata. Developing countries can benefit from the experience of these different approaches when selecting the most economic solution to their particular disposal problems.

The marine conventions and the EEC Directive on Ground Water control disposal of hazardous waste on a case by case basis (EEC, 1980). They have black lists of banned substances whose discharge into the sea or groundwater is prohibited. Another list comprises substances that can only be discharged with specific permission, while the rest are subject to general authorizations. The specific permissions are given if assessments of how the wastes behave in the environment, and the damage they are likely to do, show that the likely harm is acceptably small if appropriate safety measures are taken. The assessments, however, are necessarily based on models which cannot precisely forecast what will happen and can only make approximate predictions, because we do not yet know enough about the subject. So the permissions are based on probabilities rather than certainties of safety.

The marine conventions, coupled with measures by the International Maritime Organization to restrict pollution from oil spills, have had a positive effect. The dumping of chlorinated hydrocarbons has been reduced, if not eliminated (Norton, 1981) and partly replaced by incineration at sea. This operation releases acids which fall out into seawater and was brought under the provisions of the London Convention in 1978.

Cleaner technologies

Recent technological advances present considerable potential for the development of cleaner technologies that reduce industry's emission of pollutants (including hazardous waste) and use of energy. This includes developments in the following areas: environmental sensors to facilitate the monitoring of pollution levels; information processing technology that can help improve the dissemination of information on subjects such as cleaner technologies; advances in biotechnology that have led to improvements in the effectiveness and efficiency of treating industrial effluents; and developments in microelectronics that enable greater control over production processes and hence increased in-plant recycling of waste streams and reduced product losses, raw material consumption and pollutant emission; in addition, the possibilities for the recycling and re-use of industrial wastes in other industries or in special recycling industries are growing. For example, in Europe glass recycling has grown from about 1.3 million tonnes in 1979 to about 2.7 million tonnes in 1984. Recycling of aluminium cans in the USA increased from 24 000 tonnes in 1972 to 510 000 tonnes in 1982. In Bulgaria, the introduction of low and non-waste technologies helped reduce the discharge of industrial wastes by about 5.5 million tonnes annually (Pavlov, 1982). Increasing use is made of wastes from the chemical, pharmaceutical and food processing industries and from mining. In the GDR about 30 million tonnes of industrial wastes are recycled each year (Thomas, 1982) providing 12% of raw material required for industry. In Hungary, about 22.5 million tonnes of industrial wastes were generated in 1985; about 6.5 million tonnes of these were recycled (KSH, 1986). Scrap and paper recycling has also grown in several countries.

These cleaner technologies have achieved considerable reductions in the consumption of energy and raw materials by firms and in their discharges of pollutants. For example, a new closed ferrosilicon furnace in Norway achieves a higher yield, requires less energy and raw materials and generates fewer air pollution emissions. These new technologies are economically profitable in their own right in some cases and are undertaken for a combination of economic and environmental reasons. In other cases, the new technologies are more effective and efficient than alternative conventional treatment techniques and are undertaken to enable the firm concerned to comply with environmental regulations more efficiently.

While technological advances offer considerable potential for environmental improvement, some technological developments, coupled with changes in the structure of industry and in the types of materials used in production processes, are leading to the emergence of new types of pollution problems, for example, a shift from traditional pollutants (such as BOD) to more complex toxic pollutants such as heavy metals, toxic air and water pollutants and hazardous wastes.

References

BENNETT, B.G. (1981). *Exposure Commitment Assessments of Environmental Pollutants,* **1**, No 1, Monitoring and Assessment Research Centre (MARC), Chelsea College, University of London

BOECKX, R.L. (1986). Lead poisoning in children, *Analytical Chemistry*, **58**, 274A

BRATTSTEN, L.B. *et al* (1986). Insecticide resistance: challenge to pest management and basic research, *Science*, **231**, 1255

BROWN, M. (1979). *Laying Waste: The Poisoning of America by Toxic Chemicals,* Pantheon Books, New York

BULL, D. (1982). *Pesticides and the Third World – A Growing Problem*, Oxfam, London

BUSVINE, J. (1976). Pest resistance to pesticides, in GUNN, D. and STEVENS, J. eds, *Pesticides and Human Welfare*, Oxford University Press, Oxford

CEQ (1984). *Environmental Quality – 1984*, Council on Environmental Quality, Washington, DC

DAVIES, D.J.A. and BENNETT, B.G. (1983). *Exposure Commitment Assessments of Environmental Pollutants*, Vol 3, Monitoring and Assessment Research Centre (MARC), Chelsea College, University of London

DOVER, M.J. and CROFT, B.A. (1984). *Getting Tough: Public Policy and the Management of Pesticide Resistance,* World Resources Institute, Washington, DC

DOVER, M.J. and CROFT, B.A. (1986). Pesticide resistance and public policy, *BioScience*, **36**, 78

DOWLING, M. (1985). Defining and classifying hazardous wastes, *Environment*, **27**, 18

ECE (1982). *Market Trends for Chemical Products, 1975-1980 and Prospects to 1990*, Report ECE/CHEM/40/Vol 1, Economic Commission for Europe, Geneva

EEC (1980). Directive on the protection of ground water against pollution caused by certain dangerous substances, *European Community Official Journal*, 26 January 1980, 43

EL-HINNAWI, E. and HASHMI, M. (1982). *Global Environmental Issues*, Tycooly International, Dublin

EPA (1973). *Water Quality Criteria*, EPA, R3. 033, US Environmental Protection Agency, Washington, DC

EPA (1977). *Air Quality Criteria for Lead*, EPA-600/8.77-017, US Environmental Protection Agency, Washington, DC

FAO (1977). *Global Survey of Pesticide Resistance*, FAO Report AGP:1976/17/10, Food and Agriculture Organization of the United Nations, Rome

FLEISCHER, M. *et al* (1974). Environmental impact of cadmium, *Environmental Health Perspective*, **7**, 253

FRIBERG, L. *et al* (1976). *Cadmium in the Environment*, CRC Press, Cleveland, Ohio

FRIBERG, L. *et al* (1979). Cadmium, in FRIBERG, L. *et al,* *Handbook on the Toxicology of Metals*, Elsevier/North-Holland Biomedical Press, Amsterdam

FRIBERG, L. and VAHTER, M. (1983). Assessment of exposure to lead and cadmium through biological monitoring: results of a UNEP/WHO global study, *Environmental Research*, **30**, 95

FULKERSON, W. *et al* (1973). *Cadmium: the Dissipated Element*, ORNL NSF-EP-21, Oak Ridge National Laboratory, TN

GEORGHIOU, G.P. and MELLON, R.B. (1983). Pesticide resistance in time and space, in GEORGHIOU, G.P. and SAITO, T. eds, *Pest Resistance to Pesticides*, Plenum Press, New York

GREATHEAD, D.J. and WAAGE, J.K. (1983). *Opportunities for Biological Control of Agricultural Pests in Developing Countries*, World Bank Technical Paper No 11, World Bank, Washington, DC

GUPTA, Y.P. (1986). Pesticide misuse in India, *The Ecologist*, **16**, 36

HILEMAN, B. (1982). Herbicides in agriculture, *Environmental Science and Technology,* **16**, 645A

IARC (1976). *Monographs on the Evaluation of Carcinogenic Risk of Chemicals to Man*, Vol 2, International Agency for Research on Cancer, Lyon

ILO (1977). *Occupational Exposure Limits for Airborne Toxic Substances*, Occupational Safety and Health Series No 37, International Labour Organization, Geneva

IRPTC/UNEP (1978). *Data Profiles for Chemicals for the Evaluation of their Hazards to the Environment of the Mediterranean Sea*, International Register for Potentially Toxic Chemicals. United Nations Environment Programme, Geneva

KEAN, T. (1986). Dealing with toxic air pollutants: new initiatives, *Issues In Science and Technology*, **2**, No 4, 19

KOOL, H.J. *et al* (1982). *Organic Water Contaminants and Health Parameters: Cancer Mortality in Relation to Drinking Water in the Netherlands – An Epidemiological Approach*, National Institute for Water Supply, The Hague

KSH (1986). *State and Protection of the Environment*, Központi Statisztikai Hivatal, Budapest

LAUWERYS, R.R. *et al* (1974). Cadmium, *Archive of Environmental Health*, **145**

MERTZ, W. (1981). The essential trace elements, *Science*, **213**, 1332

MULLA, M.S. (1977). Resistance in culcine mosquitoes in California: countermeasures, in WATSON, D.L. and BROWN, A.W., *Pesticide Management and Insecticide Resistance*, Academic Press, New York

NAS (1978). *An Assessment of Mercury in the Environment*, National Academy of Sciences, Washington, DC

NAS (1979). *Lead in the Human Environment*, National Academy of Sciences, Washington, DC

NAY HTUN, M. and RAMACHANDRAN, P.N. (1977). An investigation of blood lead content and atmospheric lead levels in Bangkok, *Water, Air and Soil Pollution*, **7**, 79

NORTON, M.G. (1981). The Oslo and London dumping conventions, *Marine Pollution Bulletin*, **12**, 145

NRC (1985). *Reducing Hazardous Waste Generation*, National Research Council, National Academy Press, Washington, DC

NRIAGU, J.O. (1979). Global inventory and anthropogenic emissions of trace metals to the atmosphere, *Nature*, **279**, 409

OECD (1985). *The State of the Environment – 1985*, Organization for Economic Cooperation and Development, Paris

PAVLOV, G. (1982). *The Protection and Improvement of the Environment in Bulgaria*, CMEA, Committee for Scientific and Technological Cooperation, Moscow

PETTIJOHN, W.A. (1979). Ground water pollution: an imminent disaster, *Ground Water*, **17**, 18

PIMENTEL, D. and LEVITAN, L. (1986). Pesticides: amounts applied and amounts reaching pests, *BioScience*, **36**, 86

PISCATOR, M. (1979). Tin, in FRIBERG, L. *et al*, eds, *Handbook on the Toxicology of Metals*, Elsevier/North-Holland Biomedical Press, Amsterdam

RAINBOW, P.S. (1985). The biology of heavy metals in the sea, *International Journal of Environmental Studies*, **25**, 195

REPETTO, R. (1985). *Paying the Price: Pesticide Subsidies in Developing Countries*, Research Report No 2, World Resources Institute, Washington, DC

SARDAR, Z. (1980). The fight to save Malaysia, *New Scientist*, **87**, 700

SCHROEDER, H.A. (1971). Metals in the air, *Environment*, **13**, 18

SLORACH, S.A. and VAZ, R. (1983). *Assessment of Human Exposure to Selected Organochlorine Compounds through Biological Monitoring*, Swedish National Food Administration, Uppsala

SZEKELY, F. (1977). Pollution for export, *Mazingira*, **3/4**, 68

TAYLOR, S.R. (1964). Abundance of chemical elements in the continental crust – a new table, *Geochimica Cosmochimica Acta*, **28**, 1273

THOMAS, G. (1982). *Environmental Problems in German Democratic Republic*, CMEA, Committee for Scientific and Technological Cooperation, Moscow

WHO (1972). *Mercury*, Environmental Health Criteria No 1, World Health Organization, Geneva

WHO (1976a). *Mercury*, Environmental Health Criteria No 1, World Health Organization, Geneva

WHO (1976b). *Polychlorinated Biphenyls and Terphenyls*, Environmental Health Criteria No 2, World Health Organization, Geneva

WHO (1977). *Lead*, Environmental Health Criteria No 3, World Health Organization, Geneva

WHO (1979a). *Manganese*, Environmental Health Criteria No 17, World Health Organization, Geneva

WHO (1979b). *Environmental Health Criteria for Cadmium – Interim Report*, EHE/EHC/79.20, World Health Organization, Geneva

WHO (1983). *Management of Hazardous Waste*, WHO Regional Publication No 14, European Series, World Health Organization, Regional Office, Copenhagen

WHO (1985). *Guidelines for the Study of Dietary Intake of Chemical Contaminants*, WHO Offset Publication No 87, World Health Organization, Geneva

Chapter 6

Environmental health

All over the world, in developed and developing countries alike, environmental degradation is undermining development and damaging human health. This ill health saps the strength of the workforce and so further obstructs development, leads to greater environmental loss and causes even more disease. Yet this vicious circle can be broken – and reversed. If the environment is improved, both economies and people will become healthier.

Over the last decade the world has become healthier. Infant mortality has decreased and life expectancy increased in almost every nation. Yet gaps exist between the rich and the poor in developed and developing countries and an enormous gap remains between the two groups of countries. A baby born in a developing country is ten times more likely to die before its first birthday than one born in an industrialized nation. A European or a North American can expect to live more than 20 years longer than an African or a South Asian. People in developing countries mainly suffer from communicable diseases, largely caused by underdevelopment. People in industrialized countries and rich sectors of developing countries, by contrast, die predominantly from degenerative diseases, mainly cardiovascular diseases and cancer, which are caused, to a great extent, by ill planned development and overconsumption.

The direct causes of disease and disability include:

1. biotic factors, such as bacteria and other living agents of disease;
2. chemical factors which include inorganic and organic chemicals, and naturally occurring products of biological origin;
3. physical factors such as heat, cold, irradiation, noise and electricity;
4. socioeconomic factors such as stress, under- and malnutrition, and over-crowding; and
5. hereditary factors.

These causative factors may induce physical and mental disease, injury and death. However, the effect they have on the health of populations and individuals is highly variable, depending upon individual response and the modifying influence of other factors of the human environment.

The most widespread environmental diseases are communicable diseases that are still highly prevalent in the developing countries where, together with malnutrition, they account for high mortality and debility among the poorest people, particularly among children below the age of five. The prevalence of communicable diseases in developing countries is mainly due to the poor state of water supply and sanitation in these countries (see Chapter 3).

The present chapter deals with the three main environmental diseases – malaria, schistosomiasis and cancer – that account for a high percentage of deaths in the world. Other diseases triggered by environmental factors are referred to in Chapters 2, 4, 5 and 8.

Malaria

Malaria is a disease caused by infection from parasites of the genus *Plasmodium*, transmitted by the bite of infected anopheline mosquitoes and characterized clinically by recurrent paroxysms of chills, fever and sweating. In man, malaria is produced by four specific parasites which are not infectious for the lower animals: *Plasmodium falciparum, P. vivax, P. malariae* and *P. ovale. Plasmodium falciparum* is the parasite responsible for most cases of malaria (80% worldwide) and for the most severe, often fatal, forms of the disease. It is deeply entrenched in tropical Africa. *P. vivax* is the commonest species in Central and South America and in Asia. These two species account for most of the human suffering and economic loss arising from malaria in the world today.

Nearly half of the world's population – 2 500 million people – live in areas where malaria continues to be a health risk to some degree. Excluding Africa south of the Sahara, 8.1 million malaria cases were reported to WHO in 1980. The provisional figures for 1982 and 1983 were 6.5 million and 5.5 million respectively (WHO, 1985c). These data must be considered with caution, since screening, diagnosis and notification efforts have declined over the past 15 years. Many countries have been forced to scale down malaria control measures, thereby reducing the availability of accurate information on the disease. In areas other than tropical Africa the incidence of malaria is currently estimated to be around 20 million cases a year (WHO, 1985c). In Africa south of the Sahara some 200 million people are believed to be chronically infected and of these, about one-third suffer acute manifestations of the disease in the course of a year. The UNICEF–WHO Joint Committee on Health Policy estimated that the annual number of clinical cases of malaria in the world is about 95 million, 75 million of which are in Africa south of the Sahara (UNICEF–WHO, 1985). Accurate figures are not available for the number of deaths caused primarily by malaria, although in Africa alone it is estimated that the disease is responsible for the deaths of one million infants and young children each year.

After the discovery in 1898 of the life cycle of the malaria parasite and the critical role of mosquitoes as carriers of the disease, the primary strategy to control malaria was to drain or adjust the levels of stagnant pools and swamps where the mosquito larvae bred and to use quinine and other therapeutic drugs to treat the disease. This approach had considerable success. When DDT was first used successfully to combat malaria in 1943, optimistic proposals for a complete eradication of malaria were voiced. For a brief period in the early 1960s it appeared that malaria might soon be brought under control. Extensive spraying with DDT was reducing the *Anopheles* mosquito population and novel drugs such as chloroquine were available for treating infected patients. Twenty years later malaria is resurgent. Its causative agent, the parasite *Plasmodium*, is developing resistance to the drugs and the parasite's vector, the female *Anopheles* mosquito, is becoming resistant to DDT and other insecticides. In addition, there has been a marked relaxation in combating malaria in some countries.

The resurgence of malaria has been most dramatic in India, where the number of reported cases increased from 40 000 in 1966 to 1.4 million in 1972 and to 6.5 million in 1976 (Figure 34). Since 1976, however, the number of reported cases has dropped rapidly to about 1.9 million in 1983. Resurgence of malaria has been recently reported in several countries, for example in Thailand, Brazil, Colombia, Mexico and Sri Lanka.

In 1980, 51 anopheline species had been reported to be resistant to one or more insecticides: 34 are resistant to DDT, 47 to dieldrin and 30 to both. Resistance to organophosphates has been reported in 10 species and to carbamates in 4 species. This resistance, particularly multiple resistance, has developed in areas of great

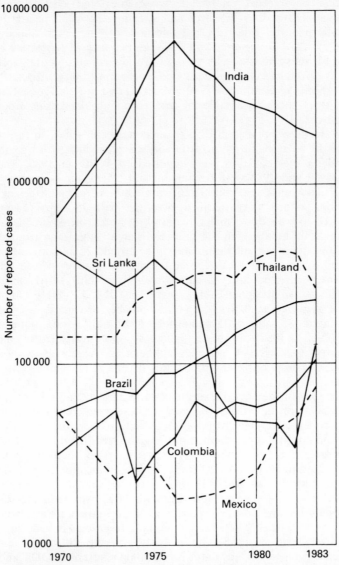

Figure 34 Trend of malaria incidence in some countries
Data from WHO, 1985c

economic importance where agricultural pesticides are intensively and often indiscriminately used for crop protection (WHO, 1985c).

Resistance of *Plasmodium falciparum* to drugs (4-aminoquinolines) has probably become the most important threat to effective control of the disease. It has arisen largely through a combination of massive antimalarial drug deployment and a failure to combat transmission of the disease. Population movements have also played a part in the occurrence and spread of resistance. Resistance of *P. falciparum* to 4-aminoquinolines was first reported in Colombia and Thailand in the beginning of the 1960s. By the end of 1984, chloroquine-resistant *P. falciparum* was present in 15 countries in eastern Asia and Oceania, 10 in South America and 15 in Africa (mostly south of the Sahara).

A global system for monitoring the spread of *P. falciparum* resistance to drugs has been set up and was incorporated into WHO's Malaria Action Programme at the end of 1983. The monitoring programme has three main objectives: to develop standard methods of recording, storing, processing and analysing drug sensitivity data; to set up a data bank; and to report periodically on drug sensitivity throughout the world. The system provides a synopsis of the geographical distribution and levels of susceptibility/resistance and calls attention to significant differences in responses to individual drugs between different geographical areas and at different times. Although a fairly recent introduction, the system will probably become the main source of data on worldwide antimalarial drug sensitivity and provide a basis for the planning of countermeasures to drug resistance.

In 1984 a new drug, mefloquine, was made available to health authorities in several countries. Mefloquine, a quinolinemethanol, is a potent blood schizontocide active against multiresistant *falciparum* malaria. The drug has been registered in Switzerland for the prophylaxis and treatment of malaria in adult males and non-pregnant females and in children over two years of age. WHO has issued a set of recommendations to ensure the optimal deployment of the drug in endemic areas and to delay the emergence of resistance to mefloquine. Qinghaosu (artemisinine), the active principle of the Chinese medicinal herb *Artemisia annua*, is a novel antimalarial. The parent compound and several derivatives have been shown to have a rapid action in the treatment of chloroquine-resistant *falciparum* malaria. The assessment of this series of compounds is in progress in some research laboratories.

The extensive use of insecticides has resulted in a number of well documented negative effects on the human environment (UNEP, 1982; El-Hinnawi and Hashmi, 1982). Although the wider environmental effects of DDT have been largely due to agricultural rather than public health use of insecticides, indoor spraying of DDT may result in undesirable effects. Domestic livestock can become contaminated: in Guatemala the yolks of chicken eggs were found to have about 30 parts per million of DDT, most, if not all of which was being picked up inside sprayed houses (Farvar, 1972). In 1970, in rural areas of Guatemala where DDT spraying for malaria control had been carried on for some 15 years, total DDT in human mothers' milk was found to be from 0.3 to 12.2 ppm (Farvar, 1975). These figures suggest that Guatemalan infants were drinking from the breast at least 15 and perhaps nearly 500 times more than the acceptable daily intake of DDT established by WHO (WHO, 1969). High levels of DDT in mothers' milk have also been reported from Papua New Guinea and Ghana. The effects of such high human exposure to DDT and other insecticides are not easy to assess. Recent evaluation of the risks to the general public suggests that excessive levels of DDT and other chlorinated hydrocarbons do affect the functions of the liver, could affect cholesterol levels and might impair the normal development and functioning of the nervous system (see also Chapter 5). Animal studies suggest that such high milk levels as were found in Guatemala and other countries might be harmful to the normal growth and development of babies. It is known that DDT and other insecticides are generally more harmful to animals suffering from protein deficiency, so it seems that the peoples of the developing world may be both more exposed to and more susceptible to damage from DDT.

Apart from technical problems, malaria control has also suffered from inflationary increases in the costs of insecticides, drugs, equipment and fuel. In contrast, government budgetary expenditure on malaria control has either not increased or, in many countries, has even been cut back. All in all, the balance favours the malaria parasite.

These difficulties facing the malaria control programmes have accelerated efforts to look for alternative approaches. Since malaria has social and ecological causes and consequences, more attention is being given to integrated, environmentally sound methods of control, with less dependence on insecticides. Several approaches have been proposed. One of these is known as 'habitat management', which involves the modification of the aquatic habitats where mosquitoes breed. Swamps and stagnant waters can be drained and their salinity can be altered; exposure to or protection from the sun can be controlled. Such steps can make the habitat unsuitable for development of mosquito larvae. A particular advantage of this approach is its suitability for self help and popular participation. In Malaysia, as early as 1901, simple drainage considerably reduced the number of deaths from malaria in two towns and many of the drainage systems built between 1920 and 1940 in Malaysia, Mauritius, India and the Philippines are still operating. In Italy, mosquitoes have been controlled by the combined drainage of marshes and use of DDT. In Mexico, where rice is planted in trenches, one species of mosquito was almost totally eliminated by making water flow down the trenches and wash away the larvae. In Portugal, another mosquito was reduced by 80% by intermittent instead of permanent irrigation (Surtees, 1971).

Another approach to controlling malaria is biological: using other organisms to limit mosquito numbers. At least 265 species of fish, for example, have at various times been tried in more than 40 countries (Gerberich and Laird, 1968). Larvivorous fish feed on mosquito larvae and this suppresses mosquito production and reduces density. The extent of larval suppression and adult mosquito density reduction depends on the species of fish, the species of mosquito to be controlled and the ecological conditions of the habitat. It also depends on how effectively an adequate population of fish is maintained during the period of mosquito prevalence. Only one fish species, *Gambusia affinis*, has been notably successful. The advantages of using *Gambusia* include its small size, prolific breeding and wide tolerance of temperature and salinity. During the 1920s, several successful results were obtained from the introduction of the fish. In the USA, a reduction of 50% in the anopheline larval density after the introduction of *Gambusia* in ponds and swamps was reported in 1925. More recently, several other countries, for example Italy and Iran, have reported similar successful results. However, there is a need for systematic evaluation of various aspects of this method of control and for scientific evaluation of the results under different ecological conditions and the resultant impact on malaria. Another variety of biological control involves the use of microbes and other parasitic disease agents to attack malaria-carrying mosquitoes (Arta, 1977; Goldberg and Margalit, 1977).

Numerous theoretical approaches to the use of genetic mechanisms for insect control have been proposed; however, except for the sterile insect method, research on development of these mechanisms for practical insect control has been limited to the selection and characterization of strains and the determination of their suitability and behaviour. The sterile insects are usually produced by direct exposure to doses of chemicals or irradiation. The sterile males mate with females and prevent them from laying fertile eggs. Field application of this method on a large scale is still at an early stage; more investigation and studies, including cost and methodology for mass rearing, environmental impact and various safety factors, are required.

The most frequently discussed requirement for a solution of the malaria problem is a vaccine against the *Plasmodium* species that cause malaria. The complex structure and life cycle of the malaria parasite and the nature of its interaction with its human host preclude any rapid solution to the vaccine problem. The stage that infects man, the sporozoite, resides in the mosquito's salivary gland and is delivered into the victim's bloodstream when the insect takes a blood meal. Within an hour each sporozoite finds its way to a liver cell. There it undergoes a complex series of transformations. Eventually a giant multinucleate stage, the schizont, fissions into small, roughly spherical merozoites.

The result is an enormous amplification of parasites: a liver cell infected by one sporozoite releases into the bloodstream from 5 000 to 10 000 merozoites. Each merozoite invades a red blood cell, where it multiplies asexually until the cell bursts and releases from 10 to 20 new merozoites that go on to invade more red cells. It is the periodic lysis of the blood cells, with concomitant release of merozoites and toxic waste products, that causes the regular fevers and chills of malaria. Some merozoites develop into male and female gametocytes (germ cell percursors), thus initiating the parasite's sexual cycle. The gametocytes are sucked up with red cells by a mosquito, mature in the mosquito gut and fuse to form a zygote. The zygote undergoes yet another series of divisions, transformations and migrations; eventually a mature sporozoite appears in the salivary gland, ready to initiate a new infective cycle.

The most striking advance in malaria vaccine research has been the cloning of the gene coding for the major protective surface protein of sporozoites of *Plasmodium falciparum*. As a result of this achievement, reported in 1984, the possibilities of producing a vaccine appear to be good. A vaccine against malaria will probably have to incorporate the dominant antigens of the sporozoite, liver stages, blood stages and even the sexual stages (WHO, 1985c,d; Godson, 1985).

Although various ecologically sound alternatives hold great potential for future malaria control strategies, no method used alone will be effective for the total control of malaria. This applies equally to chemical and bioenvironmental measures. At the present stage of knowledge and technology, some combination of effective and ecologically sound measures against larval forms and their breeding habitats, controlled application of insecticides against adult vectors and safe chemotherapy appears to be the rational approach to malaria control. The success of such a programme will depend heavily on support and participation by the affected people and community motivation is therefore an essential element. Correct land and water management for fish farming, forestry, agriculture and other practices in relation to changing human behaviour and lifestyles are also relevant factors deserving long-term attention in malaria control programmes.

Schistosomiasis

Schistosomiasis – known also as bilharziasis or bilharzia - is caused by a water borne parasite that is snail transmitted and that infects humans on contact. The disease is estimated to affect at least 200 million people and endanger another 600 million in 74 subtropical or tropical countries in Asia, Africa, the Caribbean and Latin America, creating public health problems of varying magnitudes (WHO, 1984c). Although recent figures on the number of infections are difficult to obtain, because of the lack of reliable statistical data, it has been estimated that present infections are in the range of 200 million, with half of this figure occurring in Africa. The ten countries with the highest number of reported cases of schistosomiasis are Egypt, Sudan, Central African Republic, Brazil, Nigeria, Tanzania, Chad, Mali, Zambia and Iraq (Who, 1981, 1985a,b). The peak prevalence and intensity of infection is among children 10–14 years of age. In general 60–70% of all infected people are 5–14 years of age (Mott, 1984).

Human schistosomiasis is caused by four species of flatworms, or blood flukes (schistosomes). The first species, *Schistosoma haematobium*, is found in the Eastern Mediterranean area and over much of Africa. The second, *S. mansoni*, is found in the Eastern Mediterranean region, Africa and part of Central and South America, while the third, *S. japonicum*, is found only in East Asia. These three species of schistosome have similar life cycles, involving sexual stages in man and asexual stages in various species of snails which are the intermediate hosts. The fourth species, *Schistosoma intercalatum*, may infect man, particularly in Equatorial Africa, but is of lesser significance. Species of *Schistosoma* of veterinary importance include *S. bovis, S. matthei* and *S. spindale* and have been reported in many African and Asian countries. *S. japonicum* has high prevalence in many types of wild and domestic animals (Cowper, 1971; Ree, 1977).

Methods used to control schistosomiasis depend upon interrupting the life cycle of the parasite in such a way as to break its continuity. This can be achieved by reducing the contamination of natural waters by human excreta, controlling the snail intermediate hosts, reducing human contact with infected water by provision of clean water supplies and by treating infected people.

The efficient disposal of human excreta should, in theory, be an adequate method of controlling transmission of schistosomiasis, but the socioeconomic conditions prevailing in many endemic areas make the provision of adequate latrine facilities difficult. Better health education is required so that sanitation will be accepted and recognized as desirable. Washing and laundry facilities require a safe water supply, as bathing in water containing cercariae is a common mode of infection. If adequate water is provided to meet the needs of the population, contact with natural waters will be reduced and fouling of the river or pond environment will consequently be reduced. The provision of water should be linked with ensuring adequate drainage. Unless this is done, snails may become established closer to habitations than previously and the problem of schistosomiasis and other infections may even be aggravated.

Control of the molluscan intermediate host is generally considered one of the most effective means now available for reducing transmission of schistosomiasis and its efficacy is likely to be enhanced if it is combined with other methods of control. The life cycle of snail intermediate hosts, their infection and subsequent production of cercariae and the transmission of infection, are all affected by seasonal changes. Cognizance of these relationships, together with the identification of all transmission sites, must form the basis of the timing and application of measures directed against snails in an attempt to control transmission. Failure to achieve a successful degree of control is usually attributable to a lack of basic information on the above mentioned relationships. It should also be remembered that the factors responsible for transmission may vary considerably and direct extrapolation of data on snail populations and cercariae or on the behaviour of the definitive host, from one area to another may not always be valid, even in closely adjacent areas. Reduction in the prevalence of schistosomiasis has been achieved in the Philippines through the application of methods directed against the molluscan intermediate host and based upon well founded data and sound logistics (Pesigan and Hairston, 1961).

About 10 000 chemical compounds have been screened for molluscicidal activity and the most promising ones have been further evaluated in field trials. An ideal molluscicide should combine the following characteristics:

1. It should be lethal to snails and their eggs, but harmless to other forms of animal life, especially fish and livestock and should also be harmless to crop plants.
2. It should be economical in price and light in bulk to reduce purchase and transport costs.
3. It should be simple to apply to water and harmless to the operator.
4. Its solubility should be such that it reaches the snail tissues, but not so great that it is quickly lost.
5. It should remain unaffected by the organic content of the water long enough to take effect.

The range of currently available molluscicides does not, however, meet all these requirements (WHO, 1973). Many available compounds affect plants and other non-target organisms in the snail habitat and this biocidal activity is unfortunately possessed by the few molluscicides of accepted effectiveness (Malek, 1978). The most commonly used molluscicides are niclosamide, N-trityl-morpholine and copper sulphate. Although these compounds have been effective in controlling the molluscan intermediate host, they have a toxic effect on non-target organisms, especially fish (Abdalla and Nasr, 1961; Shiff *et al*, 1967; Meredith, 1972). In addition, the long-term effects of small accumulated concentrations of these compounds (especially those absorbed on silt and clay) have not been thoroughly evaluated. Research on plants with molluscicidal properties (eg *Phytolacca dodecandra, Ambrosia maritima*, etc) is in progress to establish their active constituents and the feasibility of their use on a wide scale to control the molluscan intermediate host.

There are numerous records of the harmful effects of different parasites, predators and competitors on snail intermediate hosts and various species of bacteria, fungi, protozoa, arthropods, molluscs, amphibia, fish, birds and animals affect snails directly or indirectly (WHO, 1967; Wright, 1968). The introduction of a harmless species which might compete for the food and living space of an intermediate host species or prey upon its eggs and young snails, is in principle an attractive proposition. The ampullariid snail *Marisa cornuarietis* has been employed in schistosomiasis control programmes in Puerto Rico (Jobin *et al*, 1977). Other experiments on competitor snails include those using *Helisome duryi* (Frandsen and Christensen, 1977). Various reports of experiments with mollusc eating fish suggest that drastic reductions in snail population density can be obtained in certain habitats. Such a series of observations was conducted in Kenya; dams were stocked with *Astatoreochromis alluaudi* and observed over a prolonged period and impressive reductions in the population density of *Biomphalaria* were obtained (McMahon *et al*, 1977). Reports indicate that *Gambusia* species may also effect similar reductions in intermediate host populations in certain habitats, as does the shell cracker fish, *Lepomis microlophus*, in Puerto Rico. Successful biological control methods would undoubtedly be of economic advantage, but much more research is required into the feasibility and practicability of the application of organisms of potential value before they can be considered for use in the field (Barbosa, 1978; Van der Schalie, 1978).

The most satisfactory method of eliminating the snail intermediate hosts is the destruction of their habitats, either by removal of water or by rendering the water source unsuitable for them. Minor sites of infection can be removed by drainage or filling, but environmental control is not easy in irrigation schemes. Any large scale irrigation project undertaken in an endemic area may create a schistosomiasis problem. It is a disconcerting aspect of schistosomiasis that the disease may be spread to new areas, hitherto uninfected or of low endemicity, by dams and irrigation projects intended to increase prosperity; the incidence of schistosomiasis increases with the population density. Practices involving an occupational exposure risk such as rice growing or fish farming also tend to increase the incidence of schistosomiasis.

The principal environmental methods used to eliminate or significantly reduce the breeding habitats of snails, with or without the additional use of molluscicides, are:

1.   complete removal of all water inhabited by snails;
2.   rendering water sources unsuitable for snail breeding;
3.   enclosure of water to prevent contamination with excreta;
4.   periodic drying out of irrigation channels; and
5.   weed clearance.

The removal of water involves the drainage of swamps, fens, seepages and small lakes or ponds, and, when complete, should eliminate the snails' habitat. Obviously, this perfect method of eradication can only be applied if a safe alternative water source is available, so that the water eliminated is not required for human needs. In the case of large bodies of water the cost may be prohibitive. Small accumulations of water such as borrow pits, flooded quarries or mine workings, obstructed irrigation channels or small ponds may be drained or filled in with any suitable material available. An environment which is uncongenial for snails can be produced in a watercourse by a strong flowing current, by perpendicular or sharply sloping banks, by removal of the weeds which provide food, oxygen and a substrate for egg masses, by periodic flushing controlled by sluices, by the use of holding canals lined with cement and by various other techniques. Better still is a pumped water supply driven through closed pipes or conduits. The continued use of primitive irrigation methods such as the *sakia* (water wheel), the *shadoof* (counterbalanced bucket swinging on a beam) or the Archimedes screw, which expose the operator directly to cercariae in the water, is partly responsible for the phenomenal incidence of schistosomiasis in the Nile valley. There are examples where control of irrigation water, improved agricultural methods and adequate drainage have proved successful in controlling schistosomiasis (Yokogawa, 1972, 1974; Unrua, 1978).

Mass chemotherapy is currently thought to be an indispensable method for schistosomiasis control. Safe, effective oral drugs have become available in recent years for the treatment of *S. mansoni, S. haematobium* and *S. japonicum* infections and drugs such as praziquantel, oxamniquine and metrifonate have been used in large scale control programmes (Mott, 1984). Differences in drug susceptibilities have been observed in different populations and drug resistance has been reported, although on too small a scale to affect chemotherapy in large population groups.

Immunological approaches to schistosomiasis are currently attracting considerable attention. Laboratory experiments on animals showed that the presence of adult schistosomes reduces either the extent of, or the damage done by, later infection. On the basis of these facts, several trials are under way to produce a vaccine that confers immunity to infection (WHO, 1974, 1985a,d; Grzych *et al*, 1985); but many complicated problems will have to be overcome and an effective vaccine cannot be expected before the year 2000.

The control of schistosomiasis is an urgent requirement not only for improving health in endemic areas, but also for enhancing socioeconomic progress in these areas. While the existence of economic losses from sickness and treatment costs is generally recognized, the lack of consistent methods of estimation and of reliable data bases have led to widely different financial estimates and, hence, to some controversy over the total productivity and cost of medical care, all of which can be expressed in monetary terms, other losses are more difficult to quantify, for example, the discomfort of illness and the increase in the dependency ratio due to morbidity. Thus it appears that the economic significance of schistosomiasis is much more than has, hitherto, been estimated. Another important aspect of the economic significance of schistosomiasis is that it constitues a classical example of an economic development related disease. The increase in the number of water development projects in the last few decades has greatly increased the number of habitats available to the snail hosts, hence the rise in prevalence of schistosomiasis. In some projects, the emergence of this problem has impeded the realization of sound economic returns.

Schistosomiasis control programmes have sometimes been avoided in some countries because they have been considered too costly. However, the costs and availability of labour and the epidemiological circumstances that may occur in endemic foci vary so much that it is not usually possible to state accurately the probable costs of a control programme. In general, control programmes have been estimated to have annual recurrent costs with a range of $0.40–12.00 per capita (WHO, 1973). In St Lucia (West Indies) a two year control programme showed that chemotherapy reduced incidence of *S. mansoni* from 18.8% to 4%; snail control from 22% to 9.8%; and the establishment of adequate water supplies from 22.7% to 11.3% (Jordan, 1977). The annual costs per capita in the first two years were $1.10 (chemotherapy), $3.7 (snail control) and $4.0 (water supplies). Chemotherapy was the cheapest and most rapidly effective method of achieving disease control. Chemotherapy requires population cooperation and a stable community. Cooperation is also required for water supplies to be effective.

No single method for the control of schistosomiasis can be recommended; only an integrated approach which takes local factors into account can achieve successful results. Health education, medication and surveillance of population movements are the principal tasks to be undertaken in relation to human population. Environmentally sound water development projects, sanitation and adequate water supply are environmental prerequisites for the control of the disease. Finally, chemical, biological and environmental methods should be applied in an integrated manner for snail control. It must be emphasized that the success of any control operation depends upon public awareness and participation. It was mainly because of public participation that it was possible to control schistosomiasis in China. During the first half of this century schistosomiasis, in the most severe form of the disease, afflicted more than 10 million Chinese and probably resulted in a greater number of deaths than in any other country before or since. The blood flukes caused constant misery and even depopulation in many villages and provoked liver, spleen and intestinal diseases and early death. Since 1950 China has enjoyed a dramatic success against the disease. A national campaign against the disease utilized the country's abundant manpower to destroy the snail host. Mass drug therapy, together with proper treatment of human wastes, contributed to the successful control of the disease. Canals in the infected areas were drained, the snail infested mud was dug out and buried in dry land and snails were killed by sticks (Cheng, 1971; Anderson, 1976 and Chen *et al*, 1983). Elsewhere, endemic areas of schistosomiasis cut across politica! boundaries and the political cooperation necessary to ensure control of the disease is not always available. Migration and nomadism, still very common in Africa, increase the prevalence of the disease, since the snail hosts are generally more widespread than the infection. Persistence of effort is crucial to bringing about human behavioural changes favourable to the prevention of schistosome transmission. Although health education has seldom seriously been applied, it must rank as one of the most important basic tools for control in endemic areas.

Cancer

Cancer is a breakdown of the orderly process of cell growth and differentiation. It seems to begin with a change in a single cell, presumably a mutation in that cell's genetic apparatus. This change transforms the cell profoundly so that it begins to divide without restraint, failing to differentiate into its mature form. Eventually, this altered cell will give rise to billions of other aberrant cells, cancer cells, that invade and destroy nearby tissues. As the colony grows, some of these cells will break off, or metastasize, and be carried by the blood or lymph stream to remote parts of the body where they will invade other tissues. In connective tissues (such as bone, cartilage, tendon, muscle) cancers are called sarcomas; in epithelial tissues (such as skin, bladder, lung, breast) they are called carcinomas; and in cells of the blood system they are named leukaemias.

In the early 1970s, cancer research was galvanized by the discovery of oncogenes, specific genes that can trigger a cell's unbridled growth. Since that time, close to 30 of these cancer genes have been isolated from both human and animal cells. In laboratory experiments, the activity of a single one of them is often sufficient to transform normal cells to cancer cells. In the past few years, molecular biologists have been able to decipher the genetic code of these cancer genes. To their surprise, they found that the oncogenes are remarkably similar, if not identical, to benign genes that are normally present within the cell (Roberts, 1984). It now appears that each cell contains certain normal genes that when activated or altered in some way can start the cell on the path to cancer. Many cancer researchers suspect that all agents of cancer – radiation, chemicals and viruses – act upon these genes, somehow releasing their malignant potential.

Even before the discovery of oncogenes, it was thought that cancer was the product of interaction of genes and the environment. In 1958, it was suggested that 70–80% of cancers were directly or indirectly related to the environment (Miller and Miller, 1972). Certain agents, such as ultraviolet and ionizing radiation, some chemicals and some viruses, can initiate cancer, presumably by causing a genetic mutation. From recent work, it is tempting to think that the mutation occurs on an oncogene (Roberts, 1984). Still other external or environmental agents can promote or facilitate the process of carcinogenesis without actually inducing it.

There is now widespread agreement that roughly 85% of all cancers are caused by broad environmental factors, including lifestyle patterns. The rest, presumably, have a hereditary basis or else arise from spontaneous metabolic events. Identifying the environmental factors in cancer, however, has not been easy. Occupational chemicals are thought to be responsible for 4% of all cancers; environmental chemicals for an estimated 2%. Tobacco is by far the largest documented cause of cancer, accounting for roughly 30% of all cancers in lungs and some other sites. Recently, epidemiological studies similar to those that uncovered an association between smoking and cancer have detected a link between the foods that people eat and the cancers that afflict them. In the USA, dietary factors are thought to be responsible for 30% of cancer incidence (Roberts, 1984).

The incidence of cancer and the mortality due to cancer differ greatly from one region to another. In developing countries, where communicable diseases are still rampant, the percentage of deaths due to cancer is lower than in industrialized countries, where life expectancies extend to approximately 70 years. For example, in 1980, 4.5% of all deaths in Sri Lanka were due to cancer, while in FR Germany the figure was 22.4% and in the USA it was 21.3% (as calculated from statistical data given by WHO, 1985b). In absolute terms, however, the majority of cancers in the world occur in developing countries and rates for certain specific cancers, such as oral, cervical, gastric, oesophageal and liver cancer, exceed those in developed countries. For people in developing countries who reach the age of five years, cancer is among the three most common causes of death (WHO, 1984a,b). In addition, the cancer burden is increasing as other diseases are successfully controlled, as life expectancy in developing countries increases, as lifestyles and personal habits change and as countries become more industrialized.

It has been estimated that each year there are 5.9 million new cases of cancer in the world, more than half of these arising in the developing countries (Figure 35). The annual total of deaths from all forms of cancer is estimated to be 4.3 million, of which 2.3 million occur in developing countries (Osuntokun, 1985). Socioeconomic factors, lifestyles, behaviour and environment appear to influence the types of cancer that predominate in a particular country or region. Globally, the most common

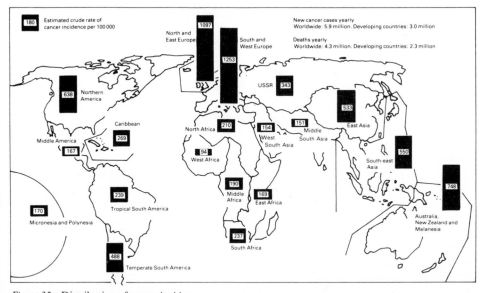

Figure 35   Distribution of cancer incidence
After Osuntokun, 1985 and WHO, 1984a

TABLE 9. The twelve major cancers: estimated number of new cases in the world in 1975

Rank	Type of cancer	Estimated number of cases
1	Stomach	682 400
2	Bronchus/lung	591 000
3	Breast	541 200
4	Colon/rectum	506 900
5	Cervic uteri	459 400
6	Mouth/pharynx	339 500
7	Oesophagus	296 300
8	Liver	259 200
9	Lymphatic tissue	220 900
10	Prostate	197 700
11	Leukaemia	175 700
12	Bladder	170 100

Source: Parkin *et al* (1984)

neoplasm is almost certainly cancer of the stomach (Table 9), incidence rates of which are high in Europe, East Asia and South America. However, the annual number of cases of lung cancer is not far behind, and this appears to be the most common tumour among males. The incidence rates for stomach cancer are declining throughout the world, while with a few exceptions those for lung cancer are rising rapidly – the USSR registered a 55% increase in lung cancer cases between 1970 and 1980, for example (Parkin *et al*, 1984). Bladder cancer is more frequent in the developed countries of Europe and North America than elsewhere, with the exception of those areas where schistosomiasis is endemic, especially Egypt (Parkin *et al*, 1984). Traditional practices such as the chewing of betel quid and tobacco or hookah smoking constitute the main reason for 90% of the 100 000 new cases of oral cancer reported each year in South-east Asia. Oral cancer is most common in Bangladesh, India, Pakistan and Sri Lanka and accounts for about a third of all cancers recorded in these countries (WHO, 1984b; Osuntokun, 1985).

Cancer can be caused by a wide variety of factors, often acting in combination with one another, over periods of many years. Evidence is growing that viruses cause certain forms of cancer. They may not act alone, but at the very least viruses are turning out to be a necessary link in the chain of environmental influences that can lead to cancer. In laboratories throughout the world, researchers are working to understand how viruses alter the metabolism of the infected cell, in the hopes of being able to block their action. In the meantime, the development of new vaccines against these viruses could prevent more people from becoming infected. Much research focuses on a virus strongly implicated in one kind of cancer: HTLV-I, the virus of adult T-cell leukaemia (Vines, 1985). Other forms of cancer are caused by hereditary factors – for example, the rare tumour of the eye in children, retinoblastoma. But the overwhelming number of causative factors which have been isolated are in one way or another environmental: they relate to the air people breathe or the water they drink, to the environment in which they work or live, to their personal diet or way of life, to habits like smoking tobacco or drinking alcohol.

Lung cancer is predominantly a disease of tobacco smoking. Active smoking habits account for an estimated 85% of lung cancer. It is now well established that (for US males) a person who smokes 10–19 cigarettes per day is more than eight times likely to die of lung cancer, and someone who smokes over 40 cigarettes per day is nearly 20 times more likely to die of cancer than is a non-smoker (Hammond,

1975). In spite of these well established facts, the global use of tobacco has grown nearly 75% over the past two decades (Brown *et al*, 1986). Although tobacco consumption in many developed countries is falling by about 1% annually, consumption in the developing countries is rising by about 2%, encouraged by changing of lifestyles and behaviour, by aggressive marketing on the part of the tobacco companies and the inadequacy of antismoking campaigns. Over a billion people in the world smoke tobacco, consuming almost five trillion cigarettes per year (Brown *et al*, 1986).

It has been argued that the risk with smoking solely affects the individual concerned and that since he alone chooses to smoke we are not dealing with a strictly environmental cancer. However, recent studies have shown that ambient tobacco smoke carries a risk of cancer to non-smokers. For example, in Japan it was found that wives who did not smoke but were exposed to their husband's cigarette smoke developed lung cancer at a much higher rate than non-smoking wives of non-smoking husbands. The risk to non-smoking wives was directly related to the amount their husbands smoked and that risk was one-half to one-third that of direct smoking (Hirayama, 1981). Such 'passive smoking' has been correlated with lung cancer in non-smoking spouses of smokers in ten other studies (Brown *et al*, 1986). Repace and Lowrey (1985) pointed out that aggregate exposure to ambient tobacco smoke is estimated to produce about 5 000 lung cancer deaths per year in US non-smokers aged more than 35 years, with an average loss of life expectancy of 17 years per fatality. A new study in the USA has found that passive smoking produces other types of cancer in addition to lung cancer. For example, leukaemia appears seven times more often among people who have spent their lives with smokers. Cancers of the cervix and breast were also strongly linked with passive smoking (*New Scientist*, 7 March 1985).

The human diet contains a great variety of natural mutagens and carcinogens, as well as many natural antimutagens and anticarcinogens. Many of these mutagens and carcinogens may act through the generation of oxygen radicals. Oxygen radicals may also play a major role as endogenous initiators of degenerative processes, such as DNA damage and mutation (and promotion) that may be related to cancer, heart disease and aging (Ames, 1983). Epidemiological studies and experiments in animals provide convincing evidence that increasing the intake of total fat increases the incidence of cancer at certain sites, particularly the breast and colon, and, conversely, that the risk is lower with lower intakes of fat. The frequent consumption of salt cured, salt pickled and smoked food tends to increase the risk of cancer, whereas the frequent consumption of certain fruits and vegetables (eg carotene-rich vegetables and cruciferous vegetables) tends to decrease it.

Certain naturally occurring contaminants in food are carcinogenic in animals and pose a potential risk of cancer to humans. Noteworthy among these are mycotoxins (especially alfatoxin) and N-nitroso compounds, for which there is some epidemiological evidence (NRC, 1982). Millions of people in Africa and elsewhere are exposed to alfatoxins, caused by fungal contamination of stored food, which can cause liver cancer (see also Chapter 5).

In the USA, nearly 3 000 substances are intentionally added to foods during processing. Another estimated 12 000 chemicals are classified as indirect (or unintentional) additives, and are occasionally detected in some foods (NRC, 1982). Large amounts of some additives, such as sugar, are consumed by the general population, but the annual per capita exposure to most indirect additives represents only a minute portion of the diet. Evidence gathered so far does not suggest that the increasing use of food additives has contributed significantly to the overall risk of cancer for humans. However, this lack of detectable effect may be due to their lack of carcinogenicity, to the relatively recent use of many of these substances or to the inability of epidemiological techniques to detect the effects of additives against the background of common cancers from other causes. Both nitrates and nitrites are widely used in the production and preservation of cured meat products and of some fish. In normal healthy individuals, nitrates and nitrites are rapidly absorbed from the gastrointestinal tract. In others, however, nitrites may react with amino groups to form N-nitroso compounds. The carcinogenic action of N-nitroso compounds in animals is known to occur in many different organs (WHO, 1978). However, so far, correlations have not been established that link cancer in man with exposure to N-nitroso compounds or their precursors, but the possible role of N-nitroso compounds and in particular their *in vivo* formation in the development of nasopharyngeal, oesophageal and stomach cancer has been suggested (WHO, 1978). Recently, it has been shown that fluoridation of drinking water is associated with increased cancer mortality rates (Bundock *et al*, 1985).

Some drugs normally used under medical supervision are now known to cause cancer. A drug formerly given to pregnant women to prevent abortion, diethylstilboestrol, is associated with vaginal cancer in their young daughters by transplacental carcinogenesis, for example, and the drug chlornaphthazine given to treat leukaemia appears to cause bladder cancer (Higginson, 1975; Hoover and Fraumeni, 1975). Medical X-rays, like radiation from nuclear industry, can significantly increase the incidence of cancer. UV radiation from the sun causes skin cancer (see Chapter 2).

Studies of occupational exposure to pollutants have revealed a great deal of information about the nature of chemical carcinogenesis (Table 10). This is partly because carcinogens are likely to be at their highest concentrations in factories, but has more to do with the existence of records of employment which have sometimes survived the long latent period – up to 40 year or more in some cases – between exposure to the carcinogen and appearance of the cancer. The causation of many occupational cancers is now known: lung cancer among asbestos insulation workers, respiratory cancer in workers exposed to arsenic in smelters and vineyards, liver cancer among workers with vinyl chloride, leukaemia among shoemakers and others exposed to benzene solvents, nasal cancer among nickel workers, are only some of the examples (Cole and Goldman, 1975). The boundary between strict occupational exposure to carcinogens, and a more general contamination of the environment outside, is a narrow one. A rare form of cancer of the lining of the lungs or the abdomen, mesothelioma, is known to occur mainly among people who had worked with blue asbestos up to 40 years previously (Newhouse and Thompson, 1965; Lieben and Pistawka, 1967). But some cases are known among the families of asbestos workers, who presumably brought the toxic dust home on their clothes, while other cases again occur with people who once lived a kilometre or two away from a blue asbestos works but never worked there.

Estimates by epidemiologists and government bodies in the UK generally put the proportion of cancer cases of occupational origin at between 1% and 5%. But it has been estimated that in the USA such cancers will constitute 20–38% of all cancers in the near future (Davies, 1984). In practical terms, the prevention of industrial cancer can be effected in three ways once a risk has been identified. First, the carcinogen in question can be removed by ceasing to use it as a raw material, by ceasing to manufacture it as an intermediate or end product or by modifying production processes so that it no longer occurs as a byproduct. Second, plant machinery, processes or handling procedures can be modified in such a way that the amount of

TABLE 10. Thirty-six chemicals or industrial processes associated with cancer induction in humans

Acrylonitrile
Alfatoxins
4-Aminobiphenyl
Aminotriazole
Arsenic and certain arsenic compounds
Asbestos
Auramine
Manufacture of auramine
Benzene
Benzidine
Beryllium and certain beryllium compounds
Chlornaphthazine
Chloromethyl ether
Cadmium and certain cadmium compounds
Carbon tetrachloride
Chlorabucil
Chromium and certain chromium compounds
Cyclophosphamide
Diethylstilboestrol
Dimethylcarbarnyl chloride
Dimethyl sulphate
Ethylene oxide
Hematite mining (underground)
Iron dextran
Manufacture of isopropyl alcohol
Melpholan
Mustard gas
2-Naphthylamine
Nickel and certain nickel compounds
Nickel refining
Oxymetholene
Phenacetin
Polychlorinated biphenyls
Soots, tars and mineral oils
Thiotepa
Vinyl chloride

Sources: International Agency for Research on Cancer, Lyon; and Davis (1981)

the carcinogen released into the atmosphere is reduced to permissible levels. Third, exposure of individual workers may be reduced to acceptable levels by the use of protective clothing and masks. Efforts to prevent occupational cancer have not been very successful (Davies, 1984). In the recent past and even to some extent today, dangerous exposure to substances that were recognized decades ago as carcinogens are still occurring; strict procedures and constant vigilance are required to make the introduction of new industrial carcinogens less likely.

From 1955 to 1975, some 40 000 compounds were screened each year in the hope of finding a few capable of killing cancer cells. Some 30 chemotherapeutic agents are now available. Their use has brought a dramatic reversal in the prognosis for some types of cancer. For instance, in 1955 virtually every child afflicted with acute lymphoytic leukaemia died of the disease, usually within a few months of diagnosis. Today the cure rate is 58%. Despite these dramatic successes, chemotherapy has several limitations. One is the ease with which cancer cells can become resistant to many of these drugs, rendering them ineffective. Another is the extreme toxicity of certain cancer drugs. Chemotherapeutic agents work by killing cancer cells and they invariably kill some normal cells as well. The cells in the intestinal mucosa, bone marrow and hair follicles are the most vulnerable to attack, which explains the common side effects of nausea, vomiting and hair loss. Perhaps more important, none of the existing agents is totally effective against the most prevalent form of cancer, the carcinomas or malignancies of the epithelial tissues, which develop in the head, neck, breast, lung, bowel and other organs. The search for new antitumour agents is continuing, as are efforts to increase the effectiveness or reduce the side effects of existing drugs. For the future, advances in molecular biology – both in the understanding of the nature of cancerous transformation and in the refinement of genetic engineering techniques – offer novel approaches to chemotherapy (Roberts, 1984). Genetic technologies may also provide methods of arresting cancer without relying on cytotoxic drugs. One approach under study would enlist the aid of some of the substances such as interferon and growth factors that cells produce to regulate their growth and provide defence against disease. It may also be possible to manipulate the immune system so that it is better able to fight off cancer. Eventually, it may even prove feasible to turn off oncogenes and halt the process of carcinogenesis or perhaps to somehow interfere with the oncogene protein product.

The total elimination of environmental carcinogens and promoters is impractical and contact with some environmental carcinogens remains virtually unavoidable. Yet a dramatic change of cancer incidence in individual organs or a steep reduction of certain occupational cancers encourages the idea of primary cancer prevention as a practical and plausible challenge. The latent period of cancer development may sometimes be measured over decades. The beneficial effects of efforts to prevent cancer cannot be achieved overnight. However, one can already see signs of victory in the decreases in lung cancer incidence and mortality in UK and Norway and to some extent in the USA, most probably as a result of the antismoking campaigns in these countries (Sugimura, 1986).

Action to combat the growing scourge of environmental cancer must, therefore, be taken at every level: in the hospital and clinic, in the workplace by public health

---

TABLE 11. **Twelve points for cancer prevention**

 1 Eat a nutritionally balanced diet
 2 Eat a variety of types of food
 3 Avoid excess calories, especially as fat
 4 Avoid excessive drinking of alcohol
 5 Smoke as little as possible
 6 Take vitamins in appropriate amounts; eat fibre and green and yellow vegetables rich in carotene
 7 Avoid drinking fluids that are too hot and eating foods that are too salty
 8 Avoid the charred parts of cooked food
 9 Avoid food with possible contamination by fungal toxins
10 Avoid overexposure to sunlight
11 Have an exercise programme matched to your condition
12 Keep the body clean

Source: Sugimura (1986)

authorities, on the local, national, regional and international scale. Government sponsored campaigns against cigarette smoking and excessive alcohol consumption, the control of chemical pollution by strict industrial and environmental regulations and other preventive methods cannot succeed without public awareness and participation. To prevent many cancers, some degree of personal involvement (Table 11) is not only possible but essential (Schneiderman, 1975; Sugimura, 1986).

References

ABDALLA, A. and NASR, T.S (1961). Evolution of a new molluscicide – Bayer 73, *Journal of the Egyptian Medical Association*, **44**, 160

AMES, B.N. (1983). Dietary carcinogens and anticarcinogens, *Science*, **221**, 1256

ANDERSON, R. (1976). The recent history of parasitic disease in China: the case of schistosomiasis; some public health and economic aspects, *International Journal of Health Services*, **6**, 53

ARTA, A.A. (1977). The developing role of microbiological agents in vector control, *Experientia*, **33**, 125

BARBOSA, F.S. (1978). Possible role of biological control measures and general manipulation, *Proceedings of the International Conference on Schistosomiasis*, Ministry of Health, Cairo

BROWN, L. *et al* (1986). *State of the World – 1986*, W.W. Norton, New York

BUNDOCK, J.B. *et al* (1985). Fluorides, water fluoridation, cancer and genetic diseases, *Science and Public Policy*, **12**, 36

CHEN, J.L. *et al* (1983). Eradicating schistosomiasis in Shanghai County, *World Health Forum*, **4**, 183

CHENG, T. (1971). Schistosomiasis in mainland China, *American Journal of Tropical Medicine and Hygiene*, **20**, 26

COLE, P. and GOLDMAN, M.B. (1975). Occupation, in FRAUMENI, J.F., ed, *Persons at High Risk of Cancer*, Academic Press, New York

COWPER, S.G. (1971). *A Synopsis of African Bilharziasis*, H.K. Lewis, London

DAVIS, D.L. (1981). Cancer in the workplace, *Environment*, **23**, 25

DAVIES, J.M. (1984). The prevention of industrial cancer, *World Health Forum*, **5**, 53

EL-HINNAWI, E. and HASHMI, M. (1982). *Global Environmental Issues,* Tycooly International, Dublin

FARVAR, M.T. (1972). Ecological implications of insect control in Central America, in *Agriculture, Public Health and Development*, University Microfilms, Ann Arbor, MI

FARVAR, M.T. (1975). Pesticides in developing countries: significance of chlorinated hydrocarbon residues in human milk from Central America, *Proceedings of the International Conference on Environmental Sensing and Assessment*, Doc No 75CH 1004-1 ICESA, Institute for Electrical and Electronics Engineers, New York

FRANDSEN, F. and CHRISTENSEN, N.O. (1977). Effect of *Helisoma duryi* on the survival growth and cercarial production of *Schistosoma mansoni* infected *Biomphalaria glabrata*, *Bulletin of the World Health Organization*, **55**, 577

GERBERICH, J.B. and LAIRD, M. (1968). *Bibliography of Papers Relating to Control of Mosquitoes by the Use of Fish – An Annotated Bibliography for the Years 1901-1966*, FAO Fisheries Technical Paper No 75, Food and Agriculture Organization of the United Nations, Rome

GODSON, G.N. (1985). Molecular approaches to malaria vaccines, *Scientific American*, May, 52

GOLDBERG, L.J. and MARGALIT, J. (1977). A bacterial spore demonstrating rapid larvicidal activity against anopheline mosquitoes, *Journal of the Mosquito Control Association*, **15**, 60

GRZYCH, J.M. *et al* (1985). An anti-idiotype vaccine against experimental schistosomiasis, *Nature*, **316**, 74

HAMMOND, E.C. (1975). Tobacco, in FRAUMENI, J.F., ed, *Persons at High Risk Of Cancer*, Academic Press, New York

HIGGINSON, J. (1975). Cancer etiology and prevention, in FRAUMENI, J.F., ed, *Persons at High Risk of Cancer*, Academic Press, New York

HIRAYAMA, T. (1981). Non-smoking wives of heavy smokers have a higher risk of lung cancer: a study from Japan, *British Medical Journal*, **282**, 183

HOOVER, R. and FRAUMENI, J.F. (1975). Drugs, in FRAUMENI, J.F., ed, *Persons at High Risk of Cancer*, Academic Press, New York

JOBIN, W.R. *et al* (1977). Biological control of *Biomphalaria glabrata* in major reservoirs of Puerto Rico, *American Journal of Tropical Medicine and Hygiene*, **26**, 1018

JORDAN, P. (1977). Schistosomiasis research to control, *American Journal of Tropical Medicine and Hygiene*, **26**, 877

LIEBEN, J. and PISTAWKA, H. (1967). Mesothelomia and asbestos exposure, *Archive of Environmental Health*, **14**, 559

MALEK, E.A. (1978). Chemical and environmental control of schistosomiasis with emphasis on side effects of schistosomiasis, *Proceedings of the International Conference on Schistosomiasis*, Ministry of Health, Cairo

McMAHON, J.P. *et al* (1977). Studies on biological control of intermediate hosts of schistosomiasis in western Kenya, *Environmental Conservation*, **4**, 285

MEREDITH, R. (1972). The assay of molluscicide: niclosamide, *Bulletin of the World Health Organization*, **46**, 404

MILLER, E.C. and MILLER. J.A. (1972). *Approaches to the Mechanisms and Control of Chemical Carcinogenesis*, 24th Annual Symposium on Fundamental Cancer Research, Williams and Wilkins, Baltimore, MD

MOTT, K.E. (1984). Schistosomiasis: a primary health care approach, *World Health Forum*, **5**, 221

NEWHOUSE. M.L. and THOMPSON, H. (1965). Mesothelomia of pleura and periloneum following exposure to asbestos in the London area, *British Journal of Industrial Medicine*, **22**, 261

NRC (1982). *Diet, Nutrition and Cancer*, National Research Council, National Academy of Science, Washington, DC

OSUNTOKUN, B.O. (1985). The changing pattern of disease in developing countries, *World Health Forum*, **6**, 310

PARKIN, D.M. *et al* (1984). Estimates of the worldwide frequency of twelve major cancers, *Bulletin of the World Health Organization*, **62**, 163

PESIGAN, T.P. and HAIRSTON, N.G. (1961). The effect of snail control on the prevalence of *S. japonicum* in the Philippines, *Bulletin of the World Health Organization*, **25**, 479

REE, G.H. (1977). Schistosomiasis, in HOWE, G.M., ed, *A World Geography of Human Diseases*, Academic Press, London

REPACE, J.L. and LOWREY A.H. (1985). A quantitative estimate of non-smokers' lung cancer risk from passive smoking, *Environment International*, **11**, 3

ROBERTS, L. (1984). *Cancer Today: Origins, Prevention, and Treatment*, National Academy Press, Washington, DC

SCHNEIDERMAN, M.A. (1975). Sources, resources and tsuris, in FRAUMENI, J.F., ed, *Persons at High Risk of Cancer*, Academic Press, New York

SHIFF, C.J. *et al* (1967). The susceptibilities of various species of fish to the molluscicide n-tritylmorphine, *Bulletin of the World Health Organization*, **36**, 500

SUGIMURA, T. (1986). Studies on environmental carcinogenesis in Japan, *Science*, **233**, 312

SURTEES, G. (1971). *Control of Mosquito Breeding in Rice Fields*, Microbiological Research Establishment, Porton, Salisbury

UNEP (1982). *The World Environment, 1972-1982*, Tycooly International, Dublin

UNICEF/WHO (1985). *Joint Committee on Health Policy, 25th Session*, JC 25/UNICEF-WHO/85. 6b, World Health Organization, Geneva

UNRUA, G.O. (1978). Design of irrigation projects to minimize the risk of schistosomiasis, *Proceedings of the International Conference on Schistosomiasis*, Ministry of Health, Cairo

VAN DER SCHALIE, H. (1978). Using ambient temperature for bilharziasis control, *Proceedings of the International Conference on Schistosomiasis*, Ministry of Health, Cairo

VINES, G. (1985). Viruses and cancer: the Japanese connection, *New Scientist*, 11 July, 36

WHO (1967). *Epidemiology and Control of Schistosomiasis*, WHO Technical Report Series No 372, World Health Organization, Geneva

WHO (1969). *Report of Joint Expert Committee on Pesticide Residues*, WHO Technical Report Series No 417, World Health Organization, Geneva

WHO (1973). *Schistosomiasis Control*, WHO Technical Report Series No 515, World Health Organization, Geneva

WHO (1974). Immunology of schistosomiasis, *Bulletin of the World Health Organization*, **51**, 553

WHO (1978). *Nitrates, nitrities, and N-Nitroso Compounds*, Environmental Health Criteria No 5, World Health Organization, Geneva

WHO (1981). The schistosomiasis problem in the world, *Bulletin of the World Health Organization*, **59**, 115

WHO (1984a). Cancer control in developing countries, *Bulletin of the World Health Organization*, **62**, 847

WHO (1984b). Control of oral cancer in developing countries, *Bulletin of the World Health Organization*, **62**, 817

WHO (1984c) Global distribution of schistosomiasis, *World Health Statistics Quarterly*, **37**, 186

WHO (1985a). *The Control of Schistosomiasis*, WHO Technical Report No 728, World Health Organization, Geneva

WHO (1985b). *Annual World Health Statistics*, World Health Organization, Geneva

WHO (1985c). World malaria situation – 1983, *World Health Statistics Quarterly*, **38**, 193

WHO (1985d). *Tropical Disease Research, 7th Programme Report,* UNDP/World Bank/WHO Special Programme, World Health Organization, Geneva

WRIGHT, C.A. (1968). Some views on biological control of trematode diseases, *Transactions of the Royal Society of Tropical Medicine and Hygiene*, **62**, 320

YOKOGAWA, M. (1972). Control of schistosomiasis in Japan, *Proceedings of the Symposium on Future Schisto Control,* Tulane University, New Orleans

YOKOGAWA, M. (1974). *The Decline of Schistosomiasis in Japan*, WHO/Schisto/74, World Health Organization, Geneva

Chapter 7

Military activity

War and the preparations for war are inimical to development because they squander scarce resources and destroy the international confidence that is essential to sustainable development and to the improvement of the environment at regional and global levels. The direct and indirect impact of military activities in the world has been greatly amplified over the years by technological progress. The total destructive power in the world's arsenals has increased several millionfold since World War II.

In spite of the great destruction and suffering caused by World War II, which claimed the lives of at least 35 million people, armed conflicts continue to erupt and destroy life and the means of life in many areas. Since the end of the World War II, about 150 armed conflicts have taken place, mostly in developing countries (UN, 1985a). Such wars have killed about 20 million people (Figure 36), have precipitated millions of refugees, and, at least 12 of these wars, have caused considerable environmental damage (SIPRI, 1976; UN, 1985a; Sivard, 1985).

Global military expenditure has increased more than thirtyfold since 1900. In 1985, the world's military expenditure was estimated to be about US$663 billion (at 1980 prices and exchange rates, or about $850–870 billion in current 1985 dollars) – about $1.7 million every minute in current dollars (SIPRI, 1986). The upward trend has accelerated in recent years. During the 1970s, military expenditure increased in real terms at an average annual rate of 2.5%. Since 1980, however, the average real rise has been 3.5% a year (SIPRI, 1985).

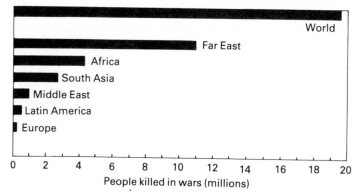

Figure 36 Number of people killed in wars, 1945–85
Data from Sivard, 1985

According to SIPRI, about 70% of the world's military expenditure can be attributed to six main military spenders (China, France, FR Germany, UK, USA and USSR – arranged alphabetically). By far the largest share in the global total comes from the two major military alliances, the North Atlantic Treaty Organization (NATO) and the Warsaw Treaty Organization (WTO). They incurred about three-quarters of world military spending in 1985.

World military research and development cost about US$80 billion in 1985 (SIPRI, 1986). The rise in its volume has been accelerating much faster than that of military expenditure as a whole. In the second half of the 1970s the average annual rise was under 1% (ie less than half the annual rate of increase in total military expenditure). From 1980 to 1983, it was 5–8% and from 1983 to 1984 it was over 10% – double the annual rate of increase in total military expenditure.

Military R and D expenditures are concentrated heavily in a few countries. The USA and USSR dominate throughout followed by UK, France, China and FR Germany (Acland-Hood, 1986). In these countries the military sector spends 10 to 20 times as much as the civil sector on R and D input per unit of output. Globally, military R and D accounts for about one-third of the total expenditure on all scientific research and development. The likely result is that the speed with which new and modernized weapons can replace older ones will be increased, creating pressures to raise military expenditures far into the future.

In 1980, the global trade in military equipment reached US$16 billion (1975 dollars). Major weapons were imported by some 90 developing countries and the traffic in arms now accounts for a significant proportion of the total trade of developing countries. The current trend in the volume of sales of major weapons, for the period 1980 to 1984, is one of decline. The arms trade in 1985 was about US$12 billion (1975 dollars). According to SIPRI (1985, 1986), the main reason for this decline is economic. The developing countries in general are deeply in debt, and have consequently been cutting back on foreign purchases, including arms. There are other reasons for this decline in trade: more production of weapons in developing countries themselves; more transfer of technology; more exports of components; and more modification and upgrading of kits.

A large share of global arms transfers is going to areas of conflict in the developing world. Thus, the countries in the Middle East region accounted for about 50% of the total weapons imported by the developing countries in the period 1981 to 1985. More than 90% of the weapons transferred all over the world were exported by six developed countries (USA, USSR, France, UK, Italy and FR Germany), with the two major military powers accounting for about two-thirds of arms exported in the period 1981 to 1985 (SIPRI, 1986). The total value of arms trade for that period has been estimated at US$66 billion (Tables 12 and 13).

Besides its colossal financial implications, military activity exerts increasing pressures on human and natural resources. Over 70 million people are estimated to be directly or indirectly engaged in military activities worldwide. This figure includes some 25 million people in the world's regular armed forces. If those in paramilitary forces or reserves were added the number might well be almost twice as high. Also making up the 70 million are about four million civilians employed in defence departments; over three million scientists and engineers engaged in military research and development, with the scientists alone numbering over 500 000; and at least five million workers directly engaged in the production of weapons and other specialized military equipment (UN, 1982, 1983).

It has been estimated that from 3–12% of 14 minerals is consumed for military

TABLE 12. Arms sales by major weapon exporting countries (1981–85)

Country	Value of sales (million US$ at 1975 prices)	% of world exports	% of total exports to Third World
USA	25 659	38.7	44.3
USSR	18 306	27.6	74.1
France	7 010	10.6	80.5
UK	3 146	4.7	66.3
FR Germany	2 662	4.0	61.6
Italy	2 501	3.8	93.9
Third World	2 434	3.7	95.5
China	1 516	2.3	95.3
Others	3 111	4.7	67.3
Total	66 345		64.1

Source: SIPRI (1986)

TABLE 13. The nine largest Third World major weapon importing countries (1981–85)

Importing country	Value of imports (million US$ at 1975 prices)	% of total Third World imports
1 Iraq	5 825	13.7
2 Egypt	4 379	10.3
3 Syria	3 316	7.8
4 India	3 146	7.4
5 Libya	2 551	6.0
6 Saudi Arabia	2 338	5.5
7 Israel	1 658	3.9
8 Argentina	1 488	3.5
9 Jordan	1 063	2.5
Total	25 764	60.6

Source: SIPRI (1986)

purposes: aluminium, chromium, copper, fluorspar, iron ore, lead, manganese, mercury, nickel, platinum group, silver, tin, tungsten and zinc (UN, 1982). For aluminium, copper, nickel and platinum, estimated global military consumption was greater than the demand for these minerals for all purposes in Africa, Asia (including China) and Latin America combined. The military consumption of pertroleum is about 5–6% of the total world consumption; close to one-half of the entire consumption by all the developing countries (UN, 1983).

The most obvious and horrifying direct effects of war are on people. But past wars have also had direct and indirect effects through the changes they have brought about in the environment, changing agriculture, shifting the margins of deserts and disturbing the balance of ecosystems.

Most wars have devastated farmlands. World War II caused a short-term reduction of 38% in the agricultural productivity of 10 nations; recovery progressed at about 8.3% per annum. In more recent wars new types of weapons, including high explosive munitions, chemical agents and incendiaries, have been deployed with still greater environmental effects. The use of chemical herbicides in the war in South Vietnam resulted in large scale devastation of crops and widespread immediate damage to the inland and coastal forest ecosystems. About 1 500 square kilometres of mangrove forest were completely destroyed and about 15 000 km^2 more damaged to various degrees; natural recovery is proceeding at a disturbingly slow rate (SIPRI, 1976, 1980, 1984a,b). The impact on the human population has included long lasting neurointoxications as well as the possibility of increased incidences of hepatitis, liver cancer, chromosomal damage and adverse outcomes of pregnancy from exposed fathers (especially spontaneous abortions and congenital malformations).

Millions of people have been killed in wars and other millions have been displaced, temporarily or permanently. In the 1970s, there were about 27 million refugees of war in the world. They have not only suffered economic and social losses, but have also increased the pressures on the ecosystems of the areas to which they migrated. In most cases, the living conditions in such areas are intolerable. Adequate infrastructure is lacking and infectious diseases, malnutrition and social disruptions have become common problems. In spite of the different international efforts to alleviate the problems of refugees, they will continue to increase with increases in tension and military activity.

There have been speculations about the possibility of causing economic or other damage to the population of an enemy through environmental modifications (Goldblat, 1975; Barnaby, 1976; SIPRI, 1977, 1984b). Environmental warfare could, at least in principle, involve damage causing manipulations of celestial bodies or space, the atmosphere, the land, the oceans or the biota. Methods of weather modification are being developed for peaceful purposes, and there is concern not only that those using them could cause accidental damage to neighbouring states, but that such techniques could have hostile applications. Thus, it appears possible to enhance the rainfall from certain clouds by 10–20%. Transport could thereby be made more difficult in enemy territory or damaging floods could be intensified. Supercooled fogs could be dissipated to reveal targets. Under certain conditions, it is possible to intensify air pollution over enemy territory by intentionally generating acid rain or smog-producing substances. Acts of this sort could perhaps even be carried out covertly in times of peace to debilitate another nation's terrestrial and freshwater ecosystems. Future possibilities for the hostile manipulation of the atmosphere include the modification of clouds to bring about hailstorms or lightning discharges in enemy territory. The dynamics and direction of hurricanes might in time be alterable for hostile purposes and it may become possible to reduce the stratospheric ozone layer over enemy territory, thereby permitting undesirable levels of ultraviolet radiation to reach the ground (SIPRI, 1984b). Manipulations of the lithosphere that would be relatively easy to achieve include the release of contained water (by rupturing dams, dikes and levees with either conventional or nuclear weapons) and the activation of volcanoes which are on the verge of eruption. In 1977 a Convention on the Prohibition of Military or any other Hostile Use of Environmental Modification Techniques was signed; the Convention entered into force in 1978 and as of January 1984 the number of parties to the Convention were 37.

The oceans and space are becoming increasingly militarized. Earth orbiting satellites are used by the military to enhance the performance of earth based armed forces and weapons. From 1958 to 1983, 2 114 military oriented satellites (Figure 37) have been launched (about one military satellite every three days). This constitutes at least 75% of all the satellites orbited (Jasani, 1984). The missions of military satellites range from navigation, communications, meteorology and geodesy to recon-naissance. The main function of reconnaissance satellites has been to obtain information on military targets.

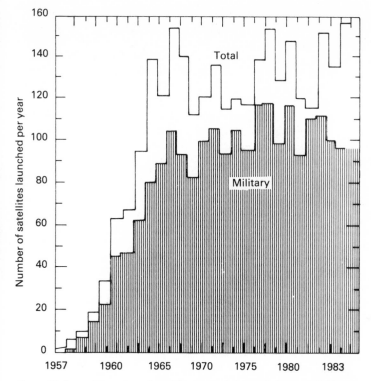

Figure 37 Annual launches of satellites around the earth between 1957 and 1983
After Jasani, 1984

The hazards of war do not end with the coming of peace. Remnants of war constitute a variety of problems in areas where military operations took place. Remnants of war refer to a variety of relics, residuals or devices not used or left behind at the cessation of active hostilities. They include non-exploding devices, unexploded land mines, sea mines and booby traps, unexploded munition, materials such as barbed wire and sharp metal fragments, wreckage of tanks, vehicles and other military equipment and sunken ships and wrecked aircraft. Material remnants of war can affect ecological balances by disturbing the soil, destroying vegetation, killing fauna and introducing poisonous substances into the environment (SIPRI/UNEP, 1985). The economic implications of the remnants of war are no less serious than the environmental ones. They are of several types, including:

1. those that follow directly from loss of life and maiming among the productive population, a reduction in livestock, and a loss of property;
2. those that prevent the use of natural resources or other aspects of the environment either because they have been damaged by the remnants of war or because their use is considered to be risky;
3. those that result from a diversion of resources from productive activities to rectifying the damage caused by the remnants of war; and
4. those that grow out of disruption of the social fabric (the disruption of families, loss of income, forced migration, and so forth).

The assessment of the magnitude of the remnants of war is difficult because often there is no exact information on the location of planted mines (Table 14). Sometimes they have been delivered by means of artillery or aircraft, in which case the ability to record their location becomes haphazard, if not impossible. Unavailability of accurate maps or geographical and meteorological conditions may also limit minefield records. The information on unexploded dud munitions is extremely vague; normally there are no records of their location, and their magnitude can be estimated only roughly. The finding and safe disposal of these remnants of war demands skills that many developing countries lack and imposes costs they cannot easily meet (SIPRI/UNEP, 1985). The safe storage and ultimate disposal of chemical and biological weapons poses greater difficulties (NRC, 1984).

TABLE 14. **Examples of remnants of war**

*	In Poland, 14 894 000 land mines and 73 563 000 bombs, shells and grenades have been recovered since 1945
*	In Finland, over 6 000 bombs, 805 000 shells, 66 000 mines and 370 000 other high explosive munitions have been cleared since the end of the Second World War
*	In Indochina, about 2 milliom bombs, 23 million artillery shells and tens of millions of other high explosive munitions did not explode as intended
*	In Egypt, following the 1973 war, about 8 500 non-exploding items were removed from the Suez Canal, and more than 700 000 land mines were cleared from the terrain near to the canal

Source: SIPRI/UNEP (1985)

Nuclear war

The introduction of nuclear weapons has added entirely new dimensions to warfare. Quantitatively it has brought an enormous increase in explosive power over that of conventional weapons. Whereas atom bombs of the type of Hiroshima and Nagasaki (Table 15) represented an increase from tons of TNT to the equivalent weight of thousands of tons (kilotons), nuclear weapons, developed decades later, represented an increase from kilotons to millions of tons (megatons). It is estimated that the number of nuclear warheads in the world stands between 37 000 and 50 000 with a total explosive power of between 11 000 and 20 000 megatons (equivalent to between 846 000 and 1 540 000 Hiroshima bombs).

Despite widespread condemnation of nuclear weapons, the race for their production continues. Concern over the proliferation of nuclear technology and the possibilities of diversion of nuclear materials for non-peaceful uses has been increasing in the world. The total number of nuclear tests from 1945–84 (Figure 38) was 1 522, of which 461 were above ground and 1 061 underground. The distribution

TABLE 15. The first atom bombs

	Hiroshima	*Nagasaki*
Date of detonation	6 August 1945	9 August 1945
Type	Uranium (U-235)	Plutonium (Pu)
Height of explosion	580 m	503 m
Yield	12.5 kiloton TNT	22 kiloton TNT
Total area demolished	13 km^2	6.7 km^2
% of buildings completely destroyed	67.9	25.3
% of buildings partially destroyed	24.0	10.8
Number of people killed (by 31 December 1945)	90 000–120 000	70 000

Source: Ohkita (1984)

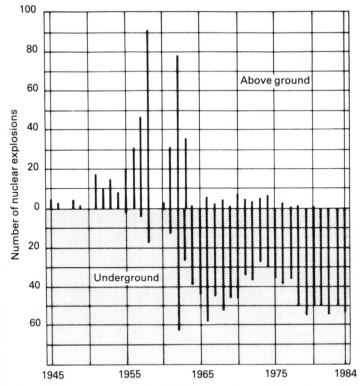

Figure 38 Total number of nuclear tests up to 1984 was 1 522 of which 461 were above ground and 1 061 underground
After Epstein, 1985

of the tests was USA (772), USSR (556), France (127), UK (37), China (29) and India (1). The Partial Test Ban Treaty signed in 1963 has banned nuclear weapon tests in the atmosphere, in outer space and underwater. It has helped to curb the radioactive pollution caused by nuclear explosions. But testing underground has continued, making it possible for nuclear power parties to the Treaty to develop new generations of nuclear warheads. France and China have carried out 41 and 22 nuclear tests respectively above ground since 1963.

Recent studies (see, for example, Ehrlich *et al*, 1983; Turco *et al*, 1983, 1984; Ehrlich, 1984; Grover, 1984; Covey *et al*, 1984; UN, 1985b; NRC, 1985; Svirezhev, 1985; SCOPE, 1985, 1986; Dotto, 1986 and Peterson, 1986) of different scenarios of a large scale nuclear war (5 000 to 10 000 megaton yield), in spite of several uncertainties, estimate that about 750 million people would be killed outright from the blast alone; a total of about 1.1 billion would be killed from the combined effects of blast, fire and radiation; and about 1.1 billion would suffer different injuries requiring medical attention. Thus, 30–50% of the total human population could be immediate casualties of a nuclear war. The vast majority of casualties would be in the northern hemisphere. Despite this devastation, perhaps 50–70% of the human population in both the northern and southern hemispheres might survive the direct effects of a large scale nuclear war. But they would be affected by what has become known as the nuclear winter.

In the aftermath of a large scale nuclear war, darkened skies would cover large areas of the earth for perhaps weeks or several months, as sunlight was blocked by large, thick clouds of smoke from widespread fires (SCOPE, 1985, 1986). The impact would be greatest over the continents of the northern hemisphere, where most of the smoke would probably be produced by nuclear ignited fires and where the average temperatures in some areas might drop some tens of degrees Celsius to below freezing for several weeks to months after the war. Climatic disturbances might persist for several years, even in countries not directly involved in the war. Rainfall in many regions of the world might be greatly reduced. Temperature and precipitation changes could also occur in the tropics and the southern hemisphere – less extreme than those in the northern hemisphere, but still significant. Tropical and subtropical

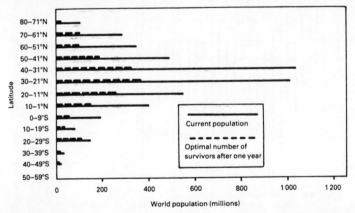

Figure 39 Vulnerability of human population to loss of food production due to nuclear war
After Dotto, 1986

regions could experience unprecedented cooling and severe cold spells, accompanied by significant disturbances in precipitation patterns.

According to the SCOPE study (SCOPE, 1985, 1986), world agriculture and major ecosystems, such as forests, grasslands and marine systems, could be severely disturbed and their plant and animal populations stressed by rapid, dramatic changes in the normal climatic regime. Crop losses, caused not only by climate disturbances but also by the post–war disruption in supplies of essential inputs such as energy, machinery, fertilizers and pesticides, could create widespread food crises in both combatant and non-combatant nations. The failure of major food production and distribution systems, and the inability of natural ecosystems to support large numbers of people, could perhaps reduce the human population of the earth to well below current levels (Figure 39).

In addition to the potential climatic effects, a large scale exchange of nuclear weapons would cause considerable devastation from the direct effects of fire, blast and local fall-out of radioactivity. Other impacts could include severe disruptions of communications and power systems; reductions in the ozone layer in the upper atmosphere which protects life on earth from the sun's biologically damaging ultraviolet radiation; intense local and long-term global fall-out; and severe regional episodes of air and water pollution caused by the release of large amounts of toxic chemicals and gases.

The arms race versus development

Over the past half decade, the living standards of the vast majority of the 2.5 billion people in the developing countries have deteriorated sharply. As the centre of this deterioration lies a crisis of almost unprecedented global proportions. In 1984, about US$895 billion in debt was owed by developing countries, a sum approximately equal to the vast amounts spent on armaments worldwide each year.

Despite the successful implementation of austerity measures in some cases, many developing countries are running to stand still and despite such efforts some are falling even further behind. They do not have the money to promote growth and to support new development projects because their current accounts are devoted to debt servicing. Meanwhile, their people are in many cases starting to resent the social consequences of these austerity plans and the lack of economic progress in their own lives. Throughout the developing world, people are protesting and even rioting. Some governments have fallen in the face of such protest while others have been elected by promising to control the foreign debt burden. Yet, it is in the developing countries, where these problems are most acute, that military expenditure, including expenditure on arms imports, is growing most rapidly. These countries are choosing, sometimes for compelling reasons of security, to spend less money than they could on economic development in order to buy weapons. Scarce scientific and technical manpower is being diverted from the development of the social and environmental foundation for prosperity to the development of military power. And world military spending is over 20 times as great as the total official development aid given by developed to developing countries.

Poverty is by far the most important cause of environmental degradation. The lack of safe drinking water for over 1 300 million people and of sanitation for over 1 700 million is the most severe form of pollution caused by poverty. The deaths, debilitation and disease caused by contaminated water have been a severe brake on development. The International Drinking Water Supply and Sanitation Decade aims at providing clean water supplies and sanitation for people in the developing countries by the year 1990. This requires some US$80 million a day (equivalent to 47 minutes of military expenditure) for 10 years. To eradicate malaria – the killer disease that claims the lives of one million children every year – some US$500 million are needed; less than half of one day's military spending. Over 1 200 million people – living on incomes of less than US$150 a year – remain undernourished. Less than 0.5% of global military spending would have been sufficient to develop agriculture in a sustainable way to approach self sufficiency in food deficit, low income countries by 1990. An allocation of about US$200 million annually (equivalent to two hours of military expenditure) would free the world of illiteracy in less than a decade. These, and other examples, underline the striking contrast between the current outlays for military purposes and the relatively modest resources required to meet the basic needs of millions of people and improve their living conditions.

Several studies on the relationship between disarmament and development (see, for example, UN, 1982, 1983, 1985c) have stressed the fact that the arms race and development compete for the world's finite resources and to command people's attitudes and perceptions. Development is a universal requirement for sustained economic growth in developed and developing countries. On the other hand, the arms race constitutes a major threat to international security and by hindering development – through the diversion of limited resources – is an important source of national and regional insecurity.

When natural resources are in short supply, people are tempted to resort to aggressive action to satisfy their needs. Although at a national level non-military approaches (market manipulation, for example) are generally used to achieve this, the reaction is different among some countries. In modern history, resorting to war to satisfy demand for natural resources has sometimes involved the forced annexation of neighbouring lands and sometimes the conquering of distant lands and conversion of them into so-called colonies. A recent study by SIPRI/UNEP (1986) indicates, for example, that the invasion in 1969 of sparsely populated Honduras by densely populated El Salvador can be attributed mainly to the latter's need for additional land. The long standing and acrimonious dispute over the waters of the Rio Lauca has, in the past, led Bolivia to sever diplomatic relations with Chile. The potential for future conflict over scarce freshwater is growing in various regions of the world. Special problem areas involve upstream and downstream water competition in arid and other regions with rapidly growing populations. Conflicts over mineral resources have also occurred. One war, from 1960 to 1964, was to a major extent a struggle for control of the copper and other mineral resources of Katanga (now Shaba) province in what is now Zaire. The Western Sahara conflict has been augmented by struggle over the rich phosphate deposits in the contested region. Numerous international disputes have arisen in recent years over fishing in exclusive economic zones, some of which have escalated to armed clashes.

There are some obvious contradictions in the attitude of the world community to the whole question of military activity. On one hand, the numerous conventions, treaties and agreements provide clear evidence of a widespread desire to prevent the more devastating forms of warfare. On the other, the evidence of mounting military expenditure around the world implies a lack of conviction in the practicability of disarmament or even of holding forces and arsenals at constant size. And there are further contradictions between the demands for agricultural, social and economic development so vital to the future of the world, in particular to the developing countries and the increasing allocation of limited resources for military purposes.

It can be stated without hesitation that the questions of disarmament, development and environmental protection are closely linked and represent some of the most important issues before the international community today. Development can hardly proceed at the required pace and a healthy environment cannot be guaranteed amid a widening and constantly escalating arms race. Moreover, development and environmental efforts are threatened by the armaments, especially nuclear weapons, already stockpiled, the use of which either by intent or in error or sheer madness would severely jeopardize mankind's very existence.

One of the most urgent tasks, therefore, is to arrest the technological spiral at the centre of the international arms race and, through substantial and substantive disarmament measures, to pave the way for major reductions in world military expenditure. A major breakthrough in the disarmament field would release vast financial, technological and human resources for more productive uses in both developed and developing countries in an international political climate of reduced tension. Even if only 20% of annual military expenditure were to be diverted, for instance, to an international fund for sustainable development projects, the developing countries would thus be enabled to attain their socioeconomic objectives more effectively.

In the environmental field, the immediate needs are first to develop means of predicting the kinds of stress various weapon systems will place upon different ecosystems and second to improve methods for the restoration of lands devastated by war. More needs to be known about the ecological disruption that could be caused through the hostile use of all weapons, especially 'mass destruction' weapons, including the deliberate dispersion of pathogenic micro-organisms, and special attention must be given to the possible military use of weather modification techniques. In addition, the restoration of farmlands and forests, provisions to secure the removal of hazardous relics of past wars and international action to ensure the safe disposal of radioactive wastes, obsolete explosives and chemical and biological weapons all merit continuing attention and effective action.

References

ACLAND-HOOD, M. (1986). Military and civil R and D expenditure, *Science and Public Policy*, February, 52

BARNABY, F. (1976). Towards environmental warfare, *New Scientist*, **69**, 6

COVEY, C. *et al* (1984). Global atmospheric effects of massive smoke injections from a nuclear war, *Nature*, **308**, 21

DOTTO, L. (1986). *Planet Earth in Jeopardy*, J. Wiley, Chichester

EHRLICH, A. (1984). Nuclear winter, *Bulletin of Atomic Scientists*, April 1984, 3S-14S

EHRLICH, P.R. *et al* (1983). Long-term biological consequences of nuclear war, *Science*, **222**, 1293

EPSTEIN, W. (1985). A critical time for nuclear nonproliferation, *Scientific American*, **253**, 33

GOLDBLAT, J. (1975). The prohibition of the environmental warfare, *Ambio*, **4**, 187

GROVER, H.D. (1984). The climatic and biological consequences of nuclear war, *Environment*, **26**, 7

JASANI, B. (1984) Outer space: militarization outpaces legal controls, *Proceedings of the Symposium on Maintaining Outer Space for Peaceful Uses*, United Nations University, Tokyo, 221

NRC (1984). *Disposal of Chemical Munitions and Agents,* National Research Council, National Academy Press, Washington, DC

NRC (1985). *The Effects on the Atmosphere of a Major Nuclear Exchange*, National Research Council, National Academy Press, Washington, DC

OHKITA, T. (1984). Health effects on individuals and health services of the Hiroshima and Nagasaki bombs, in WHO, *Effects of Nuclear War on Health and Health Service*, World Health Organization, Geneva

PETERSON, T. (1986). Scientific studies of the unthinkable – the physical and biological effects of nuclear war, *Ambio*, **15**, 60

SCOPE (1985). *Environmental Consequences of Nuclear War*, Vol II, *Ecological and Agricultural Effects*, (ed HARWELL, M.A. *et al*), SCOPE Report No 28, J. Wiley, Chichester

SCOPE (1986). *Environmental Consequences of Nuclear War*, Vol I, *Physical and Atmospheric Effects*, (ed PITTOCK, A.B. *et al*), SCOPE Report No 28, J. Wiley, Chichester

SIPRI (1976). *Ecological Consequences of the Second Indochina War*, (ed WESTING, A.H.), Almqvist and Wiksell, Stockholm

SIPRI (1977). *Weapons of Mass Destruction and the Environment*, (ed WESTING, A.H.), Taylor and Francis, London

SIPRI (1980). *Warfare in a Fragile World,* (ed WESTING, A.H.), Taylor and Francis, London

SIPRI (1984a). *Herbicides in War*, (ed WESTING, A.H.), Taylor and Francis, London

SIPRI (1984b). *Environmental Warfare*, (ed WESTING, A.H.), Taylor and Francis, London

SIPRI (1985). *Yearbook 1985*, Stockholm International Peace Research Institute, Stockholm

SIPRI (1986). *Yearbook 1986*, Stockholm International Peace Research Institute, Stockholm

SIPRI/UNEP (1985). *Explosive Remnants of War*, (ed WESTING, A.H.), Taylor and Francis, London

SIPRI/UNEP (1986). *Global Resources and International Conflict*, (ed WESTING, A.H.), Oxford University Press, Oxford

SIVARD, R.L. (1985). *World Military and Social Expenditures*, World Priorities, Washington, DC

SVIREZHEV, Y.M. (1985). *Ecological and Demographic Consequences of Nuclear War*, USSR Academy of Sciences, Computer Centre, Moscow

TURCO, R.P. *et al* (1983). Nuclear winter: global consequences of multiple nuclear explosions, *Science,* **222**, 1283

TURCO, R.P. *et al* (1984). The climatic effects of nuclear war, *Scientific American*, **251**, 33

UNITED NATIONS (1982). *The Relationship Between Disarmament and Development*, United Nations, E82. IX, New York

UNITED NATIONS (1983). *Economic and Social Consequences of the Arms Race and of Military Expenditure*, E83. IX.2, United Nations, New York

UNITED NATIONS (1985a). *Study on Conventional Disarmament*, E85. IX.1, United Nations, New York

UNITED NATIONS (1985b). *Climatic Effects of Nuclear War, including Nuclear Winter. Excerpts of Scientific Literature*, A/40/449, Report of the Secretary General to the UN General Assembly

UNITED NATIONS (1985c). *1985 Report on the World Social Situation*, ST/ESA/165, United Nations, New York

Chapter 8

Social and economic issues

Population and the environment

It took more than a million years for the population of the world to reach its first billion, whereas the second billion was added in only 120 years, the third billion in 32 years and the fourth billion in 15 years. Large additions are being made to already high levels of population over short periods of time: population growth during the last three decades has been larger than the entire world population in 1900.

At the beginning of the century there were about 1.6 billion people in the world. By mid-century there were 2.5 billion of people on earth, and by 1986 this figure had doubled to 5 billion. World population is expected to reach 6.12 billion by the year 2000. Although the rate of population growth has been steadily falling over the last few years (Figure 40), the net absolute annual addition to the number of people is expected to increase from about 78 million at present to about 90 million per year by 2000. Thereafter, with declining net annual additions, the world population may reach 8.2 billion by 2025 (according to the UN medium estimate) and reach a stationary level of 10.5 billion by 2110 (Figure 41). The low and high estimates of the stationary population level are 8 billion by the year 2080 and 14.2 billion by the year 2130 respectively.

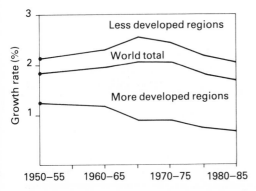

Figure 40 Average annual population growth rates in more developed and less developed regions, 1950–85 After WRI/IIED, 1986

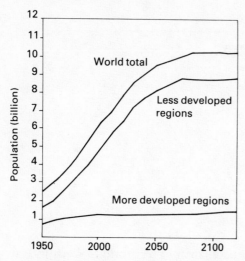

Figure 41 Population size for more developed
regions, less developed regions and world total,
1950–2120
After WRI/IIED, 1986

Population growth rates have steadily declined, both globally and in the
developing countries as a group (UN, 1985). While birth, death and infant mortality
rates have fallen consistently, life expectancies have risen in a large number of
countries. Some developed countries have already made the demographic transition
to population equilibrium, as defined by low birth and death rates and high life
expectancies. Many other developed countries and a few developing countries also,
show definite movements towards stationary populations.

In many developing countries both the rate and momentum of population growth
have been such as to produce continuous absolute increases in population every
year. Even if it were possible to reduce fertility to replacement levels, the momentum
of the population would cause it to grow for many years. This is due to the
predominance of a young age structure in most developing countries, which means
that the number of couples entering their reproductive years will, for a considerable
time, remain greater than the number moving out of that age group. Thus the
number of births will continue to be large and to exceed the numbers of deaths.

However, regional differences exist. In East Asia, South-east Asia, Central
America and the Caribbean, there have been marked declines in population growth
rates. In Africa, by contrast, there has actually been an increase in population
growth rate over the last decade. Of the 58 countries and territories of Africa, 19
show annual growth rates of 3% or more, which imply that populations will double
every 23 years or even earlier. Population growth rates have continued to decline in
tropical Latin America, apart from a few countries; but the declines have been small.
In temperate South America, population growth rates have remained nearly
constant – at moderate level – over the last two decades. In Asia, growth rates
show significant differences from one subregion to another. China, with a quarter of
the world's population, has dramatically halved its population growth over the last
decade. The Republic of Korea has, likewise, markedly reduced its population
growth rate. In South-east Asia and South Asia, the declines have been small. In view
of the already large population sizes and decidedly young age structures, the

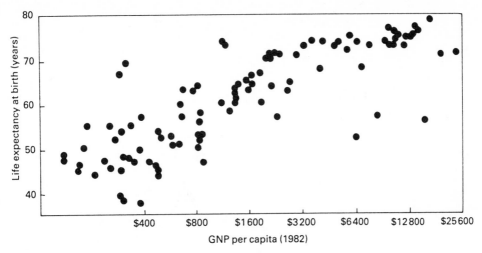

Figure 42 The relationship between life expectancy at birth and GNP per capita in 1982
After World Bank, 1985

population of several of these countries are expected to continue to grow substantially.

As for the global distribution, 80% of the increase in the world's population during the last 30 years has occurred in the developing countries. What is more, 95% of the entire projected growth to the year 2110 – prior to reaching a stationary level of 10.5 billion – is expected to take place in the countries that are currently regarded as developing (UN, 1985). It is estimated that about 86% of the world's people will be living in today's developing countries when the global population reaches its stationary level. Several developing countries will double, triple or quadruple their populations over the next 50 to 60 years. Africa's relative share of the world population is expected to more than double during the same period (World Bank, 1984).

Life expectancy, the number of years a typical individual can expect to live, given current levels of mortality, has increased greatly since 1950 and is expected to improve in the future. On a global level, life expectancy increased from 45.8 years in 1950–55 to 58.9 years in 1980–85 and according to the UN projections is expected to reach 70 by the year 2025. Present life expectancy in the more developed countries averaged 73 in 1980–85 and in the less developed regions it was 56.6; the estimates for 2025 are 77.2 and 68.9 respectively.

In general, life expectancy is closely related to economic well being (Figure 42). The countries of South Asia and sub-Saharan Africa tend to have the lowest incomes and the highest mortality rates, while the wealthier countries of Latin America and East Asia have lower mortality. The same relationship holds for infant mortality (Figure 43). Poor countries have the highest infant mortality rates. Throughout much of the world there has been a slow down in the pace of infant and child mortality improvements – already evident in the 1970s – due to economic difficulties encountered in many countries (which have resulted in the reduction of expenditure for public health and welfare). On the other hand, an important breakthrough has been made in the 1980–85 period: the introduction of the simple, effective and inexpensive Oral Rehydration Therapy (ORT) to treat dehydration in infants, resulting from diarrhoeal disease. In 1980 in the developing countries, an estimated five million children under five years of age – about 10 every minute – died as a

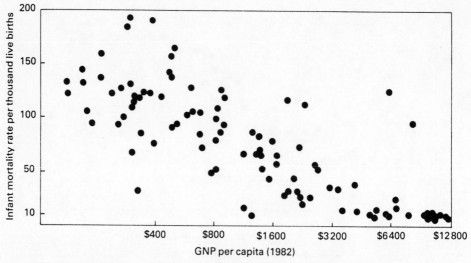

Figure 43 The relationship between infant mortality and GNP per capita in 1982
After World Bank, 1985

consequence of diarrhoeal disease. The introduction of ORT has saved the lives of millions in many countries. For example, a pilot project carried out in Alexandria, Egypt showed that the wide introduction of ORT has reduced the death rates of infants from 35.2 per 1 000 in 1980 to 20.4 per 1 000 in 1984 (UNICEF, 1986).

Population growth is outpacing the capacity of a number of developing countries to provide for their economic and social well being. The pressures thus generated are depleting natural resources faster than they can be regenerated and reducing their productivity, hence undermining development.

There is no simple correlation between population and environment. Population, environment and development factors interact in different ways in different places. Not only the pace of development, but its content, location and the distribution of its benefits determine, in good measure, the state of the environment. These factors also influence the growth and distribution of population. Environmental resources provide the basis for development just as environmental factors constitute part of the improvement in the quality of life that development is meant to bring about. Similarly, the size of population, the rate of its growth and the pattern of its distribution influence the state of the environment, just as they condition the pace and composition of development.

Population growth need not necessarily lower levels of living, impair the quality of life or cause environmental degradation. Global and historical assessments of the earth's capacity and man's ingenuity to produce goods and services have prompted some experts to project an optimistic outlook (Simon, 1981; Simon and Khan, 1984). Growth of world population has, in the past, been accompanied by a steady increase in the world's capacity to provide for the necessities and amenities of human life. People have to be fed, clothed and provided for and this is achieved by people themselves. In that process, they use and develop the resources of the environment. Yet, just as some patterns of development have improved the human environment, others have tended to degrade it, at times irreversibly.

In a large number of countries, notably in Africa, rapid growth of population over the last decade has been accompanied by a steady decline in average levels of living, as

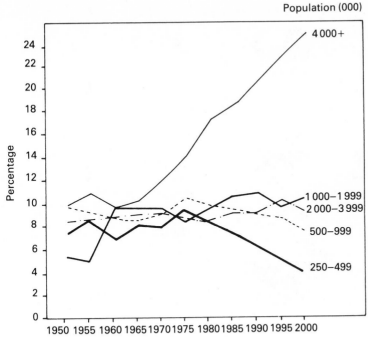

Figure 44 Urban population as a percentage of total population by size of city
(city population in 000s)
Adapted from Weiche, 1984

reflected in per capita incomes. It has also been accompanied by a decline in the
quality of life, as measured by indicators such as per capita availability of food and
nutrition, drinking water and sanitation. Furthermore, the last decade has witnessed an
increase in the number of people with inadequate or no access to essential services
(such as health care) or amenities (such as shelter) in Africa, Asia and Latin America.

On the other hand, even though, over some stretches of the decade, rates of
economic growth appeared to be satisfactory in some developing countries, they did
not necessarily bring about noticeable improvements in the levels of living of the
majority of their people. Environmental conditions in rural as well as urban areas in
many developing countries have deteriorated as their populations have grown.
Generally speaking, the quantity and quality of their natural resources, which
provide the foundation for sustained development, have steadily declined
(World Bank, 1984).

Human settlements

Throughout the world, the single most frequent form of human settlement is the
village. Cities and towns are far fewer than villages; they are more concentrated in
the more developed regions of the world. In these regions, the proportion of
population living in urban areas was 66% in 1970 and had increased to 73% in 1985.
On the other hand, in the less developed regions, the proportion of population living
in urban areas was 25% in 1970 and reached 32% in 1985 (UN, 1985). On a global
basis, the percentage of people living in urban areas increased from 37% in 1970 to
42% in 1985 and is projected to reach more than 50% by the year 2000 (Figures 44, 45).

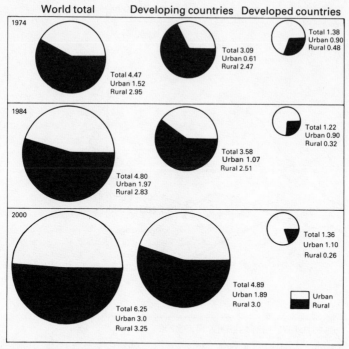

Figure 45 Population distribution in urban and rural areas (billions)
After UNCHS, 1976

The pattern of urbanization in the less developed regions has been quite different from that which took place in more developed areas. Whereas urbanization in the industrialized countries took many decades, permitting a gradual emergence of economic, social and political institutions to deal with the problems of transformation, the process in developing countries is occurring far more rapidly, against a background of higher population growth and lower incomes. The transformation involves enormous numbers of people: between 1970 and 1980, the urban areas of developing regions absorbed about 320 million people; between 1980 and 2000, the increase is projected to be more than 1000 million.

Such a remarkable increase in urbanization in the developing countries has been accompanied by a rapid expansion of the number of very large cities. It was estimated that in 1975 there were 95 cities of more than one million inhabitants in the developed regions and 90 in the developing regions; a median projection of growth to the year 2000 showed 155 and 284 in both regions respectively. In 1950, only one city in the less developed regions (greater Buenos Aires) had a population over 4 million. In 1960 there were 8 cities that had reached or exceeded that size, compared to 10 cities in the developed regions. In 1980, there were 22 cities in the developing regions with more than 4 million population each, whereas in the developed regions there were only 16 such cities. It has been estimated that by the year 2000, the developing regions will have about 61 cities of or above this size, compared with about 25 in the developed regions. Eighteen cities in developing countries are expected to have more than 10 million inhabitants by that time.

Rapid urbanization has been sustained by the combination of high rates of natural population increase and rural to urban migration. The relative contribution of each to urban population growth varies, but in the majority of cities natural increases are the primary contributing factor. However, the two sources are intertwined, for a large proportion of those leaving the countryside are in their reproductive years and therefore may be partly responsible for the high rates of natural population increase in urban centres.

The increasing concentration of people in urban centres has strained the capacity of most governments to provide basic services. Illegal settlements (eg slums, squatter settlements etc) are common. In such areas people are usually deprived of access to the basic facilities of drinking water and waste disposal. They are frequently forced to use open water for washing, cleaning and the disposal of waste in unhygienic ways and to live in makeshift shelters surrounded by accumulating domestic waste. Unhygienic living conditions in slums often spread diseases such as typhoid, cholera, malaria and hepatitis through entire settlements.

Low incomes and weak purchasing power are manifestations of the poverty that characterizes most families living in slums and squatter settlements. The cause of this poverty lies in the lack of sufficient opportunities for steady and gainful employment. The major problem for most families is underemployment and the low, fluctuating incomes which this entails. Underemployment rates for slums and squatter settlements can reach more than 60% (UNCHS, 1982). Despite the great variety of occupations cutting across all sectors of the urban economy, most slum and squatter settlement residents work in the informal sector and in the lower paying categories of work in the formal sector. Comparatively few are engaged in occupations requiring higher levels of skills and training.

The economically precarious conditions of most slum and squatter settlement residents trigger an increasing number of social hazards: an increase in the number of conflicts among residents of these settlements; an increase in the number of riots and the extent of crime and drug addiction (which in turn tends to increase the crime rate); and, ultimately, increasing mistrust and alienation between slum dwellers and other urban dwellers.

People in the crowded squatter settlements in the developing areas are most prone to the effects of natural disasters: floods, tropical cyclones, etc (El-Hinnawi, 1985). Recently, such populations have also been tragically affected by industrial accidents. In November 1984 a massive explosion at a liquefied petroleum gas storage facility in the crowded San Juanico neighbourhood in Mexico City killed 452 people, injured 4 248 and displaced 31 000. The blast illustrated the precarious nature of a city where many of the 17 million inhabitants live cheek by jowl with a variety of potentially dangerous installations. In December 1984 methyl isocyanate leaked from a pesticide plant on the outskirts of Bhopal, India, killing more than 2 500 of the people living in the slums nearby. More than 20 000 were seriously affected by the gas and at least 200 000 people had to leave their homes to take temporary refuge elsewhere. Both disasters illustrate the non-existence of appropriate urban planning, which is a common feature in most developing countries, and the hazardous environments that have been created by rapid urbanization.

Environment and the economic dialogue

The world economy in 1985 was characterized by modest expansion of production and disappointingly slow growth in international trade, after the significant but uneven increases observed in 1984. The growth of world output fell back by nearly one-third from the rate of 4.6% reached in 1984. The growth of world trade was only about one-third of the near 9% observed in 1984. Expected rates of growth of world output for 1986 and 1987 are of the order of 3.5%. The rate of growth of world trade is expected to be somewhat above 4% on average in 1986 and 1987 (UN, 1986).

Although the economic performance of the developed market economies in 1985 was well below the expectations of a year ago, for most countries in the group the recovery continued. For several countries, it entered its fourth year in early 1986. A remarkable feature of this recovery, aside from its durability, is that significant expansion of output has taken place simultaneously with a sharp reduction in the rate of inflation in nearly all countries in the group. In the period 1983–85, for the group as a whole, real output grew by 10.5% while the inflation rate fell by 3 percentage points (UN, 1986).

Although the economic expansion of the developed market economies continued in 1985, in comparison with 1984 the real rate of growth of their combined GDP fell by more than 2 percentage points to only 2.7%. There was greater balance in patterns of aggregate demand and output growth rates, particularly in comparison with the great unevenness of 1984; but the convergence was around a much lower average rate of expansion.

In general, events in 1985 demonstrated once again the vulnerability of many developing countries to external events, which has increased partly as a result of inadequate external financing. The slow down in the growth of the developed countries was costly and untimely for all those developing countries whose fortunes are closely tied to international trade. After some progress in 1984, these countries suffered a major setback in 1985. The rate of increase in their export volume fell significantly, their terms of trade worsened and for many of them interest rates in real terms (ie nominal rates adjusted by the rate of change in their export prices) rose sharply. For the developing countries as a whole, the growth rate of GDP remained below 2.5% for the fifth year in a row. Growth of net energy exporters remained insignificant and that of net energy importers fell from 3.8% in 1984 to 3.3% in 1985 (UN, 1986).

Aggregate growth figures mask the extent of the difficulties of the developing world, because there was a great diversity of experience between larger and smaller countries. Some of the largest developing economies (eg Brazil and India) grew at substantially higher rates than the average; but in the rest of the developing world the gains that were made in 1984 were nearly wiped out in 1985. Nearly 60% of the developing countries, representing just under a third of the total population and located mainly in Africa and Latin America, had either stagnant or falling real per capita GDP in 1985.

While the state of the world environment is not directly dependent on short-term economic fluctuations, it cannot be considered to be isolated from them. Owing to the financial strains to which the developed countries have been exposed during the years of recession, there has evidently been less readiness and capacity on their part to deal with the problems of environmental improvement in the developing countries – or indeed in the developed countries themselves: the concern over foreign trade balances has led many developed countries to accelerate the shift from gas and oil towards coal, thus potentially aggravating acid rain and other forms of air pollution.

The world community is confronted by a closed cycle: economic problems cause environmental despoliation which, in turn, makes economic and structural reform more difficult to achieve. Breaking the cycle requires a new earnestness from nations in their approach to environmental cooperation. Two major causes of environmental destruction should be tackled now. First, the arms race, with its insatiable demands on global financial, material and intellectual resources, must be slowed (see Chapter 7). The second requirement is to alleviate the appalling debt burden of many developing countries. The debt burden and regressive terms of trade place pressure not only on the economic surplus produced by the developing countries, but also, and increasingly, on resources, which have to be overexploited to ease the debt burden. For instance, for one Latin American country it took 9.8 times as much beef to buy a barrel of oil in 1981 as it did in 1973. Similarly, at the end of the 1970s, profits from the export of one ton of bananas were enough to purchase only half the steel they would have bought 10 years earlier.

The expectations for multinational cooperation raised at different fora over the past decade have so far not been realized. The call for an immediate launching of global negotiations remains unrealized. The results of the Sixth United Nations Conference on Trade and Development have been disappointing for many, particularly developing countries. A similar disappointment has been felt over failure to translate the prescriptions for global economic recovery expressed in the Williamsburg Summit Declaration into concrete action.

In the field of the environment, the preparedness of governments to translate good intentions into action has been more positive. The trade in endangered species, wetlands and world heritage conventions have provided major instruments for cooperation between and among developed and developing countries. The favourable international reception afforded the publication of the UNEP state of the environment reports, the World Conservation Strategy and the World Charter for Nature is a further illustration of international support for environmental protection. The conviction that environment can provide a fertile area for intergovernmental cooperation is borne out by experience. The years after Stockholm witnessed an increase in environmental cooperation among different nations in different regions.

It can be seen, then, that environmental problems have been present in the overall dialogue between and among developed and developing countries. But it must be stressed that relative to the preoccupation with apparently more pressing economic, financial and fiscal questions, the environmental dimension has not been afforded the priority it merits. It may be argued, indeed, that the present economic crisis cannot be overcome without establishing new, less wasteful and environmentally sound resource use patterns. There is, thus, an urgency now for the dialogue, implicitly, to take proper account of the close relationship between economic activity and the state of the environment. Indeed, the point has now been reached where the dialogue must be followed by appropriate action.

In this context, the nature and time perspective of some environmental issues also need to be taken into account. Some important environmental issues, with pronounced implications for the international and national economies (for example, climatic change, soil degradation, desertification and forest depletion), tend to be longer-term and in terms of both their causes and their manifestations are not easy to fit into the standard frame of reference of international economic negotiation. Indeed, the whole negotiating process, as presently conceived, is often ill suited to dealing with such prospects as threats to the health and genetic heritage of future generations, the degradation of ecosystems, the projected disappearance of some tropical forests in 25 years time or the long range transport and synergistic interactions of pollutants. Such environmental issues are often inconspicuous, are not felt immediately, are difficult to quantify and, like issues such as health, education and social benefits, are not easily reducible to the standard cost–benefit equations, methods and objectives that guide countries, negotiators and decision makers in how they think and what they do. And they often involve sacrificing today's tangible economic benefits for tomorrow's intangibles. Yet, difficult though it may be to deal with short-term and long-term issues in the same process with the same sense of urgency, many issues with long-term consequences do require short-term actions.

Furthermore, environmental issues may need to be dealt with on different time scales. In other words, they may arise, and/or require action, at the global, regional, subregional or other levels. Problems of global concern, including those of the joint management of the global commons and of environmental interdependence, can be dealt with in the overall setting of multilateral international negotiations. A case in point is the law of the sea. There are also clearly identifiable issues characteristic of given geographical settings and countries, which are best dealt with regionally, subregionally or nationally, even though many of these have a broader significance. The overall frameworks and economic and political environments at the international level do affect, and should be supportive of, the actions required at the regional, subregional or national levels.

Relevance of issues in the economic dialogue to the environment

The dialogue is intended to bring about the equitable economic and social development of all countries, with the linkages between the welfare of the developed and developing countries being explicitly recognized and used to support the achievement of this objective. There are aspects of the present situation which have negative consequences on the environment and these negative consequences, in turn, make equitable economic and social development more difficult to achieve. This results in destructive, self-reinforcing cycles. The issue of interdependence, which has been considered in economic terms in various fora in recent years, should also be seen in terms of environmental concerns.

Poverty is by far the most important cause of environmental destruction. It degrades the human environment and in so doing obstructs development. If the dialogue is to achieve much, it will have to provide for the establishment of the economic means needed to deal with the water, nutritional, human settlements and other poverty related issues of the developing world.

Overconsumption and wasteful use of resources by the developed nations and the privileged strata in the developing world pose a threat to the environment comparable with poverty. The build-up of carbon dioxide in the atmosphere and industrial pollution are only a few manifestations among many. However, the global problems created by inequitable development go far deeper. The demands of the developed countries for resources from the developing nations add to the pressures on their environment. The commitment of increasing amounts of the most fertile land in the developing countries to grow cash crops for consumption in the industrial countries provides an instance. Unsustainable demands on fish resources and tropical forest cover are two more.

Thus, the effect of population increases and people's patterns of consumption and production has been to upset the balance between people and resources, hence leading to deterioration of the environment. The economic future of developed and developing countries is not dependent only on the laws of trade and finance, but on environmentally sound development cooperation. To be beneficial, such cooperation should deal not only with the relations among man, but also with the relations between man and nature.

Food production and trade are becoming major global issues because of the growing food deficit of a large number of developing countries. While the world as a whole is producing enough food to sustain the present level of its population, the inequality in food distribution leaves millions of people undernourished (see Chapter 3). The current situation in which exportable surpluses are produced in high cost developed regions while developing nations have no means to pay for such surpluses works to the benefit of neither the industrialized nor the developing countries. It is therefore important that agricultural production and subsidizing policies in the developed countries do not discourage agricultural development in the developing countries.

The world commodity issue and the demand for rationalization and control of commodity markets might look at first sight to be almost exclusively economic and only derivatively social. The often stated objective is to stabilize the markets in such a way as to obtain remunerative prices and higher incomes for primary producers. But the issue has important environmental aspects which have not entered directly into the negotiations. The instability of commodity markets leads to irrational and wasteful allocation of resources: periods of high prices and demand lead to an expansion of the area under cultivation for a particular crop, which is then in oversupply during the periods of falling prices and demand. And as the environment cannot adjust as quickly as the markets change, the environmental damage persists.

Major environmental problems also occur because of the unchecked use of often environmentally imprudent technologies or of the use of technology in a manner inappropriate in the light of current knowledge. Examples of such problems are toxic wastes, threats to the ozone layer and to coastal areas, effluents from feeding lots, possible climate change etc. The economic effects – worldwide – of such environmental problems could be severe. Indeed, technology is crucial in terms of the impact, positive and negative, its use has on the environment. In the industrialized countries, the capacity to ascertain and evaluate this impact is growing. However, only a small percentage of the world's scientific and research capacity is found in the developing countries. The current pattern of technology use has therefore been elaborated in the economic, social and environmental conditions of the developed countries. The environmental soundness of any particular technology in the local conditions for which it is intended should be a fundamental element in deciding upon its appropriateness.

Careful consideration is also needed of other economic issues which enter into international economic relations. Almost all these issues have important environmental aspects which, if taken appropriately into account, can only reinforce the likelihood of successful environmental policies. Developing countries are facing increasing difficulty in their efforts to find adequate resources, particularly foreign exchange, to step up their pace of development. This has often compelled them to focus on shorter-term aspects without giving adequate weight to longer-term considerations. The high real interest rates prevailing in the last few years have tended to reinforce these effects, since high interest rates tend to skew cost–benefit assessments unduly towards short-term benefits. Environmental issues, the impact of which is felt over a longer period, are discounted by this forced short-term perspective.

A 1% increase in interest rates adds approximately $5 billion to the debt burden of developing countries (World Bank, 1983). To have increased its export earnings (not profits) by one billion dollars in 1981, South America as a whole would have had to increase its banana exports threefold, Ecuador fivefold and Colombia ninefold, while cotton exporters like Egypt and Turkey would have to double and triple their cotton exports (FAO, 1981). This would have meant bringing millions of additional hectares into production to grow these export crops.

Where programmes of adjustment are imposed that require sharp falls in living standards, increased exports and reductions in domestic investment, it is proving increasingly difficult to give adequate attention to longer-term concerns. In many countries, the distortion towards the short-term leads to a balancing of accounts in which the rate of return on investment has to be unrealistically high and measures of environmental protection are seen as diminishing such returns.

The current economic situation, which would appear to call for more cooperation among developing countries, in fact makes it more difficult to achieve as the lead which ties developing countries' economies to developed countries' economies is tightened, giving developing countries less room to manoeuvre.

Another factor is that the world is undergoing a period of rapid technological evolution owing, among other things, to a growing understanding of the energy and resource use and environmental impacts of current technologies. Thus, many new technologies, developed with such understanding, tend to be environmentally more benign than those they supplant, while a number of others, for example, in electronics, are inherently less resource-intensive. The extent to which developed countries apply such new technologies is affected on the one hand by their commitment to existing industrial patterns, and on the other by their greater economic capacity to invest in them; developing countries, on the other hand, are less committed to existing industrial patterns, but lack the economic capacity to invest in new technologies or to evaluate technologies adequately. For developing countries to be tied to environmentally inappropriate technologies is ultimately counterproductive not only for their environments and for the global environment, but also for their economies. Increased transfer of technology to developing countries should be accompanied by the provision of data which would permit informed choice in the light of local conditions and the capacity of these countries to evolve suitable technologies should be strengthened.

In concluding this section, it can be said that traditional economic and industrial approaches are often incompatible with sustainable environmental development. As a result, resources have often been wasted. There are many examples of devastation of both renewable and non-renewable resources (forests, minerals including underground fuels, soils etc) which can be shown to have arisen from false political and economic assumptions, often based on short-term calculations. The cost of overexploitation is not carried by the exploiting enterprise and its immediate region alone, but is often spread widely and over several generations. And the environmental side effects are 'internalized' by the national economies of the countries concerned through deterioration of income, national wealth or conditions of life.

Where a commitment to conservation is generated, for instance in energy consumption in many parts of the world, it is clear that higher levels of production per unit of energy use can be achieved. There is a lesson here for the use of other natural resources. While productivity in terms of output per person/hour is an important economic yardstick, thought given to output per unit of resource use would possibly prove illuminating. A basic question is whether equitable development for all could be achieved on a sustainable basis were resource-intensive patterns of production and consumption to be generalized.

The central question today, therefore, is not whether to choose between development/industrialization and environment. It is how to select patterns of development that not only minimize adverse impacts, but are actually designed to stabilize and improve environmental, and hence economic, conditions. International economic cooperation is vital in this context. What is required is a more integrated approach towards evolving an international economic system which responds adequately to the financial and other development needs of developing countries in the context of an equitable and efficient adjustment process.

Relevance of environmental issues to the economic dialogue

The systems nature of the global environment is highly relevant to a set of issues such as depletion of stratospheric ozone, long range transport of pollutants, climatic change resulting from carbon dioxide accumulation, marine pollution, the movement of hazardous products in international trade and disposal of toxic waste. Such problems are now seen as likely to have significant consequences for the development and well being of the developing countries, which have not in the past, for historical or other reasons, taken a sufficient interest in their resolution (although they are now increasingly aware of the implications). Developed countries, in turn, domestically and within their own regional groupings, have been engaged in an intensive search for solutions, and for ways of resolving the potential or actual differences arising among them on account of these new phenomena. Their actions in turn also have significant effects on the developing countries. The global environmental system, therefore, is not self-contained: environmental issues are closely linked to the effort to bring about the equitable economic and social development of all countries.

It must indeed be recognized that environmental problems have global, as well as regional and local dimensions. Environmental problem solving has created its own natural selection process. Some problems – threats to the ozone layer, carbon dioxide build-up – can only be tackled by way of coordinated multilateral and worldwide action. A separate category can be more effectively treated at the regional level – protecting enclosed seas, managing river basins. Other problems lend themselves to the various forms of national action. Examples are tree planting, urban renewal programmes and national environmental protection laws. At none of these levels, however, can actions be effectively applied if environment is considered to be a separate item. Acceptance of this fact will add a new dimension to global negotiations.

The interdependence of environmental concerns

Halting and reversing ecological degradation has been identified as a major priority in a growing volume of major national and international studies and reports, including many where the principal concern was national and international economic development. For example, the report of the Independent Commission on International Development Issues entitled 'Common Crisis: North-South Co-operation for World Recovery' (1983) stated:

> Growing pressure on land, increasing use of chemicals, desertification and deforestation are reducing the productivity of soils in many parts of the world. The removal of forest cover, incautious use of chemicals and fertilizers, and soil erosion are destroying the soils and agricultural potential of scarce land resources and causing severe environmental damage ... We emphasize the need for resources to halt and reverse these processes of ecological degradation, which now assume emergency proportions.

Such reports (see, for example, *World Conservation Strategy*, 1980; *The State of the World Environment*, 1982; and OECD, 1982) have contributed to a much greater awareness and understanding of the interdependence among species and among nations. They have drawn on a fast expanding knowledge of the interrelatedness of the environment. Advances in environmental monitoring and biological sciences combined with harsh experience in national economic development have given an insight into the nature and workings of environmental linkages. This new understanding has helped to bring into sharper focus the two sided reality of interdependence. In many areas there are opportunities for improved international cooperation by all members of the international community; equally, there are also increasingly severe disadvantages for all if international cooperation is not strengthened.

Environmental standards and their relation to international investment and trade

Foreign investment and trade play a major role in global economic development and in the national economic development of both developing and developed countries. In developing countries during the past decade, 60% of industrial investment originated from outside, much of it coming from multinational enterprises. A large proportion of the foreign investment in developing countries went into the exploitation of natural resources such as fuels, minerals, timber and fish, largely for use in developed countries.

Recent studies by OECD and UNCTAD indicate some evidence of a trend to site primary industries in developing countries in order to take advantage of lower labour and other costs of production, including lower costs for meeting pollution abatement and environmental protection standards. This seems particularly applicable to certain traditionally heavily polluting industries such as steel, non-ferrous metals, asbestos and some toxic chemicals. Very few non-ferrous smelters, for example, have been built in developed countries in the last decade.

Nevertheless, differences in environmental standards between developed and developing countries do not generally appear to have been a major factor in location decisions so far. On the one hand, for multinational enterprises the principal considerations motivating investment in a particular country have included the characteristics of the resource, the size of the internal market, and labour, energy and transport costs. One the other hand, for developing countries negotiating agreements with multinational enterprises, environmental protection has not been as high a priority concern as such issues as taxation, foreign exchange earnings and the employment of host country nationals.

As a consequence of these and other factors, agreements between developing countries and multinational enterprises often ignore, or contain only limited references to, environmental concerns. In one survey completed in 1977 of 21 mining agreements, 9 lacked any reference at all to environmental protection. The provisions in the other 12 agreements were fairly general, and none contained unambiguous statements of positive obligations on the part of the enterprise to prevent environmental damage or to repair any damage that might occur.

Nor have differing environmental standards apparently been a major competitive concern in international trade between developed and developing countries. There does not seem to have been any significant pressure to date from developed countries to reduce the possible trade advantage of the generally lower environmental standards in developing countries. However, if differing environmental standards become a more significant factor than at present in international industrial location and investment decisions, the subject is likely to emerge first as a competitive concern among developing countries, before becoming an issue between developed and developing countries.

Consequently, to avoid or at least reduce the negative impact this issue could have on the natural resources, environment and economies of many developing countries, as well as on other areas of cooperation among them, it would seem timely and prudent now for developing countries to attempt to develop together at least some basic common principles and guidelines for resources use and environmental protection.

Guiding Principles concerning International Economic Aspects of Environmental Policies, including the polluter pays principle, were adopted a decade ago by OECD countries to reduce the potential for conflicts among themselves while at the same time respecting the need for environmental protection. That principle reflects their conviction that economic efficiency would be promoted and distortions of trade avoided if the pollution control policies of OECD countries required polluters to internalize the external costs. There are exceptions to the principle, or special arrangements for implementing it, in some OECD countries, but these are permitted only as long as they do not lead to significant distortions in international trade and investment.

In sum, foreign investment and trade have played a major and often crucial role in the economic development of many developing countries, but have also been increasingly associated with heavy inroads on both exhaustible and renewable resources, with avoidable and sometimes even irreversible damage to the environment and the essential ecological basis for sustainable economic development. Consequently, there are many disadvantages to avoid and mutual advantages to be secured through timely joint action and cooperation among developing countries on, for example, basic common environmental principles and guidelines regarding international investment and trade. Complementary steps could be taken with or by developed countries to strengthen the existing codes and guidelines for multinational enterprises, as developed countries also have a responsibility for, and an increasing stake in, supporting and assisting developing countries in their efforts towards better natural resources management and environmental protection.

Environmental economics

Production is the basis for the existence and development of human society. Human needs are constantly growing and in order to satisfy these needs, man interacts with and affects the natural environment in a variety of ways, both positive and negative. At the same time, the natural environmental resources of water, soil, plant and animal life constitute the natural capital on which man depends to satisfy his needs.

Until recently, land and natural resources could be exploited without restraint, and wastes could be discharged freely into air and water, which nobody owned. Natural resources were considered inexhaustible because many of them have the capability for self regeneration. However, it has recently been realized that the process of self regeneration is a rather slow and complicated one; if some natural resources are overexploited, the stock will fall rapidly, leading ultimately to the complete destruction of the resource. It has also been realized that air and water have limited assimilative and carrying capacities and that pollution control measures must be instituted to safeguard the environment and the quality of human life.

It is therefore important, if sustainable development is to be achieved, to evaluate the environmental costs and benefits of any development process. But such evaluation is not easy. Some of the environmental effects of development can be easily identified and evaluated quantitatively; others cannot. Nevertheless, an economic analysis of the environmental effects of alternative development processes, partial though it must necessarily be, is important because it creates awareness of the fact that natural resources ought not to be treated as free goods. Good management of the environment should be based upon avoiding wastage of resources and pollution. This is more appropriate and certainly more efficient than redressing environmental degradation after it occurs.

Environmental costs arise either through the damage done as a consequence of resource exploitation or through the effort expended to redress the damage. Much of the debate about environmental economics in recent years has centred on the fact that the costs of environmental damage may fall on people different from those benefiting from the actions by which the damage is caused, and on means of ensuring that the costs incurred in preventing unacceptable damage are borne by those benefiting from the action liable to create it.

The best available data on damage costs that could be put into monetary terms relate to oil spills in the sea, industrial catastrophes and floods. For example, clean up costs of oil spills have been estimated at $US1 000 per barrel of oil spilled (EPA, 1978). In 1974, a huge oil tank in the Mizushima refinery on Seto Inland Sea, Japan, developed an 8m rupture and spilled about 50 000 barrels of oil into the sea. The total cost of the damage incurred from the spill and from the cleaning operations was about $US160 million (Nicol, 1976; Hiyama, 1979). The costs of large oil spills since Torrey Canyon have been estimated at more than $1 billion (Schiff, 1980).

The accident at Seveso chemical plant in Italy caused damage estimated at $US150 million. The costs of rehabilitation of the damaged Three Mile Island nuclear power station (after the 1979 accident) was about $US2 billion; and the costs of the recent accident at Chernobyl nuclear power station in the USSR have been estimated at more than $US5 billion.

Even without accidents, large quantities of pollutants enter the environment as a result of human activities. Several studies attempt to estimate the economic costs of damage caused by such pollution, for example the loss of production due to illness (or death), health expenditure or losses to agriculture and productivity. The cost of air pollution damages in the USA has been estimated to vary between $US2 billion and $US35 billion per year (CEQ, 1975; OECD, 1985). Generally speaking, the economic cost of pollution damage in developed countries varies between 3% and 5% of the GNP; this cost has kept on growing in absolute value (or at best has stabilized) during the period from 1970 to 1980. The results of a French study on 24 pollutants indicate that the cost of pollution in 1978 was between 3.4% and 4.2% of GNP. One quarter of this damage was due to air pollution and another quarter to noise (Theys, 1978). Comparable figures have also been reported in Canada, Italy and the UK. A study in the USSR estimates the cost of health expenditure and decreased work efficiency due to air pollution at the equivalent of $US38 per capita and the cost of damage to pasture and crops as the equivalent of $US130–135 per hectare (Balazkii, 1979).

Damage costs may also be imposed in the process of development, through the destruction of certain types of renewable resources, eg the large scale loss of tropical forests, soil degradation due to salinization, imperfect cultivation of submarginal lands etc (Kneese, 1977). Some 30 million km^2 (19% of the earth's land surface), with a population of about 80 million, are threatened with desertification and consequently with huge economic and human losses.

It should be noted that this costing of the damage due to the irrational use of natural resources and/or pollution is far from being complete. Environmental damage is often selective and unequally distributed in time and space and among societies. Many of the physical, biological and socioeconomic consequences of large development projects are inadequately known and some can be quantified while others cannot. Examples of the latter are when landscape or historic monuments are threatened with irreversible change. Even if all the consequences could be enumerated and their likelihood assessed, placing a price tag on them would pose further difficulties. Consider, for example, the problems of placing a value on a human life. The traditional economic approach has been to equate the value of a life with the value of a person's expected future earnings. Many problems with this index are readily apparent. For one, it undervalues those in society who are underpaid and places no value at all on people who are not in income earning positions. In addition, it ignores the interpersonal effects of a death which may make the loss suffered much greater than any measurable financial loss.

Like damage, benefits are difficult to compute. They include direct and obvious elements like the profit to industry on the products sold or the gain to a country from the products exported and the employment provided. But they also include important elements like the stimulus a worthwhile job gives to individuals.

In developed countries, the cost of environmental policies has been estimated to range between 1% and 2% of GNP (OECD, 1985). Most of this expenditure is for pollution abatement and natural resources protection. In developing countries, the expenditure is much lower and and is mainly directed towards drinking water supply and sanitation. Expenditure for pollution control varies from one developing country to another and in order to control pollution effectively in the Third World it would be necessary to allocate between 0.5% and 1% of GNP for that purpose (Leontieff, 1977). These figures should be seen in the light of the cost of pollution damage in developed countries, which amounts to 3.5% of GNP.

The costs of environmental policies are generally more than compensated for by the benefits accrued from reducing the damage. It has been estimated, for example, that the health benefits from 60% reduction in air pollution in the USA would amount to a total annual saving of $US40 billion (CEQ, 1980). The US EPA has estimated that the 12% decrease in particulates alone achieved between 1970 and 1977 provides $US8 billion in health benefits each year, compared to the total 1977 expenditures on controlling all air pollutants from stationary sources (the primary source of particulates) of $US6.7 billion (CEQ, 1980). In the developing countries, the costs of improving the quality of the environment and of protection of natural resources are far outweighed by the benefits accrued to society. For example, the construction of drinking water or sewage systems in Third World countries could reduce the incidence of infectious diseases such as typhoid, dysentery, cholera and schistosomiasis by 50–60% or even more (Saunders and Warford, 1976). Such an improvement in human health would lead not only to an increase in productivity and time on the job (both of which contribute to increased GNP), but also to less expenditure on goods and services delivered by the medical sector, most of which are imported.

Environmental awareness and the introduction of strict environmental control measures in some countries have encouraged the development of alternative technologies, for example, recycling and low waste and non-waste technologies. From an economic point of view, such technologies could lead to substantial savings. Thus in Norway, strict measures to control atmospheric pollution have led to innovations in the production of ferrosilicon which have reduced production costs by 8–12%. In Sweden, changes in the pulp industry from the sulphite to the sulphate process and recycling of waste led to reduction in water consumption, production costs and wastes discharged. A similar trend has emerged in several other countries, for example China, Finland, France and the USA (see UNEP, 1982).

Although many of the environmental effects of human activity cannot be measured in economic terms, it is important to assess, in broad economic terms, at least some of the more tangible impacts that various policies have on the quality and quantity of natural resources. Such assessment constitutes an aid to judgemental decision making. One of the areas in which the costs and benefits of environmental protection are most evident is tourism.

The environmental costs and benefits of tourism

Tourism, with its different categories – international, intraregional and domestic – has become a major industry dependent on the continued availability of a number of generally renewable resources. There are certain basic characteristics of these resources which are distinctive and which in turn give a special character to tourism and its problems. First, there is the varied nature of the resources – pleasant climate, beaches, mountain scenery, wildlife, historic towns and villages, museums, art galleries, cultural events, the way of life of the people etc. Second, there is the geographically diffuse nature of the resources. Certain parts of a country may be more generously endowed with resources and as a result contain the bulk of the tourism industry, but all parts of a country have tourist resources and to a greater or lesser extent tourism is present generally throughout a country. Third, tourist resources are rarely the resources of the tourist industry alone – the terrain which as scenic landscape is a tourist resource is also the resource for agriculture; coastal and inland waters have economic use; historic towns and villages are homes and places of work of local people.

Tourism, by its diverse and diffuse nature, is so integrated into the life and fabric of a country that developments within the industry affect for better or worse, society, the economy and the environment generally. The planning of tourist development, therefore, requires a comprehensive approach which will consider the various aspects of tourism as they act and interact within the industry; and tourism itself as it affects, and is affected by society, the economy and the environment in the national, regional and local context.

The economic, cultural, social and environmental aspects of tourism have been recently reviewed by UNEP (1982), Haulot (1985) and Salm (1985). These analyses reveal a picture of increasing tourist activity with both negative and positive impacts. It is clear that in many areas the limits of desirable tourist influx are being reached and planning and management for a new balance between costs and benefits will be a challenge in the future. Those meeting it will be helped because during the 1970s the factors determining whether the impact of tourism on the physical and sociocultural environment of the receiving country or area will be beneficial or damaging were more clearly defined. The most important appeared to be the nature and carrying capacity of the receiving area; the type, intensity and pattern of tourist development; the approach to planning, design and management; and the ideology and types of tourists.

Where environmental damage was caused by tourist developments, it was most often due to poor planning of individual tourism schemes and of the overall growth of the industry. In some cases the increase in visitors outpaced infrastructure development. Such damage is ultimately counterproductive for the industry itself. Authorities have sometimes been inclined – perhaps under commercial pressure, perhaps from inexperience – to take a short-term or limited view of planning, with the result that a later generation or a particular segment of society pays an undue price in environmental damage. As for any other sector, it is the responsibility of the government and the public authorities to ensure that there is proper planning and supervision of developments, with due regard to the assessment of likely environmental impacts, so that profits for the industry are not made at the cost of wider environmental and social loss.

A key principle advocated by those who seek a balance between tourism and the environment is that the type and scale of tourist development and activity should be related to the carrying capacity of tourist resources (see Pearce and Kirk, 1986; Jackson, 1986; Salm, 1986; Western, 1986; Lindsay, 1986; Singh and Kaur, 1986). Such an idea has an obvious relevance to, say, the airlines or water supply systems serving a particular tourist resort. But the principle applies equally to the social system and the physical or cultural resources that may form the basic attraction to the tourist. The social system – the population and its workforce – may absorb and serve a certain number of tourists before strains begin to appear. The physical resources, such as beaches, ski slopes or African game reserves, may take a certain load of tourist activity, but show signs of deterioration if that load is exceeded. Assessment of carrying capacity and the balancing of levels of tourist development and activity with that capacity, are thus crucial means of preventing environmental damage, protecting resources and securing the continuance of tourism itself on a 'sustained yield' basis.

Public perception and attitude

The public's attitude towards the environment changed considerably after the Stockholm Conference. While remaining concerned about pollution, people became more alert to the scarcity of some natural resources, the necessity for conservation and the relationship between environment and development.

Public attitudes can affect the quality of the environment in at least two important ways. First, individuals can mobilize support for particular issues and exert political pressure that causes changes in public environmental policies. Second, public attitudes can affect the way individual members of society act in relation to the environment. The first is best illustrated by the flurry of pollution legislation regulations that have been formulated and implemented in many countries over the past decade. The second has been important, for example, in promoting energy conservation in several countries and in the protection of wildlife and some other resources in others.

Public opinion surveys coordinated by OECD on environmental issues were made between 1981 and 1984. Such surveys showed a significant common pattern in the USA, Japan and Europe. For example, despite the economic problems experienced by several OECD countries in that period, only about 27% of the public was willing to sacrifice some degree of environmental improvement for economic growth when offered the choice in a trade-off question (OECD, 1985). Expressed concern has been higher for national and global environmental problems than for local problems. The surveys indicated that 45% of the public were concerned about damage from oil spills, 45% about nuclear waste disposal, 43% about industrial waste disposal, 38% about transfrontier pollution, 35% about water pollution and 35% about air pollution (OECD, 1985). These surveys pioneered the measurement of opinion about several global environmental problems: the findings suggest that concern about these issues is quite high. For example, 36% of the public expressed concern about extinction of some plants or animal species in the world, 36% also expressed concern about the depletion of the world forest resources, while 30% of the public have been concerned about possible climate changes brought about by increase in carbon dioxide and other greenhouse gases (OECD, 1985).

The surveys carried out by OECD also indicated that public opinion supporting environmental improvements has remained remarkably strong over time. Where public opinion polls have asked the same questions about environmental issues over a period of years, there has been little or no softening of support for stonger programmes in spite of either observable improvements in environmental quality or adverse economic circumstances. In the USA, for example, the support for stronger programmes has actually increased since 1980. In addition, polls in the USA, Japan and Finland show that large numbers of people believe things have worsened rather than improved over the past 10 years. In a 1982 USA survey, 41% said the quality of the environment had 'grown worse' over the last 10 years compared with 29% who believed it had 'improved' and 28% who felt it had 'stayed the same'.

On the other hand, public perception and attitude towards the environment in the developing countries vary widely from region to region and from country to country. A common feature, however, exists: concern is more focused on local and national problems rather than on international issues. People are more concerned about water pollution, air pollution, municipal solid wastes, noise and to some extent about industrial wastes.

In general, awareness of human impact on the natural environment has grown rapidly since 1980. It has been manifest in countless conferences, meetings, publications, and debates. News media and non-governmental organizations have been instrumental in promoting this increasing awareness. Many countries have now instigated television and other mass communications programmes to inform their citizens about specific environmental issues and about their environmental responsibilities. In some countries these efforts are sponsored substantially by the government, while in others non-governmental organizations have taken the lead.

National responses

The task of designing and implementing environmental protection programmes rests with national governments. As present, nearly all countries have environmental machinery of some kind. Some countries have established ministries for environment and/or natural resources; others have established environmental protection agencies and/or departments either as independent bodies or affiliated to particular ministries. The responsibilities of these environmental bodies vary from one country to another. In general, their responsibilities are to design programmes that aim at national environmental protection by enacting the necessary legislation; establishing standards for levels of emissions from different sources; creating monitoring programmes to identify where the problems are most serious and to measure the success of the control programmes in dealing with them etc. In some countries, periodical reports have been published since the early 1970s describing trends in air and water quality. Such environmental quality reports have been further developed by time to include other aspects of the environment and amount, at present, to national state of environment reports. Over the past five years, an increasing number of countries have produced such reports under different titles, for example, environmental quality, state of environment, environmental data or environmental statistics. However, few of these reports are comprehensive, providing time series data that can be used to establish trends in environmental quality. In addition, these reports provide information that is difficult to compare. UNEP (1985) has recently published guidelines for the preparation of national state of environment reports in an attempt to harmonize, as far as possible, the preparation of such reports in order to facilitate intercountry and interregional comparisons.

Although several countries formulated legislation to improve the quality of their environment decades ago, most of these environmental protection laws were amended in recent years or clarified through modifications of regulations. In some cases these were required because problems were found to be more serious than had originally been thought. In other cases, adjustments were to make the environmental protection programmes more effective. However, the implementation process of environmental laws has not been easy. Sometimes the environmental machinery in a country does not have sufficient information to know the extent to which polluters are or are not in compliance with rules and permits. Some countries have been unable to keep pace with the agendas they have established for implementation of environmental laws. This is particularly true in developing countries, where environmental laws are hardly implemented.

Recently, some adjustments have been made to environmental laws and programmes in some countries. One approach was to adopt market-type economic incentives as part of the environmental control programmes. Such schemes may improve both the effectiveness and the efficiency of the existing laws. Under such a law, German industrial companies had to begin paying taxes on their waste water discharges in 1981 (OECD, 1985). Several countries have implemented taxes for aircraft or disposal charges for waste oil. The USA has allowed emission limitations to be traded among different sources in order to allow the most abatement to take place at the sources where it is least expensive and has also attempted to set non-compliance penalties to offset any cost savings that enterprises may make as a result of being in infraction.

Several countries have been attempting to integrate their environmental protection programmes more closely with other programmes, for example, development programmes, natural resources management, conservation programmes etc. Harvesting timber, for instance, can cause soil erosion and water pollution, eliminate scarce wildlife habitat and diminish the quality of recreation. Recognizing these conflicts, several countries are increasingly managing their natural resources in the light of a multiple use concept that takes account of these different environmental values. In some countries, such as France, Hungary and Bulgaria environmental programmes are included in economic plans. Others such as FR Germany, the Netherlands, Canada, USA and the Nordic countries include environmental analyses, to varying degrees, in the development assistance they provide to developing countries.

Another important development in recent years is the increase of public participation in the decision making process, especially in developed countries, through what has been known as environmental impact assessment processes. Although the details of these processes differ substantially from one country to another, they usually require that the environmental implications of a proposed action be analysed thoroughly and that they are described in an impact statement made available to the public. They also include opportunities for the public to react to such proposals and require that the agency responsible takes these reactions into account. Most of the legislation in OECD countries includes, at present, provisions for undertaking such environmental impact assessments. On the other hand, environmental impacts assessments, including public participation, are hardly implemented in developing countries.

One important conclusion that came out from the UNEP report *The World Environment, 1972-1982* was that the environmental data base is of very variable quality and that there are startling gaps and a special lack of reliable quantitative information about the environment in the developing world. In addition, there has been a marked lack of time series data and, therefore, the establishment of trends in environmental quality has been very difficult. The OECD has recently pointed out that one of the most serious problems facing OECD countries as they attempt to implement their environmental programmes is the lack of information on current and past environmental conditions and incomplete understanding of why some of the more serious environmental problems are occurring and what can be done to solve them. The OECD further pointed out that there is a substantial need for more research and monitoring to allow more efficient responses, in order to keep better track of the progress being made and to allow better anticipation of emerging problems.

Recognizing this need, several OECD countries have enacted special environmental research and monitoring statutes and established environmental research centres. Most countries also have large government supported environmental research programmes. It has been estimated that in 1981 the OECD countries spent about US$700 million on environmental research. Expenditures on environmental research vary in different countries and are generally between 0.3% and 3% of total R and D expenditure (OECD, 1985). Although some environmental research is being carried out scattered in research centres and universities in developing countries, no data are available for expenditures on such research, since these are commonly embodied under other areas or in the overall R and D expenditure.

References

BALAZKII, O.F. (1979). *Economics of Pure Air*, Nankara Dunika, Kiev, USSR

CEQ (1975). *Sixth Annual Report*, Council on Environmental Quality, Washington, DC

CEQ (1980). *The Global – 2000 Report to the President of the USA*, Council on Environmental Quality, Washington, DC

El-HINNAWI, E. (1985). *Environmental Refugees*, United Nations Environment Programme, Nairobi

EPA (1978). *Energy/Environment Fact Book*, EPA-600/9-77041, US Environmental Protection Agency, Washington, DC

FAO (1981). *Trade Yearbook*, Food and Agriculture Organization, Rome

HAULOT, A. (1985). The environment and the social value of tourism, *International Journal of Environmental Studies*, **25**, 219

HIYAMA, Y. (1979). Survey of the effects of the Seto Inland Sea oil spill in 1974, *1979 Oil Spill Conference*, American Petroleum Institute, Washington, DC

JACKSON, I. (1986). Carrying capacity for tourism in small tropical Caribbean islands, *Industry and Environment*, **9**, 1, 7

KNEESE, A.V. (1977). *Economics and the Environment*, Penguin Books, New York

LEONTIEFF, W. (1977). *The Future of the World Economy*, United Nations, New York

LINDSAY, J.J. (1986). Carrying capacity for tourism development in national parks of the USA, *Industry and Environment*, **9**, 1, 17

NICOL, C.W. (1976). *The Mizushima Oil Spill*, Environment Canada Report, EPS-8EC-76-z, Ottawa

OECD (1982). *Economic and Ecological Interdependence,* Organization for Economic Cooperation and Development, Paris

OECD (1985). *Environment and Economics*, Organization for Economic Cooperation and Development, Paris

PEARCE, D.G. and KIRK, R.M. (1986). Carrying capacities for coastal tourism, *Industry and Environment*, **9**, 1, 3

SALM, R.V. (1985). Integrating marine conservation and tourism, *International Journal of Environmental Studies*, **25**, 229

SALM, R.V. (1986). Coral reefs and tourist carrying capacity: the Indian Ocean experience, *Industry and Environment*, **9**, 1, 11

SAUNDERS, R.J. and WARFORD, J.J. (1976). *Village Water Supply*, World Bank, Washington, DC

SCHIFF, D. (1980). The costs of oil spills, *Environment International*, **3**, 189

SIMON, J.L. (1981).*The Ultimate Resource*, Princeton University Press, Princeton

SIMON, J.L. and KHAN, H. (1984). *The Resourceful Earth*, Blackwell Scientific, Oxford

SINGH, T.V. and KAUR, J. (1986). The paradox of mountain tourism: case references from the Himalaya, *Industry and Environment*, **9**, 1, 21

THEYS, J. (1978). *Environmental Assessment of Socio-economic Systems*, Plenum Books, New York

UN (1985). *Population, Resources, Environment and Development*, Population Studies E.84.XIII.12

UN (1986). *World Economic Survey – 1986*, E/1986/59.ST/ESA/183

UNCHS (1976). *Global Reviews of Human Settlements – Statistical Annexe*, document presented to the United Nations Conference on Human Settlements, Vancouver, May-June, (A/CONF 70/A/1/1 Add 1) Table 1

UNCHS (1982). *Survey of Slum and Squatter Settlements*, Tycooly International, Dublin

UNEP (1982). *The World Environment, 1972-1982*, Tycooly International, Dublin

UNEP (1985). *Guidelines for the Preparation of National State of the Environment Reports United Nations Environment Programme*, Nairobi

UNICEF (1986). *The State Of the World's Children*, UNICEF, Geneva

WEICHE, W.H. (1984). *Life Expectancy in Tropical Climates and Urbanization,* Report presented to the Technical Conference on Urban Climatology for Tropical Regions, Mexico City, October

WESTERN, D. (1986). Tourist capacity in East African parks, *Industry and Environment*, **9**, 1, 14

WORLD BANK (1983). *World Development Report 1983*, World Bank, Washington, DC

WORLD BANK (1984). *World Development Report 1984*, World Bank, Washington, DC

WORLD BANK (1985). *The World Bank Atlas – 1985*, World Bank, Washington, DC

WRI/IIED (1986). *World Resources – 1986*, Basic Books, New York

Index